Chronicles of a Reluctant Widower

Gerry Pelser

A Memoir on Love, Death, & Life.

A portion of the profits of this book
will be donated to breast cancer research.
Play with boobs.
It may save a life.

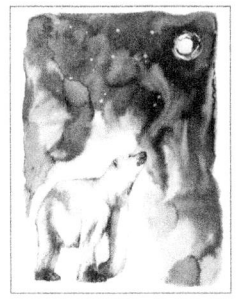

A STAR CALLED PRIM

THIS BOOK IS DEDICATED TO

Prof Dr Carol-Ann Benn

&

Dr Ronwyn van Eeden

THE WOMEN WHO GIVE UNWILLING SUPERHEROES THEIR CAPES.

"He who laughs at himself, never runs out of things to laugh at."
    - Epictetus

"What cannot be said, will be wept."
    - Sappho

Note from the Editor.

Dear Reader,

It's me, Tamsyn. Otherwise known as 'the editor'. Since you decided to pick up this book, and I'm thrilled that you have, I figured we should have a wee chat before you dive in. In the grand scheme of things, how this manuscript landed in my hands is of little importance, but what does matter is that it did. What also matters is how I approached it, simply because it required a really tough decision on my part. Let me caveat this by saying that I'm not arrogant enough to believe there aren't editors who are more skilled, or experienced, or better qualified than I am who could have done a better job. Yes, I've been in the industry for almost a decade, and I have a very expensive piece of paper that took me three years to obtain just so I can call myself 'qualified', but no two editors will edit the same way. Which brings me to the decision I had to make: I was about a third of the way into *Chronicles of a Reluctant Widower* when I called Gerry to give him an update. By this point, I was torn between doing what I've been 'taught', and what I knew was right for this story. And if I were to follow my own instincts and follow through on what I believe the story deserved, there was a chance the book itself could be what I call 'slammed' for poor editing. Gerry took my call, and rather than beat around the bush, I was honest: "I can rip this story apart and put it back together for the sake of technicalities, and craft, and story structure, and grammar, and all the other things I 'fix' when I'm editing a manuscript, but with this story, I don't want to." Now, Gerry is an incredibly gifted storyteller, of this I am aware, but this isn't just another story to him, and I needed to honour that. Of course, my worry was that once Gerry saw what I did (or didn't do) to his manuscript, he'd be wondering what he paid for, and I was honest about that too. To have ripped this story apart would have taken away from the very thing that gives it life: magic. And worse still, I would have changed Gerry's voice. It isn't my job to do that. I'm the one who makes it better, and helps a writer hone their skill, but I simply told Gerry, "I won't change the way this story is written. I refuse. And if anyone complains about the editing, you can send them straight to me." Gerry, of course, was surprised (I don't know why), but I went on to explain that this story is an experience, and the love he feels for his wife, Andrea, is punctuated by how he has penned this story. The events aren't chronological, and there are many Gerry-isms that not only bring comedic relief, but also exemplify his vulnerability, and were I to throw a style guide at this the way I would any other manuscript, I'd take the very things that make this story so beautiful, away. And now, dear reader, I will tell you what I told Gerry: This story is stunning. It is unlike anything I have ever read, or edited, and it left me speechless. It is both breathtaking, and heartbreaking, and makes you laugh when you want to cry, and cry when you want to laugh. It's a love story so poignant, and authentic, there is nothing I can do to make it better. Clean it up? Yes. But make it better? No. Because this story, and how it was written, is the ultimate metaphor for how Gerry loved Andrea – some parts are messy, some parts don't make sense, some parts are hilarious, some parts break your heart, some parts are ridiculous, and some parts are pure love. And I made the decision to keep all of it, the way it is, because life isn't editable, and neither is losing the love of your life and writing about it. My hope is that you will have the same experience reading this story that I did. That it'll move you, make you laugh, make you cry, and make you sit back and reflect. Gerry, it was an absolute honour, and privilege, to work on this, and to experience your journey with Andrea, and yourself, through your eyes. I will never be the same after reading this, and I hope everyone who picks this up, will feel the same.

Tamsyn

Foreword.

BY DR MARLENE ARNDT, CLINICAL PSYCHOLOGIST

*"The secret source of humour is not joy but sorrow;
there is no humour in heaven."*
- Mark Twain

There is a difference between authors who set out to write a novel and authors who set out to tell a story. At once touching and devastating, the book explores a love-story and the effect of death and gut-wrenching grief on a personal and intimate level. The author writes with a personal voice that feels more like a having a conversation than reading a book. This book is centred around loss and grief; however, it is also a story of a joyful and unique partnership. Parts of his experience may have been told before, but never with such honesty. The author does not shy away from talking about the good times as if to avoid pain.

Of course, it's one thing to experience grief and quite another thing to write about it. With humour, laughter, and gratitude, he navigates his personal grief process. And, because humour draws us in, it is an ideal way to give the reader an intimate look at the grieving man. If you are fortunate enough to be present when a grieving man expresses his pain in this way, and if you do not know what to say, say nothing. If you have ever wondered what it was like to walk in a reluctant widower's shoes, then this is an unflinchingly honest place to start.

This is a book I will continually refer to and gleaning wisdom from, especially in times of grief and in seeking to be a comfort to others.

Dr Marlene Arndt, August 2021

Author's Foreword.

Well, hello there, Gentle Reader. Thank you for picking up this book. Just you reading this paragraph shows courage. Why? Because what lies ahead is a remarkable yet disturbing story. My story, to be sure. But ultimately it is about my wife, Andrea, who died of breast cancer in December of that *annus horribilis* which was 2020. But it ain't about cancer and a self-indulgent tale of 'poor-me' woe.

So, what is this book about, then? It's a story about love, about death, and then, at the end, a story about stumbling over silver linings and finding meaning, even if the meaning only comes tomorrow.

Not gonna lie, this is a harrowing book. Some depictions are graphic, but I hope not gratuitous. What can I do? It's a harrowing tale.

And paradoxically, hilarious.

You are about to enter my living room. Just you and me in the intimacy of my house. Kick off your shoes, grab something cold — or something hot — and get comfy. I'm about to tell you a story about the loser who got the troubled yet inspiring girl, how he lost her, and how he managed to get out the other side.

And if you persist in your courage, Gentle Reader, I'm sure you can too. Let's begin.

Wedding Bells
Joburg – 3 February 2015

Part One:
ON LOVE.

Chapter 0 - The Beginning. Sort of.

1

I am that guy you tell your friend 'He has a nice personality'. That classic euphemism for 'he has a face like a bowl of lumpy mashed potatoes and teeth like crazy-pave'. A face for radio and a voice for print. Redeeming features are scarce. Vanity is not my strong suit.

I do have a nice ass, though.

Think I'm exaggerating?

The first time I got laid was at the age of twenty-eight. This was when some of my pals had been divorced already, not going to nightclubs and wondering like Beavis and Butthead when were they ever gonna score. Look, I can tell you why, and make an appreciable song and dance of it, but that would be indulgent. And would miss the point.

The point is that it was a Saturday evening in December 2005, and I was shitting myself. A few months ago, my second girlfriend and I ran aground after a mere four months (Michelle is a lovely girl, we just did not click, nobody's fault). A failed relationship did my already badly-battered self-esteem no good, and here I was: trolling the murky waters of internet dating sites, looking for someone whom I can at least get along with. This was before Tinder. Thank heavens. When one fills in internet dating site details, they ask about your habits and preferences. Smoking (no), drinking (yes), and children (love them slow roasted with garlic sauce, but I can never eat a whole one). One presumes the dating company then uses an algorithm to match like-for-like to give you a potentially grand match. I mean, this is only logical. You don't want a screaming militant vegan paired up with a guy who has seven hunting rifles and all the Rambo movies on VHS, do you? Anyway, I get a hit: there is a potential match! I click the link, and sure as heck, we match like chicken wings and beer. Bloody carbon-copies of each other, we are. So perfect, in fact, that I get suspicious. Back then, I earned my measly living as a freelancer, designing and coding websites. This was back when a 'web developer' was still a novelty and one could make okay money from it. I started this solo endeavour with the name Orange JellyBean. That's another long and irrelevant story, but that silly and odd name stood me in great stead: people forgot NetActive and *WebCraft* and all the millions of generic quasi-tech-sounding names the moment someone introduces themselves. When I introduced myself as 'Gerry from Orange JellyBean', no one ever forgot.

So, what would be the handle of this perfect match on the internet dating site? Blue Smartie.

Yeah, right. Pull the other one.

I contacted said *Blue Smartie* on MSN (youngsters, ask your parents) and blatantly asked her, "who put you up to this?"

Smartie's response, predictable in hindsight, was, "What the hell are you talking about?"

My riposte: "You're not real. You're one of my buddies playing a mean joke on me. Your profile is too perfect, you're like my own teenage fantasy of what my perfect girlfriend would be. You are everything I'd ever want in a woman. The only way this makes any sense is if someone is playing a practical joke on me. I mean, even your *name* is a bad impersonation of my business. A colour and a candy."

Yeah, she was *that* perfect. She convinced me she was very real. Turns out, she only joined the internet dating site because she saw an ad for the internet dating service on a news website headlined 'Dare to Date Me,' and my profile was the random pick which *pinged* on her screen. She somehow clicked on the pony-tailed head of yours truly, was intrigued by what she saw, and sent my profile off to one of her mates, who told her, "Fuck, he looks perfect for you! Are you sure he is real?" I am the only reason she paid to join the dating website: to get my contact details. Assured of each other's mutual realities, and with a silly grin on my face, we commenced chatting up a storm via MSN, and soon afterwards, the phone calls started. I remember the first time we spoke telephonically. Her voice came over the line, soft and husky. She had the most awesome and beautiful voice. Just her saying my name was enough to create a stirring in my otherwise dormant nether regions. Later on, we jokingly called it her 'Phone Sex' voice, and we've used it to great success on those lonely nights when she was off on a business trip. And when we needed a service provider to deliver something. With her speaking into the phone with *that* voice, people paid attention. I think if Andrea pursued a career in voice acting, she would've made a fortune. The conversations, both via MSN and telephonically, continued, and the mutual intrigue grew.

Not too long after our first chat, about a week before Christmas 2005, we set a date for our first face-to-face meeting. We were to meet at an upmarket-ish pub and grill at a shopping mall — it was the Dros in Cresta, okay? — and I was crapping myself. Anonymously, over a phone or internet relay chat (youngsters, ask your parents), I can hold my own. But face to face? This is where my confidence runs away screaming, and hides quivering in the bushes. So far, I really liked this girl. A lot. A real lot! I did not want to fuck this up, and if history is anything to go by, I fuck up hard and often. I had no looks, no style. Phil Collins even wrote a song about me: *I can't dance, I can't talk…*

I arrived at the mall, parked my car, and made my way to the Dros. I arrived at the escalators, and descended a level, and as I made my slow way down, she came into view. A short and chubby dark-haired girl, and she was absolutely beautiful. 'Pretty' is a term that did not apply to Andrea, for 'pretty' is too girly. Neither was she 'striking', that's reserved for the models I would work with later in my career. But by God, she was beautiful.

I know you won't believe me, but I swear on my Peanuts collection this is true: as she slowly came into view from my position on the escalator, a strangely calm thought entered my head. *So, that is the woman I'm gonna marry.*

I had no idea just how profoundly right I was.

2

I told you I have a good ass.

It may be my only redeeming physical feature, but it looks great in jeans. Out of jeans, it has shape, but is just way too hairy.

A week before this first-ever meeting, I was in Mozambique on a diving trip. Fun in the sun, endless beaches, sickly sweet cocktails. And men with too much money and testosterone throwing their four-wheel-drive penis-extensions around on the dunes. Very few things are as chest-thumpingly masculine as taking your Ford Ranger and scaling terrain angels would fear to fly across. I did not have a four-wheel-drive Ford back then, (now I do, albeit only a tiny little EcoSport), but I had a Laurentina beer in my hand and was happy to sit on the back of one of these grunt mobiles and drink while the dive instructor's version of the Camel Rally takes place on the Mozambican dunes. We arrived at a ditch, and the only way over it was for the driver to floor it. Which he did. The first bump threw me up in the air, and I landed with my right butt-cheek on the floor of the pick-up truck, cracking a pelvic bone. Immediately on impact, we hit the second bump, and I was airborne again. This time I came down on my left side on the tailgate and broke a few ribs. I was the lucky one. The lady who was drinking beer with me on the back of the Ranger had a compression fracture of her spine and spent many months in a plastic body-cast.

We both held onto our beers, though.

The net result of this misfortune is I had a purplish-black bruise the size of a dinner plate on my right butt-cheek. It was quite impressive, even if I say so myself.

So, there I was in the Dros, telling Andrea this story about my recent mishap on the back of a four-by-fuckoff, when she said, "Show me." I know she meant it as a joke, but I have a sense of humour and no shame. I got up and pulled down my pants, exposing my hairy bruised ass for her — and everybody else — to appreciate. (To thunderous applause and several drinks sent over…no, not quite, but surely you concede my ass deserves it.)

She often joked afterwards and said that's what did it for her. She liked my mind, and she liked my sense of humour, but it was the ass that sealed the deal.

3

Her name wasn't Marcie — name changed to yadda yadda, you know the drill — and she was smokin' hot. Refer to my definition of 'stunning' above. Also, an internet date.

And boy, was she kinky. This tall and slim redhead with a penchant for bondage was quite something. She sure got my dials spinning. Before I left for my bruising scuba trip, she came over for dinner and during small-talk, she sat on my armchair, smoking a Cartier cigarette in a way which put *that* Sharon Stone scene to shame. We never did the deed, because I'm not the type to hump on first dates, but she sure as hell made me happy for those seven minutes in the shower. *Ooh, the possibilities!* Not-Marcie had a value system much like my own when it came to deviances, and one never says 'no' to that, does one?

The week between Christmas and New Year's, Andrea and I went on our second date at an avian zoo near a casi — oh, screw it, it was the bird gardens at Montecasino. It was a beautiful summer's day, and I was thrilled that my wit, charm, and bruised ass managed to get a second date with Andrea. I have to admit, I did not have the guts to make the first move, but when we walked, Andrea took my hand and interlaced her fingers with mine, and it made me very happy. The bright summer sky above me, a beautiful girl's hand in mine. What could possibly be better?

Sure as God made little black puppies, we rounded a bend, and there she was, the woman not named Marcie. We made eye contact. Ten days ago, we had a very promising date, and here I was holding the hand of another. At that moment, I needed to choose. The stunning, slim redhead with a mind as kinky as a pocket full of earphones, or the short and round beautiful black-haired girl who was as vanilla as ice cream?

It was a no-brainer. I never spoke to not-Marcie again.

That was also the day I met Andrea's mother, Missus H. I had been warned that my future mother-in-law was quite eccentric. Now that's the understatement of the century.

Naomi Heidgen was loved by all. She brought people into her life and heart by sheer force of kindness. Andrea led me into the smoking area of the casino, and there she found her mother somewhere in a dense fog of Benson & Hedges, playing a slot machine. This incredibly thin old lady with sharp eyes and a cynical smile and cigarettes for fingers shook my hand at the introduction. Her first words to me? "What's with the hair?"

To be fair, she had a point. At the time, I had a long and luxurious ponytail... No, not quite right. I had a backwards comb-over that resulted in a ridiculous little rat's tail in the nape of my neck, the remnant of what had been a rather luxurious ponytail before Mother Nature started expanding my face upwards. I was disinclined to cut the damn thing. I loved my hair, dammit! Even if nobody else did.

Later on, Andrea told me her mother liked me, but being Jewish, wanted to know if I was circumcised. Well, luckily for me, my mum had a Jewish paediatrician, so I had my calamari-ring sliced off at seven days. It was so traumatic I couldn't walk for a year, but this pleased Missus H to no end.

I only saw Missus H one more time.

4

Neither Andrea nor I were particularly religious. Her heritage was a mix of German Catholicism from her father's side, and semi-orthodox Judaism from her mother's. I was at that stage lapsed Dutch Reform, on a slow but certain and painful journey towards full-blown atheism. Neither of us had this ridiculous 'no sex before marriage' rule, but both of us were rather discerning as to whom we shared our bodies with. And Andrea was adamant: you want nookie, you better be prepared to go steady. She wasn't someone who would just put out. She only humped boyfriends, not one-night stands. I loved that about her. I'm all for sexual liberation and I'm by no means a prude. I will never look down on those who had more sexual partners than I've had warm meals, but it's not my style. I'm a monogamous kinda guy. As of the afternoon of Friday the 13th of January 2006, I had as many lovers in my life as Germany has World Cup wins today. Four. On the evening of Friday 13th of January 2006, I upgraded to Brazil.

And, what's even better, I got myself a girlfriend.

Score one for the little guy!

It was the beginning of a fifteen-year relationship that had its literal unbelievable ups, its heart-wrenching downs, and ended in the greatest tragedy that I'll ever experience. This is not a spoiler. You know the title of this book. You read the blurb.

Forgive me if I skip the heart-wrenching downs, okay? They had no bearing on the ultimate outcome of this story. Every relationship has its tense moments, and Andrea and I were no different. Our relationship nearly ended twice. But the fact is, it didn't. To delve into those tense moments would only be a distraction on what I really want to say. But let me be clear: I was never unfaithful. I was never a 'bad husband' to her, and God knows I've had the opportunity. In my line of work, occasionally one comes across the type of person who is so randy and eager to do the dirty that Ron Jeremy would tell them to calm the fuck down. But my pants always stayed zipped. I was not about to risk the most precious of things for twenty-seven minutes of ego — and other — stroking. The last time I had sex with someone who wasn't my wife was with my second girlfriend, Michelle, back in October 2005.

Regardless of our issues, both of us had the determination — and ultimately, the love for each other — to make sure the relationship did not end. It got hairy once or twice, but the relationship survived.

I'd like to humble-brag with this, though: we never had a fight. We never raised our voices. Our most heated arguments were just two people gently talking to each other, as if the greatest thing each of us had was at risk. Because that is prezactly what it was. Our relationship was sacrosanct, and worthy of saving at all costs. We never risked it in its most fragile moments through ill-chosen or harshly spoken words. Shit, maybe we should've had a proper all-out screaming-match fight once in a while. I've heard make-up sex is awesome.

5

99.94

To the world, it's just a number, but to the cricket fan, it is the most iconic — if not poetic — number in the entire world of cricket. If you are a lover of the bat and ball and oval pitch, from Jamaica to Johannesburg, London to Lahore, you will know this number is Sir Donald Bradman's batting average. You see, cricket is life, and the rest is detail. There are few pleasures as satisfying as watching a well-drawn five-day cricket game. It's full-contact chess. A game of physical and mental fitness. Look, I get it. If you did not grow up with it, it can never be explained to you. To the unbeliever, to see twenty-two guys dressed in white stand around for six hours a day for five days in a row, only to shake hands on a Tuesday afternoon after no winner has been declared would seem like the ultimate pointlessness of life. But to those of us who relish in the sound of leather on willow, and cucumber sandwiches — not to mention lovers of cricket — it is the godliest of sports. Fair to say I fucking love it. I've spent many a happy hour at the Wanderers and Centurion cricket stadiums getting lost in the magic of the game in white. And when I could not be there, it was on the telly. And when I did not have a telly, it was on the radio. Sitting alone in my tiny flat coding a website with the radio droning on in the background as South Africa takes on an adversary on the pitch…I'll tell you there is no better way to do a day's work. And the good Lord I do not believe in had bestowed upon me a woman who loved cricket more than I do. Andrea did not just know Sir Don's poetic batting average; she could tell who was coming out to bat purely by the way he walked. She would get up at ridiculous o'clock to watch England take on Australia in the Ashes. When the Indian Premier League was held in South Africa in 2009 because India was in an election year, I think it may have been the highlight of her life. Seeing Sachin Tendulkar and Kumar Sangakkara and Adam Gilchrist and Chris Gayle all on home soil, all at the same time, was bloody cool for me. But it was nearly reverential for Andrea.

But I digress.

Ricky Ponting's 2005/2006 Aussie team was — is — legendary. Undoubtedly not just the best team on the planet at the time, but arguably the best cricket team *ever*. On the 1st of April 2006, Andrea and I had our first ever cricket-date. We had tickets on the grandstand of the Wanderers, and we sat there in beer-and-hot-dog fuelled cricketing bliss. Merv Hughes sat three rows in front of us. It was to be the last 'normal day' this young couple was to have.

My grandfather had died a few days earlier. The fact that I did not lead with this tells you just how not-loved the old man was. He was a cantankerous racist of a bastard, and there weren't many tears at his death. When the obligatory impromptu family reunion happened the morning of his death, Andrea met my family for the first time. The awkwardness of meeting your boyfriend's family exponentially exacerbated by the fact that the patriarch of the family had just kicked the bucket. It was weird, but it was okay. Now at least my new chick knew just how dysfunctional my family was. Anyway, on the 2nd of April, sunburnt and happy after a day at the cricket, her brother phoned up: The previous day, while we were basking in cricketing heaven, Missus H had toppled from the top of the stairs and had lain all night on the landing with a broken hip. Oh. Fuck. I lived in Roodepoort and Andrea in Hyde Park (which sounds fancy, but the 42 square metre bachelor flat was anything but), and Missus H was lying sixty kilometres away, in an intensive care ward in Pretoria. This is where I think our three-month-long stint as probationary boy-and-girlfriend got cemented into something permanent. Andrea hurriedly packed some clothes and sped up north to go crash at her mother's flat. I had a choice to make, so I made it. I packed my suitcase — and with it my computer, still a desktop with a bulky CRT screen — and joined her. I'm still of the opinion that my decision to join my girlfriend in her time of need in the next city over was the ultimate decider. I set up my computer on the dining room table, lived out of a suitcase on the bedroom floor, and stayed with Andrea and her brother for the next several weeks while we waited for the inevitable. Naomi Heidgen, as said, was a scrawny woman with cigarettes for fingers. She hardly ate, instead subsisting on a diet of Coca-Cola and nicotine. For a woman in her condition, a broken hip was a death sentence. It wasn't too long after the fall that we all knew Missus H's last home would be the ICU ward at Unitas hospital. This was the second — and last — time I saw my mother-in-law. We all knew she was going. Even she did. I respected the family perimeter. It was not my place to visit Missus H in hospital, it was my duty to provide comfort to her daughter. I did not enter the ICU ward, instead sat patiently on the linoleum-covered benches for the hour the family could visit. But one night, Andrea invited me in. One can only surmise why. The end was neigh. I entered the ICU, and greeted Missus H with what I hoped was a confident and solemn smile, and she gave me a death stare as if to say 'if you hurt my baby, I'll send a special envoy from hell just to torture you'. I made her a promise that I'd make sure her daughter was well-loved.

I'd like to pat myself on the back that I kept that promise. She was.

This is also the first time I've met a man who would later have a great influence in my life, Andrea's cousin, Norbert. (Norb's mother was Andrea's father's sister, for those of you keeping score.)

Norbert is a tall guy with soft eyes who outgrew his hair. He is an incredibly gentle and soft-spoken man. Just the way he talks lets the attentive listener in on his best-kept secret: he is wise, but would never flaunt it.

Norb and his wife, Astrid, and their two adopted boys, live about 8,800 kilometres away, in a farming village near Cologne, Germany. (PS: Norb's house in Germany is the inspiration for Giulia Hoffmann's home in my second novel, *Defining Giulia*. Thank God Norb's family is not the inspiration for Giulia's Simpsonesque ancestry.)

Anyway, I remember the night Andrea called up her favourite cousin to tell him that his favourite aunt was dying. I held her hand, and it was a heart-breaking conversation to be partisan to. Andrea did not ask him to come, but less than twenty-four hours later, we fetched Norb from OR Tambo International Airport. He had dropped everything and flew half-way around the world to be with his aunt and cousin. Being part of the family at such an intimate and sad moment was a privilege, and maybe even prepared me for what was to come one-and-a-half decades later. Shortly after midnight on the 13th of April, Unitas hospital phoned, and I held on tightly as my bereaved girlfriend cried for her mother. She had lost her father to a drunk-driver when she was eleven, and now, at age twenty-nine, she was an orphan. She was a strong woman with an intimidating finance degree and a professional career. She did not need anyone to take care of her. But I took care of her anyway.

And for the fifteen years after that, she took care of me.

Chapter 1 - Hounds and Homes.

1

Andrea and I were both independent people. Introverts. Loners. I had my place; she had hers. I lived in a garden cottage in a suburb of Roodepoort, and she lived twenty clicks away in her townhouse simplex unit, which was so small that if you wanted to change your mind you needed to go outside. At first, we mostly saw each other only on weekends. Gradually, 'weekends' expanded from Friday to Sunday evenings to include Thursday evening and Monday morning. Sometimes she'd come to me, other times I'd go to her. And sometimes I'd knock on her door on a random Wednesday evening and tell her surprised face, "I was just nowhere near your neighbourhood."

Those were good days, but it lacked a certain something. That x-factor that one cannot quite put your finger on. Turns out our x-factor was of the canine variety. Andrea loved dogs more than she loved cricket, and I think I impressed upon you just how much she loved cricket. She had a keychain with a metal fob which read 'I love dogs', and she could not pass a dog in public without petting it. Even police dogs and guard dogs, who would normally take your face off, rolled over and purred like kittens when Andrea appeared. She just had the 'touch'. She would reminisce for hours on end about her childhood canines: Lassie and Shnuff (Border Collies), Lady (A stray, mixed breed of questionable but multitudinous heritage), and Makhatini (A Scottie). She spoke of these dogs with love and fondness. Like the time Makhatini ate a spider and slept for three days. The way one of the Border Collies would share vienna sausages with her when she was a toddler. Andrea would sit on the kitchen floor with a sausage, take a bite, and then offer it to the dog, who would then take a nibble. Then Andrea, then the doggie, then Andrea, then the doggie…The dog knew instinctively not to gobble up the whole sausage. Dogs, man. Dogs are awesome. The last of Andrea's dogs, Lady, had shuffled off — after twenty-one years — mere months before Andrea and I met. And to further illustrate how much she loved doggies: we don't have any children, no progenies we could leave our earthly belongings to after we die. Her solution? She was going to use her posthumous fortune — which she planned on being substantial — to establish a trust to look after dogs. She would generously give to dog charities, never passing by an opportunity to make sure a canine could have a home and a meal. In this regard — and many others — she was generous to a literal fault. She would spend so much money on canine charities buying balls, blankets, and dog food for doggie shelters, that during our broke days we hardly had food ourselves. I am happy to say that I was often a beneficiary of Andrea's legendary generosity.

But I digress.

I, too, am very fond of pups. I did not have dogs when I was small, but as I grew older into my late teens and early adulthood, I had three doggies of my own. First came a brindle English Bull Terrier named Brezhnev who could play wicket keeper (And here the Brits thought only Jack Russell could play wicket keeper…). After Brezh died of skin cancer, a second brindle Bullie named Sam, who could climb trees (seriously!), and after Sam died of suspected poisoning, a yellow Labrador named Jakes who would help with the gardening. My mom was an avid gardener. The only time you would find the indomitable Ria Pelser on her knees was when she was busy pottering with her plants. She seemed to have infinite patience with gardens — a trait I most certainly did not inherit. When my mom gardened, and she needed to scoot three paces to the left, Jakes would pick up the gardening tools and bring them to her so she would not have to get up from her kneeling position. He would then wait patiently for the next move, and he would happily bring his mom her tools. Thanks Jakes! Saved me a lot of hassle when all I wanted to do was sit in my room and draw. (By the way, the name 'Jakes' would later on make a cameo in my first novel, *Discovering Leigh.*).

Tell you a great story: when I lived in my two garden cottages after I left home, having pets was not an option, and I missed the damn yappers! A life is not complete without a dog. However, in my first home after home, my landlord — who loved rugby more than anything else — had a little Miniature Pinscher, who, for some bizarre reason, he did not allow in the house, and so Nikita lived outside. Nikita fell pregnant, which excited my landlord greatly. He, paradoxically, had a shimmer in his eyes when he thought of all the new puppies. One night, I heard Nikita howl. I went outside and saw her nestled in the soft plants in the garden. It was time. I gave her a blanket and some water, and sat with her and comforted her while she birthed those puppies. It was an awesome experience to play midwife (or was that mid-tenant?) to those little doggies.

I obviously had no philosophical objection against man's best friend joining our lives to make a house a home. In fact, I loved the idea. There's only one tiny issue: I am actually highly allergic to cats and dogs. Animal dander is not kind to me. A cat once put me in hospital — that was scary — and most dogs have my chest close up like a liquor store during a riot. I was allergic to my own Bull Terriers to the extent that I broke out in hives and had to have a bronchial dilator anti-wheeze pump on me when I played with them. Besides, between my garden cottage and Andrea's townhouse, getting a pet that wasn't a goldfish or a cockroach was just not feasible. Then Andrea introduced me to Lenny.

Lenny was nothing but a photo of a dog from one of her two-dozen-odd books on dogs, and the coolest photo of a dog I'd ever seen. Lenny belonged to a breed I've never even heard of: a Hungarian Puli. And he just looked so damn cool! For those of you who never heard of a Hungarian Puli either, let me break it down for you: it's a small-ish doggie, a bit larger than a Scottie but a bit smaller than a Lab. Obviously, it hails from Hungary, and is a working dog, a sheep dog. (Allegedly) very intelligent, and, get this, hypo-allergenic. Why? Because of the Puli's most striking feature: their dreadlocks. This dog looks pure Rasta! Their coats never stop growing, and during their lifetime, forms into dreadlocks that one does not expect on a dog, and it just looks so damn cool! The net result is that these dogs do not have that highly allergenic dander stuff that would have me wheezing like a piston on a steam locomotive. It just looks so damn cool! Did I mention that? These dogs look damn cool. So, the dream began: we would one day get a house, one with a big lawn, we'd move in together, and we'd turn the house into a home with the addition of two Puli pupsels. Insert pastoral scenes from *Little House on the Prairie* here. Just call me John-boy!

Andrea was the undisputed queen of Google. She could find anything. When Larry Page was in doubt, he asked Andrea. And sure enough, she found the one and only Puli breeder in South Africa. Buying a rare-breed pure-bred dog is not as easy as buying a bar of soap. It doesn't just happen. These things take time! But we might as well get the ball rolling, right? Prepare for the 'one day' that will certainly come some undetermined time in our future. It was in June 2011 when I phoned the breeder to 'just find out'. You know, get to know the process, the costs, what needs to be done and not done. All the usual so we could 'one day' go get ourselves some puppies. Uh… Problem! The breeder just had two litters! And guess what? She stopped breeding; these would be her last litters. If we wanted, it was now or never. And most of the pups were already spoken for.

Oh, hell. 'One day' turned out to be today. On a Wednesday afternoon, we set off to the breeder and there they were: about ten of the cutest little nunus you ever saw! Tiny black baby-puppies huddled against each other in the winter cold. Some of their eyes were not even open yet. I chose a boy and named him Laszlo. Andrea chose a girl and named her Gizi. And then we paid the GDP of a mid-sized Central American nation for them.

But fuck, what now? Andrea cannot keep them at her townhouse. Not even 'just for a while'. There were no gardens to speak of and 80 other tenants in the densely packed complex. The only solution was my pad. With my tail between my legs, I approached my landlady. Now, picture this: Auntie Ann was a retired schoolteacher, and while her heart was of solid gold, her brain was well-oiled cast iron. She was an extremely strict and 'proper' woman in her late seventies/early eighties (now 91 and still going strong!), ramrod straight, went to the gym three times a week, and even in her old age, she once climbed over her own garden gate when she accidentally locked her keys inside. She could strike fear into the heart of an All Black lock-forward by merely *looking* at him. But boy, could she bake! Stereotypical of her generation and upbringing, I know, but stereotypes exist for a reason. Auntie Ann could bake to soothe the savage keto fanatic. But I digress. My lease on my garden cottage clearly stipulated 'single occupancy, no pets'. That I had a girlfriend who would do the mortal sin of *sleeping over* was already too much for her puritanical heart to take, and now I want to bring pets in? I mentally prepared myself to get shot. Or worse: evicted.

Side quest: Andrea was a consultant who did the bulk of her work on a laptop from home. This baffled the octogenarian Auntie Ann to no end. Having literally never missed a single day of work during her teaching career, she could not understand how someone could not go into the office every day. One worked! That's what one did. She almost understood my home-bound career of web design, but only after I painfully explained it to her. She initially scoffed that Andrea was 'lazy', because she did not 'work'. At least, not in the traditional sense. Until the day Andrea arrived in a brand spanking new Mercedes Benz…Yeah, the unemployed classes regularly purchase those, huh? Auntie Ann threw her hands in the air and claimed not to understand the youth. Her kids were farmers, engineers, orthodontists. They worked! They did not sleep till ten and then muck about on a laptop for a few hours. The indignity of it all!

Anyway, this 'single occupant, no pets' landlady needed to be approached. And placated. I expected the worst. Heck, in my mind, I was already borrowing suitcases from my dad and pilfering boxes from the greengrocers to pack my shit. Yet, somehow, even the ultra-strict schoolmarmish Auntie Ann's wiles were not immune to the charms of our puppies, and we had ourselves a home. This is how Andrea and I officially moved in together, more than five years after we initially started dating. I mean, after five years most couples are married — if not filing for divorce already — not only just moving in together. But it has to be said, I think for about three years before the official cohabitation, we never spent a night apart, one of us always sleeping over at each other's. Bloody hell, we should have done it sooner to save on rent, but yes, eventually, we moved in together. Andrea and Gizi and Laszlo and I; one big happy family living in a cramped garden cottage on the outskirts of Roodepoort, ready to start our lives together.

2

A sad interlude: Gizi did not last long.

About two weeks after we got the puppies, Gizi would not come out of her crate. She was a very loving little puppy, keen to be with her humans, while Laszlo was a bit more shy. She was the Alpha Dog of the two pups. When she would not come out of her crate that morning, not even for a treat, we knew something was amiss. We took her to a vet, who kept her overnight for monitoring, and the next morning when we went back, they told us that her kidneys had failed, and that the best, kindest, course of action would be to euthanise. I collapsed against the wall in the vet's office that day. The body-blow was almost too much to handle. I offered to sell my car to pay for whatever treatment they could do to save her. They said it happens. Sometimes new-born animals just die. There is no obvious reason for it, they just do. There was nothing they could do to save her, not for all the riches of Croesus. I cried like I have never cried before. It had been the saddest moment of my life, including the death of my grandmother. Andrea and I held onto our little girl and we both repeated to her: 'you are loved, you are loved' as the barbiturate overdose took our girl-puppy away. Her ashes are now mixed with potting soil underneath a topiary bush in the back yard. It was, at that stage, the worst day of my life. As it was for Laszlo. The poor boy who had literally shared his entire life with his sister was now alone. The breeder gracefully offered to replace Gizi and gave us Peaches. Sadly, Peaches did not adapt, and continually bullied the submissive Laszlo into a state of panic where he would refuse to eat. We returned her, leaving Laszlo a lonely boy, and Andrea and I heartbroken.

We needed to get Laszlo another sister. For which he had to wait a year, because the only place we could find another Puli was…bloody Denmark! The breeder who supplied Laszlo and Gizi's breeder is situated in Copenhagen, of all places. This is not just 'up the road', you know. This is not 'pull up, take a pup, and go home'. This took planning and energy and the GDP of a large continental European nation, but almost a year to the day that Gizi died, Laika arrived via cargo plane from Copenhagen. A tiny twelve-week-old puppy with a tail that wagged like a helicopter propellor. The first thing I said to her was, "Hello Laika, I'm your new daddy" and her tail went berserk. As did Laszlo's! Both the dogs are with me in my office as I write this. Laszlo is a wise and mischievous dog. He loves to 'play games', like hide his sister's ball, and he is an 'old soul'. Laika is much more energetic and, frankly, dumb as a brick. But boy, is she a loving puppy who would lick you to death if given the chance. We joked by saying Laika is made of hair, love, and play-gland.

I thank them for keeping me sane.

And for giving us a home.

And for giving Andrea the unconditional love only dogs can.

3

We did not stay at Auntie Ann's place for long. Before Andrea moved in, *I* did, though. When I moved out of Auntie Ann's place, I had been there for close to eight years. To date, the longest I've ever stayed in one place. We first found ourselves a two-bedroom rental place, which I loved. It had more of the chilled, laid-back feeling of holiday lodgings rather than a house. It was perfect for us. Andrea had found — shock, horror — an office job! I still built websites from home, but now also added professional photography into the mix. We needed a place to sleep, cook, watch telly, and for me to work. That was it. We need not have a large place, and for a while, the two-bedroom rental house was our little slice of heaven.

Another side quest: this is also where I learned about the strange faculties of dogs. Andrea's boss, Kerron — who shall become pertinent later — wasn't too fussed about trivialities such as 'office hours', only about delivery. Which meant that when the heat was on, Andrea would come home at eleven at night. And when it was not, at eleven in the morning. Which is a long way of saying she had no specific routine. However, whenever Andrea was about to come home, Laszlo would get up and wait at the gate. This dog had a sixth sense about his mother. Laszlo would amaze me by abandoning his position next to my desk to go wait at the garden gate for his mother to arrive. Andrea would phone to tell me she's ten minutes out, and I'd say, "I know, Laszlo just went to the gate." We tested this sometimes by her *not* telling me she was coming, and still, sure as hell, Laszlo would get up and go to the garden gate, and ten minutes later the Benz would pull up. Many people have postulated many theories why this happens. None of them hold water. The only explanation a reasonable and rational atheist like me can offer is that there was a certain spiritual bond between the scruffy boy and his mother. Dogs know, man. Dogs know. We were in this house for less than a year when Laika arrived, and yes, we named her after the first doggie in space. This is also important, because this is where I tell you Andrea was a bit of an amateur astronomer — not to be confused with astrologer. (Auntie Ann could never quite distinguish between physics and superstition, and the uber-Christian Auntie Ann always looked at Andrea with a critical eye whenever Andrea took out her Celestron for a journey through the nightly heavens).

The Celestron telescope is one of the few truly great moments in Andrea's life. The stars and planets and nebulae fascinated the daylights out of her, but we were too poor to afford a proper scope. The best we could do was a big set of binoculars, which we mounted on my camera tripod. It wasn't much, but they were strong enough to make out the rings of Saturn. I still have them on the bookshelf.

Anyway, every year — on the rainiest, cloudiest, most miserable day they can find — the Astronomical Society of Southern Africa organises their showcase event: Scopex. An annual event of celebrating stargazing with deep-space photography, lectures, exhibitions, and boffins showing off their incredible home-made telescopes.

It *always* bloody rains on that day. Even when they moved it from September to avoid the early spring rain into the heart of winter in order to guarantee the stereotypical crisp and clear Johannesburg winter skies, it bloody rains! Want to break a drought? Organise a day dedicated to observing heavenly bodies. One year there was a lucky draw, where first prize just happened to be a 115mm Celestron Newtonian telescope. What an Alfa Romeo does for Jeremy Clarkson, that scope did for my wife. She bought a ticket, and promptly forgot about it. Several weeks later she called me, all a-flush and a-flutter. She won! It was the only thing she had ever won in her life. I can count that day as one of only half a dozen where I've seen Andrea blissfully happy. When we indulged in beer-and-wine-fuelled daydreams about building our perfect house, having a viewing deck where we could set up a scope was always on Andrea's list of needs.

Which is a long way of saying it was absolutely no surprise that the second girl-doggie we would get would be named after the Russian stray who sacrificed her life so that humanity could pioneer an era. (Laika, my girl, you have big shoes to fill...)

4

It was while we were living in this house that Andrea and I made a decision which would change both our lives forever. It was an extreme risk, but one worth taking. With vital assistance from Microsoft Excel, Andrea calculated she could make more money working for herself than she was making working for a boss, all while doing the same job. It would take the proverbial blood, sweat, and tears, but it could be done. She tentatively approached a client, who said yes, and she then handed in her resignation. Sidus Consulting was born. 'Sidus' being the Latin word for 'constellation', or sometimes more poetically, 'the night sky'.

Andrea's bold move to start her own company had a profound impact on my personal and professional life. As she got busier and busier, my own work took a back seat, until close to the end of the whole mess, I was no longer working at all. My web development almost totally ceased to be, and I only had the odd sporadic photography client. I was just too busy supporting my wife. I had become a de facto house-husband; a role I absolutely relished and flourished in. Andrea would spend her time behind the laptop or seeing clients, and I would ply her with breakfast, lunch, dinner, and about three million cups of tea. She brought home the bacon, and I cooked it. We settled into a very comfortable symbiotic relationship where our individual skills supplemented the other's needs. She made more money than I'd ever make on my own, and I could take better care of her and the daily household tasks than she could do on her own. In short: it was perfect. My mother always said I'd make a good wife. Seems she was right.

Thus, we entered the comfortable golden years of our relationship. As said, I'll pass over the bad parts because they have no bearing, but all in all, it was what life should be. Peaceful, quiet, serene: pastoral life replete with dogs and cricket. We did not stay in that two-bedroom rental for long, because now Andrea needed a home office, and she bought a three-bedroom house with a slightly larger garden for the pups.

5

It was also during this period at the two-bedroom rental where I earned my marital nickname.

All couples have pet-names for each other. From sickly sweet things like 'Schnookie' to the juvenile and somehow grotesque 'Babe', no couple in love call each other by their first names.

Andrea was always 'Sweetie' or 'Sweetie pie' (pronounced 'Sweediepai'), and I was the more generic 'Love'.

Until one day.

A constant in the life of suburban Johannesburg, for those who do not know, is that every available surface is claimed by posters and stickers for every service you can find. From auto repair to hair replacement, from window blinds to satellite TV installations, from penis enlargement to 'legal' abortions, from get-rich-quick schemes to fortune tellers, these omnipresent bills are so ubiquitous as to not even be seen anymore. We were on our way somewhere, and she was driving. Waiting at a red light, I examined the clutter of bills covering the back of a road sign, and I saw one for 'House Planks'.

"What the heck is a house plank," I asked.

"A what?"

"A house plank," I replied, and pointed out the sign. She snorted laughter. "You. You are a house plank! Read again. It's house plans." Well, duh. Blame dyslexia, but since that day I became Andrea's Houseplank.

To give context for my international friends: a 'plank' is a derogatory term often used by English-speaking people to describe a certain type of Afrikaner. Certainly not all Afrikaners, but there is a subset of my culture which is very, how can one say, 'common'. Backwoods people, under-educated and over-alcoholed; comparable to trailer trash or hillbillies. These people are looked down upon with distaste, and often referred to as 'planks'.

I am certainly no plank (at least, not by my own estimation), but the nickname stuck. I became a Houseplank the way Dobby was a house-elf. To such an extent that on the occasion where I had to declare my occupation on a form, I would put down 'Houseplank'. Not many people noticed. And to make matters even more hilarious: I used my graphic design skills to draw up a menu which she could consult when she was stuck for meal options. I headlined this menu: *Ristorante Chez d'Hôuseplanque.*

But vengeance is mine, because my nickname for her was 'Cheeken'… To which she would comically pout and say, "No! I'm not a poultry!" And I'll tell you something, when somebody rubbed me the wrong way, Andrea would get quite defensive: "Nobody messes with my Houseplank!"

It's silly things like this which are the touchstones that turn relationships to gold. Speaking of names: you'll find I sometimes refer to Andrea as 'Prim'. This was her late father's pet name for her. This came about because she was a premature baby and kept in an incubator for a while after birth. She was in a paediatric ward with all the other premature babies, whom the nurses collectively referred to as 'premmies'. Her middle brother — three years old at the time — heard this 'premmie' term thrown about, pointed to his baby sister in the broiler, and proclaimed "Prim!"

Job done. Mister H never referred to his daughter as 'Andrea' again.

Andrea referred to herself as 'Prim', and only the chosen few were allowed to call her by that name. She was Andrea. Except when it came to me, her family, her dearest friends, and herself. It became so weird, actually, that saying her name to her face was odd. I could — and can — easily speak of 'Andrea' to anyone else, but *calling* her that seemed wrong. She was 'Prim'; a duality of monikers I'm not sure I understand, even after I explained it. And as these things go: when all was fun and games, I was 'Houseplank'. Generically, I was 'Love'. And when I was in trouble, it was 'Gerry'.

Yeah, that's how I knew I'd mucked up: "*Gerrraaayyyyy!*"

Oh, fuck…what did I do now?

Andrea, of course, was always 'Prim', 'Primcess' (with an *m*), or 'Sweetie', or sometimes 'Primcess Cheeken'. She was the woman of the house, and would never, ever, be in trouble.

God forbid.

Chapter 2 - interlude: Previously on...

1

I guess some exposition is in order. This book is all about the most wonderful person I've ever known. And of course, Andrea... Okay, jokes aside. This is actually a very difficult book to get a handle on. As any ecologist or botanist or palaeontologist will tell you, it is impossible to describe an organism without also describing its environment. The two are so intertwined that the organism describes the environment, and the environment describes the organism.

I was Andrea's environment.

So, in order for you to get a better handle on my wife, I need to tell you a bit about myself and my past. Relax, I'm not gonna go all Freudian on you and pull the old 'Tell me about your childhood' indulgence, because boy, if I tell *that* story, my print costs would skyrocket! But I would not be faithful to the gist of this story if I do not at least tell you some backstory.

2

Her name was Marlize. Yes, that's her real name. However, I just fondly called her 'Mary'. She is half the inspiration for the character 'Scary Mary' in my novels *Discovering Leigh* and *Defining Giulia*.

Now, here's the ugly truth: nobody would have ever accused Mary of being good-looking. She was a heavy-set woman, a full head taller than me. A behemoth. And as I said, yeah, let's just call her 'homely'. But by God, she just *oozed* sex appeal. I'd be in a bar, having a beer with the ugliest girl there, and people would tell me just how damn lucky I was... I'd agree; I was the lucky fucker who was the beneficiary of that abundance of sex appeal.

I met her in 2002 on an IRC chatroom (educate the youngsters) euphemistically called 'Truth or Dare', but should actually have been named 'Bondage and Fetish'. I wiled away many a lonely hour in that chatroom. I've made a great many pals there, a handful of whom are still in my life, twenty-odd years later. It was an absolute blast. 'Truth or dare'... yeah, right. It was an excuse for 'kiss and tell' kinky adventures. Oh man, it was fun!

So, I click with this chick. We just laugh and talk crap and we just find ourselves on a wavelength. And as I said in the beginning, the first time I got laid was when I was twenty-eight years old. So, put one and one together, will ya? At this stage of my life, I'm still a bloody virgin!

Gerry Pelser, friend of all, lover of none.

Anyway, on 8 March 2003, Mary invites me over to her house for some real-life face-to-face kink, fetish, and bondage games. How do I remember the date so accurately? Well, because while Mary was lying hog-tied and gagged on the living room floor, I was drinking beer watching Zimbabwe lose to New Zealand in the 2003 Cricket World Cup.

I told you cricket is life, and the rest is detail. But did you believe me? Nooo....

And so began a kink adventure with a stranger who became a friend who, on a sunny Sunday afternoon in June, popped my cherry.

I finally got laid!

And what's even better: I got laid in my own bed with a woman I loved. I had a dinkum girlfriend for the first time in my life, and I fucking loved it! And Jesus, we could hump! If there was ever a mixed doubles team to send to the Humpolympics in Peru, Mary and I were it, hey. We were virtually assured of a gold when it came to the Kinky Sex disciplines. Shoo...

And when we were not humping, we had a lot of good, clean, kinky fun together. Shit, the stories I could tell.

The point is, I loved this woman. I really did. They say you never forget your first love, and y'know, I never will.

However, there was a problem. Mary was a divorced mother of two. Her kids were still small, and there was always a bit of an 'undercurrent'. Mary was number one in my life, but I would — rightfully — never be number one in hers. The kids would always come first. I have ideologically no problem with that. Your duty as a parent is to always put your kids first, and Uncle Daddy needs to come in after that. However, *being* Uncle Daddy kinda sucked. When you constantly put someone as your number one, but you are at best number three in her life, no amount of good, clean, kinky fun can make up for that emotional disparity. The whole kids thing finally became too much, and Mary and I broke up on Christmas Eve.

How is that for depressing? Christmas day, my father — who assumed he was going to have the traditional Christmas lunch at his elder son's girlfriend's place — and I drove around town looking for an open shop to buy food. We eventually found vetkoek at a petrol station. Christmas 2003 was a rainy day with my father and I having vetkoek with Bully Beef for lunch.

Yeah.

(For my international friends: Vetkoek with Bully Beef = fried bread with tinned corned beef.)

3

Do you know what is awkward? Awkward is taking your brand new girlfriend to your first love's funeral.

Andrea and I just started dating when Mary's cousin called me: she had been in an accident, in intensive care, and things were looking grim. A week or two later, the cousin called again: Mary's gone. She was thirty-three.

Even though we had broken up more than two years prior, she was still my first love, and I still had — maybe, even have — a soft spot for her. I was sad. I have to admit, telling Andrea my ex had died, and that I wanted to go to the funeral was odd. But asking Andrea if she would join me? Well, that was downright strange. I did not cry at the funeral. But only just. It would not have been fair to Andrea to have her brand new boyfriend cry for his ex on her shoulder. However, Andrea had a different take on it. "Imagine the shoe on the other foot. If Steve died, would you have a problem if I went to his funeral?"

"Of course not!"

"Would you come with me?"

"Of course yes!"

"Would you have a problem if I cried on your shoulder?"

"No, duh!"

"Then why do you think it is weird for you to cry on mine at your ex's funeral?"

See, this was the empathy and understanding of Andrea.

But again, I digress.

Often, I reminisce about the past and tell stories about the crap Mary and I got up to and the adventures we had. Ah, fun times.

But I'll never author a book about her.

4

This one's gonna sound creepy, but I promise you it ain't. If it was, I would not talk about it so openly.

In July 2010 I had a gig to be the photographer at a 'paparazzi party' for a sixteenth birthday party: the daughter of one of my pals and her schoolmates, a gaggle of about a dozen girls.

On the couch was a mousy but insanely beautiful girl — if one can reconcile those two seemingly contradictory things. She absolutely *owned* the camera when she was in front of it, and she did not even know it. As shy and mousy as she was, she had a presence there none of the other girls had, and a spunk that set her apart. Her name was Michaela, and she was only fifteen. I have no interest in younger women. In fact, I preferred older women, but these days 'older women' are my age. But the professional in me could recognise that this girl would set the world on fire as a model when she grew older. After the shoot, for marketing and tagging purposes, all of us exchanged Facebook details, and that was that. I forgot about her for several years.

Until in January 2013, when she popped up on my message box. She wanted photographs. She's out of school now, eighteen years old, and — for a reason she did not specify at first — she was dead set on getting nude photography done. This was a bit troubling, because I was pals with her mother, and taking nudie pics of your pal's kid is a bit odd. However, I know the photography industry. For every legit photographer out there, there are half a dozen perverts who would just love to take gratuitous and salacious pussy pics of a beautiful and nubile — not to mention gullible — eighteen-year-old for their personal spank-banks. I reasoned that if I'm not gonna do it, she's gonna go somewhere else, and if she lands in the hands of one of *those* guys…

If she wasn't a daughter of a friend, I would have said no. The world's problems are not mine to solve. So, I agreed.

And if all this sounds like the opening chapters of my second novel, *Defining Giulia*, that's because it is.

Over the course of the next two years, Michaela and I formed a friendship that I never would have thought possible. Andrea is the best friend I've ever had. But Michaela, fondly known as 'slinky' (lower-case s), comes in at a close second.

We all know the story about how the Greeks have four words for love. *Storge, eros, philos, agape…* all those mean different things in trying to describe what type of love — specifically — one feels for another human. The Greeks have the right idea, but I fear even their rather expansive descriptors fall short of the mark of the relationship slinky and I had. Look, I'd describe it if I could, but I'm not a good enough writer to give you an adjective or a noun as to what the love I had for her was like. One thing it wasn't though, was 'eros'. We did not hump. 'Romantic love' or 'erotic love' wasn't it. And it was a lot more intimate than 'brotherly' or 'parental' love. Truth be told, I tried to make sense of it in *Defining Giulia*, and fell short. The best way I can describe it, is that slinky and I spoke the same native tongue; one neither of us were aware of until we heard the other one talk. The old cliché of 'cut from the same cloth' comes to mind. We just understood each other on a fundamental level where explanation was unnecessary.

There are several reasons we never graduated to a session between the sheets — or the pool table in my photographic studio. Topmost of these is the obvious: I was in a happy and committed relationship with Andrea. Second was the twenty-year age gap. Third was the fact that she batted for the other team. So, even if I wasn't in a relationship and I could forgive the two-decade age difference, we still would not have played mattress tennis. This does not mean we did not have a shitload of fun and shared soul secrets.

Shortly after her twenty-first birthday in 2014, slinky committed suicide. It was at the time the worst thing that has ever happened to me, and remained the worst thing until 9 February 2020.

Slinky's death shattered me. I was an absolute broken man. I never quite got over it. I never quite got over her. A photo of her — butt-naked and luxuriously smoking a cigarette as she leans over a balcony-railing in the afternoon sun — is hanging framed above my bed. I loved that woman profoundly, and the day she died, a little part of me died with her. When I heard of her death, Andrea held me as I wept. A week or so later, at her memorial service, I held onto Andrea as she wept.

Remember I said above that for all the fun Mary and I had, I can never write a book about her? Well, *Defining Giulia* is my book about slinky.

5

In my life, I have loved three people, and the universe had taken all of them from me.

I have carried to their graves the coffins of uncles, aunts, grandparents. Those I can handle. They were all on the older side of life where one can start to expect to depart on the cruise ship down the River Styx. But none of these women lived to see forty-five.

I am way too intimately acquainted with death.

Sometimes I wished I was religious so that I can spit in the eye of God and tell him what a cruel and cowardly asshole he is. If this offends some of my more devout readers, well, tough shit.

Laika
16 December 2018

Chapter 3 – Effing the ineffable.

1

How does one write an homage — or indeed, compose an ode — to someone like Andrea? Words simply fail me, and now I'm going to spend the next several pages telling you why.

To be fair, I'm sure everyone who has ever loved someone this deeply can spend pages singing the praises of their loved one. I know and appreciate this, but hear me out.

Let me start by saying that she moved in a way that would make the oceans jealous, she spoke in a voice of the angels, and had a way of reorganising your priorities in such a way you thought it was your idea in the first place. She was big of brain, heart, and bosom. She was an all-round woman.

But a thing about Andrea is that she was 'independently inspirational'. So, what the hell does that mean? Well, let me give you some context.

Sadly, my wife did not have the best of lives. In fact, she lived a very sad and unhappy life, and she had seen and experienced her fair share of trauma and sadness. My life was no picnic, but it was a cakewalk compared to some of the shit she had to endure. At eleven, she lost her father to a drunk driver. This sent her mother on a downward spiral that saw Andrea and her brother often left home alone for days at a time while the mourning Missus H wiled away days in casinos, which she euphemistically called 'spas'. This was in the days before cell phones. Andrea would come home from school to a note on the kitchen table: 'at the spa', and that was that. Not which 'spa', or for how long. It could be hours. It could be several days. The Heidgen siblings would then need to figure out for themselves how to get food on the table. At the same time, the loss of his father sent Andrea's brother into a protracted violent period; a spell in which he terrorised his sister. An anecdote: they each received a slab of chocolate. Peter gobbled his up, Andrea saved hers, eating it piecemeal. Then, of course, Peter got jealous because Andrea still had chocolate left. In order to get her to tell him where she hid the chocolate, he beat her up. When she still did not relent, he put a knife to her throat. She dared him. Fortunately, he showed himself as the coward he was and did not cut, but just continued to beat the living shit out of her.

And her mother's response? "Don't provoke him."

To be clear: that was just an anecdote. A singular example of a teenage wherein abuse was a daily torment. But there's an even better one. Peter squandered his inheritance from his father on two motorbikes. Andrea saved her money. Peter put a knife to her throat — again — and demanded she loan him money because he wanted to buy a gun. A Glock, specifically. "You mean you're threatening my life for money so you can buy a gun? Uh, no."

It is fair to say there is no love lost between Andrea and her middle brother.

Note I said middle; there is an older one too. Johnny. He made one brief appearance in the fifteen years Andrea and I were together, and therefore this one singular appearance in this book. When we knew that Missus H was dying, and Andrea called Norbert in Germany, she also called her older brother to tell him his mother was dying. Johnny was living in Cape Town at the time. His response? "What has that got to do with me?" and "Who is going to pay for my plane ticket?" This is not a man who is destitute, but one with a fairly successful career as a brand manager for an international beverage company.

When Andrea heard she was terminal, she asked me not to notify her brothers. "They had no part in my life, they should not get to be part of my death," she said. To this day, neither of Andrea's brothers know their little sister has died. And that is only right and fair.

When Andrea's mother died, all her family in South Africa died along with her, leaving Andrea with no relatives she cared for — or who cared for her — in South Africa. The closest family she had was her cousins in Germany. Which will make for an interesting story later.

As one can imagine, having lost your father, and then having your brother physically abuse you, and your mother being absent — and non-caring when she was not — took its emotional toll on Andrea. And if you were ever a kid, you will know the cruellest thing on this planet is a child who can smell weakness in another. Is it a surprise then to tell you she was gang-raped? She was at a sleepover at one of her friends, and two teenage boys — the friend's brother and a mate of his — took it upon themselves to defile Andrea. They stuffed a sock into her mouth and took turns; one holding her down while the other one had his merry little way with her. The good news is one of these prats killed himself a few years later. One can only hope it was in guilt. When she confessed to her mother what happened, Missus H just shrugged and said, "Deal with it, where do you think Johnny comes from?"

And then you wonder why so many rapes and sexual assaults go unreported… And I'm sure by now you can see that Andrea's relationship with her mother was a troubling one.

As teenage grew into adulthood — and she got to escape the turmoil of the familial home when she left school — she fled across the country to the University of Cape Town. It was as far away from home as she could get at the time. South Africa was welcoming a new era of hope, and Andrea moved to the southern tip of Africa to find her new spiritual home in Cape Town. During the next several years, Andrea flourished. At least, emotionally. She was in an environment that was not merely non-threatening, but downright supportive! She found herself among intellectual peers, and made some damn good friends, some who would remain for life. She even got herself a boyfriend. Steve.

Of course, everything went well until it didn't. The bough broke on a road trip between home and university, a thousand miles of open road. On a long and lonely stretch of road, a tyre burst. Not too big a deal. Andrea steered the car onto the shoulder as to not obstruct the road. Except there was an unseen culvert. The car went into the ditch and injuries were had. No deaths, thank goodness. By sheer luck, a police car was not too far behind them, saw the whole thing, and ambulances could be hailed. Else, God knows how long the four students would've been trapped. The most serious of these injuries was a broken back. (He is okay now, he is walking and fully recovered). Andrea had a stiff neck. Not too much to worry about, right? Right?

She went back to Pretoria to recuperate from the physical and mental stress of the crash, but her neck remained sore. Days later, she could not stand it anymore, and drove herself to hospital. Missus H accused her daughter of overreacting and would not take her to the hospital for medical care. So, Andrea drove herself. Yeah, there's a reason blood of the covenant is stronger than the water of the womb.

A medical exam was done, and… Panic stations! She had broken her neck. In particular, C2. Yep, the medical ones among you would know this is the 'hangman's fracture'. They told her that if she sneezed hard, she could have died. Fortunately, she did not have a propensity for hay fever… She spent months in an assortment of neck braces and traction, and had to undergo years of physiotherapy.

But as said, this is where the bough broke. Shortly afterwards, a myriad of medical conditions cumulated. PCOS. Adrenal insufficiency, which led to an Addisonian crisis which led to Cushing's syndrome. And due to her work: ganglions, carpal tunnel, and ulnar nerve entrapments. She had several surgeries on her hands and elbows to release nerves and repair damage. And let's not forget the neurological: Shortly after the accident, she was diagnosed with temporal lobe epilepsy. It is impossible to say if she sustained an injury which caused this condition (probably not), but I have to put it here for the sake of completion.

As a child, she only missed three days of school: when the family flew to Germany to bury her father. She was the picture of wellness. But she was not a very healthy grown-up. The childhood traumas and the adulthood illnesses turned her into a melancholic person. While she was diagnosed with clinical depression, she was not 'morose', merely one of those 'sad' people that others write love songs about. She was a lonely person, even in the company of others. Heck, some may say *especially* in the company of others.

2

Which is why she was just so damn inspiring! I've now given you the context of Andrea's sad life in an edited highlights (or is that lowlights?) reel. I could expand even more, but why jump the shark? I think I have made the point.

Despite Andrea's myriad of things to complain about, she hardly ever did. Wherever she went, she left a mark. She impressed the pants off colleagues, clients, friends. Friends of friends.

The second time I ever saw Andrea was at a party a week or so after I showed her my ass at the Dros. I was with a bunch of mates and their mates at a house party, getting drunk on cheap beer and expensive champagne. It was great fun, and maybe it was Dutch Courage, but I messaged her and asked what she was doing. When she replied 'not much', I invited her over. The more the merrier, right? She arrived, this girl whom I'd met face-to-face only once, and I introduced her to my pals. She had them eating out of her hand in half-an-hour flat. "Gerry, I don't know where you found her, but she's a keeper!"

But yeah, your pals *should* tell you that, right? It's hardly an unbiased opinion. A neutral party needs to make that proclamation for it to have any validity. So, how about, I don't know, the President of the country?

Long story as short as possible: Andrea graduated in business science, with an honours in finance and a minor in accounting. She just fucking loved numbers. She once said she loves numbers because numbers never lie. She also loved puzzles. She loved 'figuring things out', and I'm convinced that should she have cared to learn the games, she would have made one hell of a poker and chess player. Instead of applying her mathematical and problem-solving skills to a deck of cards, she applied it to her work, where she excelled. So much so that she ended up consulting for a law firm who, in turn, consulted to government. The Thabo Mbeki government, to be specific. The First Lady at the time, Mma Zanele Mbeki, convened an organisation, 'South African Women in Dialogue', an organisation that specifically looks at women's issues in South Africa, and within *SAWID*, an offshoot, 'Young South African Women in Dialogue', to deal with intergenerational issues. Word about Andrea's insight, competence, and esteem got around, to the extent that Mma Mbeki herself invited Andrea to join her organisation. And even Thabo commented on what an exceptional woman she is. You know what, Prez, as unexpected as it may be, we actually agree on something!

And to prove her professional esteem even more: a year or three after she started her own business, she was just too swamped to do everything herself. She needed help. She convinced Kerron, her old boss, to resign from the global conglomerate he was working for and join her company as a director. That's how you do it: resign, start your own business, and then get the guy you worked for to come work for you. Wherever she went, she inspired, commanded respect, and in my case: awe. I still cannot fathom the depth and capacity of this woman. One of life's greater mysteries is how I just got so damn lucky. An even greater mystery is how she loved an underachieving schmuck like me. She's a number's person, I'm mathematically illiterate. She's logical and analytical, I'm creative and a dreamer. She is structured, I'm impulsive. She's administratively competent, I write notes on Post-Its never to be seen by human eyes again. She's driven and I'm lazy. She makes a mean bolognaise and I chow all of it. But our value systems were in sync. I can speak about how we like the same type of TV shows and movies, how we enjoy cooking, and how we like '80s music. But those are superficial things. On a much deeper level, we agreed on how life should be lived, even if 'could' was often times a bridge too far. We both strived for (if never achieved) an elegant simplicity in life, living simply for the sake of living beautifully. I have come to learn there is actually a word for this quality of 'elegant simplicity': 'shibumi'. While I have made my peace with the fact that I'll never discover the illusive quality of 'shibumi', I'll keep on trying. It seems a worthy ideal.

The point is that Andrea and I were both complimentary *and* supplementary to each other. A Yin and a Yang making a whole greater than the sum of its parts. She was my greatest champion and my fiercest critic. She kicked my ass when it needed kicking. She tended my wounds when they needed soothing.

I loved the man I became during our relationship.

It was awesome having someone to live for.

3

All of us carry with us remnants of our childhood. Whether it be the traumatic issues we speak to our psychologists about, or a love for cheap ghastly overly sweet chocolates, some things from our childhood will never go away. And now I'm to invoke the ire of my late wife by telling you about the childish remnants she brought with her, and in particular, the case of one Felicity Watermeyer. If I'm lucky, Andrea will come haunt me tonight for what I'm about to write. Sorry, Sweetie.

Andrea was 160 cm tall, and every inch a woman, but she was never a girly-girl. She wasn't into pink and barbie dolls and makeup and frilly and fancy clothes. I think in the fifteen years we were together, I saw her in make-up less than two dozen times. She was more than happy to step out into the world without lippy — I'm sure several of you ladies cringe at merely reading this.

But Andrea's girly thing: cows. And sheep. Especially white cows with black spots on them. Not real ones, mind you, but stuffed ones. Over the years, she had literally collected hundreds of stuffed cows and sheep, each of them with their own name, each of them with their own made-up backstory. There's Clyde, who she got in Clyde, Scotland, there's Charles, so named because of his big ears. There are two Russells, a Lambert, a Shirley, and a host of others. She called them 'The Children' and they were all displayed on a shelf. All? Not quite. We could not fit all the children on a shelf. Some were obviously more special than others, and those of prominence got the top shelf. King of the Hill naturally was Shaun, as in Shaun the Sheep from the eponymous Aardman Animations. I think she had three or four of him. And along with that, cow-spot *anything*. If something had cow-spots on them, she went moggy. This elegant, graceful, and sophisticated woman had magnetic cow-spots for her refrigerator! Naturally, this indicated her love for Gary Larson's *The Far Side*, not just for the intellectual if obscure humour, but because Mr Larson featured cows more often than not in his strips. Several 'Cow Side' cartoons were clipped from newspapers and magazines and held onto the fridge with cow-themed magnets.

Which brings me to her pyjamas. Elegant, graceful, sophisticated.

Erm...

She loved her jammies. Fluffy jammies with cartoons on them, accompanied by bunny slippers. The peak of which was — duh! — the cow-spot set(s). White pj's with black cow-spots dubbed... 'The Moo-suit'.

(Segue: along with cricket, Andrea was also a huge football fan, a love I could not quite cultivate. Her teams were Arsenal and Germany. Many a night we would be in front of the telly, with her yelling in frustration at Arsenal, and me watching bemusedly at my wife going through alternating stages of apoplexy and bliss in the space of ninety minutes. Her favourite player would, of course, hail from where the love for club and country intersected: Mesut Özil, the Arsenal and German midfielder. Or, as she called him: *Moo-suit* Özil. Mr Özil, should you ever hear this: Andrea referring to you as 'Moo-suit' was the greatest honour she could bestow upon you.)

The moo-suit was Andrea's natural habitat, and she went through several sets in our relationship. I wonder what all her high-end clients would think if they had seen what I saw: this incredibly educated and experienced and competent consultant doing high-level corporate and/or governmental work: not in a high-powered business suit sitting in a luxurious corporate office, but sitting behind her laptop in her home office, wearing cow-spot pyjamas, surrounded by several cows and sheep with cricket on the telly. Usually drinking tea from a bovine or ovine mug.

It was actually hilarious, and it made shopping for Christmas and birthday presents a breeze.

Which brings me to the most important 'person' in Andrea's life: Felicity Watermeyer.

I found 'Licity one day circa 2008. She was sitting on a shelf in a discount homeware store, and the moment I saw her, I just knew this was Andrea's best friend. I picked her up from the shelf and poked Felicity's head around the corner where Andrea was browsing for sheets.

"'Allo!"

Andrea looked round and rolled with it. "Well, hello. Who are you?"

I made the name up on the spot. "I'm Felicity Watermeyer," Felicity said. "This shop sucks. I'm coming home with you."

The conversation fades at this point, but this is how a generic, off-an-assembly-line, toy hippopotamus entered her — our — lives. She is now a Stuffed Petite Baby Hippo, and she lives in the living room in a custom-made hammock we made. Along with Felicity, is her 'posse': Russell (a walrus. As in 'Wal*rus*', get it?), Klaus (a cow), Bastian (A pig, named after Bastian Schweinsteiger), Thomas (A really tiny hippo, a Zen master, and the ultimate embodiment of 'shibumi' — his perch is on top of Felicity's hat), and Ozzy (A reindeer, named after the Oseberg Viking ship at the Oslo Viking Museum where we procured him.)

So began arguably the strangest aspect of 'Little Andrea': her relationship with this Stuffed Petite Baby Hippo named 'Licity. I would use Felicity as a ventriloquist would use a dummy, and Andrea would have entire conversations with her, and we'd piss ourselves laughing at 'Felicity's' antics. We constructed a whole backstory and personality for her, and it turns out Felicity loves cricket too, and adores MS Dhoni. We would dress Felicity up in a superhero cape made from the South African flag, and put a yellow mask on her to hide her true identity, and take her to the cricket as a mascot named 'Velocity'. We always left the telly on the cricket channel so Felicity could watch, even if we did not. Andrea would get very grumpy with me if I left the telly on a channel other than cricket, because Felicity would want to watch. (Felicity had a super-power, you see, where she could watch cricket even if the TV was off – Pronutro vision.) Every year on Andrea's birthday, 'Felicity' would buy her a gift and a birthday card, which I would write using a crayon in my left hand. I even cobbled up stories we would amuse ourselves with: '*Prim and Felicity go to the cricket*'. '*Prim and Felicity make pancakes*'. 'Curious George' type stories where a little girl seen only from the knees down and her friend, a Hobbes-esque hippo of questionable reality, would get into all kinds of adventures and mischief. Often, Felicity would muck up.

"Oh fuck," said Felicity, having dropped an egg on the floor.

"Felicity," Prim yelled out. "Language!"

"That's right. I *am* using language."

You see how absurd this could go? We often spoke about publishing those stories, even setting up an Instagram account for Felicity, but at the end of the day, it was the stuff Andrea and I shared, and it was special to us.

When Andrea heard that she was terminal, she told Felicity to take care of me. I still leave the telly on the cricket channel, even if I'm not watching. I still have conversations with her, and *through* her. Felicity is my gateway to the Andrea I know and loved: a mass-produced polyester children's toy which evolved into something 'real' and developed more personality than most people I know. When my brother and father come to visit, they say hello to Felicity. They know.

This was the contradiction of my wife. Refined and supremely intelligent and rational, with scary qualifications doing high level consulting work. With a love for cows, sheep, and a Stuffed Petite Baby Hippo named Felicity.

When Andrea went to chemo, Felicity went along (Felicity even had her own covid mask!) to comfort her. And when Andrea died, Felicity was right there on the bed with her. It could not have been any other way.

Should the house burn down, I'd grab Felicity first.

Felicity Watermeyer

Chapter 4 – Edited Highlights

1

There's more than enough really heavy shit in the chapters ahead. So, let's have a bit of fun, shall we?

I'm the only guy I know who got Rick-Rolled in real life. You know what Rick-Rolling is, don't you? It's an internet bait-and-switch prank where you lure someone to a very interesting and/or funny video clip, only for Rick Astley's seminal song, *Never Gonna Give You Up*, to start playing. I guess it could be mildly funny if you are of the lowbrow type.

But it's downright hilarious when it happens in the flesh.

Andrea had a fetish for '80s music the way I have a fetish for chicken wings and beer. And who can blame her, really? I mean, the '80s were bloody awesome! It was superior to everything ever, before, or since, in every conceivable way. Well, apart from the fashion, the hair, the makeup, and the human rights violations, that is. But everything else was just *awesome*. In my own life I can look back at 1985 and declare it as the singular best year ever for music. Ah, they don't make them like that no more!

In the summer of 2012, Andrea's musical wet dream presented itself: an eighties revival concert, right here on home soil in South Africa, in her hometown of Pretoria. All the big stars of our late childhood and early teenage were to perform live on stage. Not Madonna-big or Eurythmics-big, but, well, big! Nik Kershaw! Tony Hadley of Spandau Ballet! The Human League! And... my own musical wet dream: one Ms Belinda Carlisle. I mean, let's face it, there was no heterosexual male over the age of six alive who did not have a crush on Belinda Carlisle. I'd leave a light on for her any day of the week, and twice on a Sunday.

We went the whole hog! She dressed up in day-glo neon, replete with side-pony and fishnet fingerless gloves. I got a wig and a white George Michael *Choose Life* T-shirt. I still have it. And Andrea made sure the life we chose was great with Golden Circle tickets. Sunshine! Beer! Live '80s Music! And my woman looking super cute in her neons and side-pony…

Late afternoon the MC comes on stage and introduces the first act: Leee John! (Yes, that is Leee with 3 e's — Google it if you do not believe me.) And Gerry gets into the groove of it. Then it's Nik Kershaw, who sang that he won't let the sun go down on him exactly as the sun went down, which was kinda poetic. And then it was ABC's Martin Fry who sang about what he hears when Smoky Sings. And then… and then… Hold my beer! Belinda Carlisle is live on stage, every bit as beautiful as she was in my early teenage fantasies. Yes, heaven is indeed a place on earth. Sorry, I need a moment.

And then it happens. In all his gloried aging-in-reverse splendour and his ubiquitous suit, looking for all the world like Ed Sheeran's college-educated brother, comes the man himself. Mister Rick Astley: who had my wife swooning and throwing panties. Yes, he did sing that he was never going to give her up or let her down, and there I was, grinning like the village idiot because of it. He even winked at her when she yelled at him: "I love you, Rick!"

He replied: "Well, don't just scream at me, love!"

Gotta love it.

After my childhood in the glory days of the '80s, came my late teenage years, and I made the jump from pop to alternative rock. My bands (and therefore T-shirts): New Model Army. Nick Cave and the Bad Seeds. Sisters of Mercy. The Mission. You know, *serious* music. Not this upbeat preppy vapid pop bullshit. What's next? Modern-fucking-Talking? My idea of 'vapid' is Violent Femmes, and that's how low I'll go.

Yet I loved every minute of it!

You get into the vibe, you go with the flow, you go down memory lane when life was different. Not necessarily better or simpler, but different. But most of all, I loved — and still love — how Andrea just exploded into joy. I watched her instead of watching the stage. If she only had that level of happiness more often.

And I can say I got Rick-Rolled in real life, and I'm proud of it!

2

More Music!

Remember I said Andrea and I had similar value systems? This also applied to our theory of music concerts. You have two options: either you are right up front, front-row-centre getting your vital organs squashed against the crowd-control barrier, or you go right up to the back of the house nosebleed seats. Option one puts you right there with the person you paid a fortune to see, up close and personal. And if you are lucky, even some interaction. (This is how Michael Hutchence from *INXS* kissed me, but that is another story entirely).

Option two has you comfortable, able to see the entire spectacle, and have easy access to beer and bathrooms. This is how we went to watch U2 and Bruce Springsteen. Good thing too. Anyone who has ever been to a Springsteen show knows the geriatric fart can rock people half his age under the table, and he carried on for an excess of three hours. Glorious. Exhausting. I cannot imagine being up against the rails. One would pee blood for a week after such a marathon. And thusly, another of Andrea's favourite musicians comes to town, Mister William Martin Joel. Now, I've a liking for Billy myself, and I'd consider *Piano Man* one of the finest songs ever written; makes my personal top-20 any day. And *We Didn't Start the Fire* is a cracking tune. But I'm not going to go gaga over Billy Joel. He's okay and all, but he falls into the cheap-seats category quite easily. Andrea, however, disagrees. She has all his *Best of* CDs, as well as a myriad of others. She really digs Billy Joel, and she wants to be up front. Well, since she's buying the tickets, why the hell not, right? So, we rock up (South African for 'arrive') at the stadium early, secure our front-row-centre places, and wait. Eventually, up comes Billy Joel, looking for all the world like my uncle Koos. And it's great! With a few notable exceptions, Billy is not really a rocker, you know. He is more of a balladeer, and I can honestly appreciate his musical capacities. He has very complex songs; the antithesis of three-chord rock. One of these complex songs is of course the very intricate and beautiful and haunting *She's Always A Woman*. Which just happens the be the fourteenth song performed on the night (thanks, setlist.fm). At this moment, I decide to hell with Billy Joel, and I turn to Andrea. I ask her if I may have this dance. And so we did. We did a slow, clumsy and crowded slow-dance up against the barrier to Billy Joel himself serenading us. At the end of the song, Billy looked at us, made eye contact, smiled, and bowed his head in acknowledgment.

It was awesome.

And true. Because Andrea will always be a woman to me.

That's why I married her.

3

Ah, language. Or more accurately, vocabulary. As these things happen to those who spend large amounts of time together, sharing beds, meals, and bodily fluids, we developed a language of our own. It became such a weird little secret language which we took for granted in such a way that we'd converse with other people in it, and they'd look at us as if we were nuts. Which we were, of course.

A common, and understandable, one is 'I'm coming round the mountain' when one of us were on the way home, and about ten minutes out. "Hi Sweetie, I'm coming round the mountain." Cool, it meant I would be home shortly. Yawn.

But then there was 'Zim,' and it was posed as a question: "Zim?"

This one is Andrea's doing, and I nearly dumped her on the spot for it. I was lounging, staring off into space, getting planning permission for castles in the air, and she went "Zim?"

Huh?

"You look lost in thought," she said. "I'd offer you a penny for your thoughts, but your thoughts are not worth that much. I can offer you one Zimbabwean cent." Which was worth about $0.00002.

'Zim' became the de facto verbiage for "what are you thinking about?"

I'm still thinking about how useless she thought my thoughts were.

Humpf.

A funnier one was our invention of a fictional punk-ska band named the Taxidermy Ducks. I cannot quite remember the context, but there was a guy being interviewed on TV, and in the background: a green-head mallard duck, stuffed and on display. "Why does [person] have a taxidermy duck?"

We both found it hilarious, and I said that's a great name for a punk band, and so the Taxidermy Ducks were born. The very next day, right behind Andrea's car's rear wheel, was an old discarded electrical plug, rusted to heck and gone. How it got there, nobody knows, but had we reversed over it, we would have written off a tire. "Look! We've got a rusty plug here…" and so 'Rusty Plug' became the lead singer of our imaginary band. For the rest of all eternity, whenever something funny was being said or overheard, or if something could be taken out of context to mean something different, it became a Taxidermy Ducks song. Like when I overheard her on the phone to a client: "…we need to get to quantifying uncertainty." I was like "what the hell is quantifying uncertainty?" and she explained it is a term used in risk management. But 'Quantifying Uncertainty' became the first Taxidermy Ducks album to have a cover designed, printed, and stuck up on the fridge. It still amazes me to think how many people thought it was real. And the odd looks we received when, in the middle of conversations, either of us would interject with, "Wow, there's a Taxidermy Ducks song for you" when someone said something that sounded completely corny when taken out of context. I wish I kept a list of all the 'songs' and 'albums' we came up with. It could have been funny. Then again, maybe not. Just arbitrarily obscure.

'Arbitrarily obscure'? Hey, there's a Taxidermy Ducks song for you!

Then there is 'Vexicle'.

Vexicle? Read it as if you are pronouncing 'Mexico' in Spanish. It's not Mec-si-co, it is Me-hee-co. Ve-hee-cul. This came because of a police roadblock, and I made fun of my fellow Afrikaners, overdoing the stereotypical dumbed-down Afrikaans accent so prevalent in those who cannot quite speak English: "Please sir, would you step out of your ve-hee-cul." We killed ourselves laughing in that rare but delightful crazy feeding-on-itself hilarity that ensued, repeating the word 'vexicle' to each other and busting a gut, nearly crashing our own vexicle into a lamp post in the process. Okay, funny-ish. Then one day I had a hiccough, and Andrea asked a philosophical question: "When someone sneezes, you say 'bless you'. What do you say when someone hiccoughs?" I answered deadpan: "Vexicle." From that moment on, whenever one of us had a hiccough, we would respond with 'vexicle'. Eventually, we took it for granted, but gained us the oddest 'are you quite mad' looks from others who did know the private lingo.

We have this green metal jar opener, which became simply 'the green thing'. "Pass me the green thing" meant "Excuse me, would you mind getting the jar opener for me." We were at a friend's house one day and they had the exact jar opener. But with one tiny difference: "Hey, Sweetie, look at this! Their green thing is blue!"

'Man-Panties' became the term for my Jockeys. Which in turn led to 'woman-man-panties' for her undies.

We bought a Lazy Susan for our dining room table. Andrea could not quite find the word for 'Lazy Susan', and she gestured frantically in frustration: "You know, that thing that goes around, the... the... the turn bastard!" So now the Lazy Susan is known as 'the turn bastard'. Hey, I never said it had to make sense!

'To part'. A portmanteau of 'falling to pieces' and 'falling apart' and came as an unintentionally funny moment during a time of emotional distress.

Andrea was weepy and wanted to say she was 'falling apart' or 'falling to pieces' and she said, "I'm falling to part." She saw the funny side, and we laughed about that one. 'To part' entered the household lexicon and stayed with such permanence that I often use it in conversation and in my writing. An editor once pinged me on a 'to part' in a manuscript, and for a minute I was genuinely baffled as to what was wrong with it. We had a similar problem with 'shortly' and 'forthwith' which became 'shortwith'.

Even food! Entire meals had one-word descriptions. Like 'boob-soup', but that's a story for later. 'Cousin Boneless' was our name for one of my specialty boneless chicken meals. Parmesan cheese became known as pasta sugar. Chili sauce was referred to as 'paint stripper'. Microwave meals? 'Buzz-pings'. 'Galli-lunch' was a combination of 'gallivant' and 'lunch'. "Sweetie, we had cousin boneless last night, I'm a bit chickened out, and not in the mood for a buzz-ping. What do you say we go gallilunch? I can do with some paint stripper prawns." And she'd order a bowl of spaghetti and ask the confused waiter for extra pasta sugar.

And then there was the word 'wanker'. For legal reasons, I shall not name the person this term refers to, but a prominent public figure of particular distaste to both Andrea and I had the surname of Smith. He became known as Wankersmith, later abbreviated to just 'Wanker'. Let it be known that whenever we saw someone with the name 'Smith' we automatically read it and said it as 'Wanker'. We never stepped in the shit with this one, but we had several near misses. Sometimes I wonder how the hell we communicated with the outside world at all. And if I think that I must navigate the rest of my life without 'our' special language, it makes me want to fall to part.

4

I am racking my brain for more good stories. Sadly, not many are forthcoming. Or, at least, not many I can tell. A few more cool stories will rear their giggly heads later, but nothing worthy of its own subchapter. Oh, I can tell you about that time we got invited to a friend of a friend for a party, and we went to, erm, 'initiate', the host's laundry room. I can tell you about a sunny Christmas day when we were at my uncle Koos' house (who looks uncannily like Billy Joel. My uncle, not the house). With the entire family present, we bonked in the pool while my father kept watch to make sure nobody interrupted us. (My father is really cool. 72 years old, drinks like an automatic pool cleaner, smokes like a diesel pick-up with worn piston rings, has a mind as open as a barn door and as filthy as a pigsty. I love the old man). I can tell you how I spanked Andrea — to great approval of the bar patrons — with a wooden shooter-tray at the Berlin Pub in Ruimsig. Is it my fault that the shooter tray looked like a good, solid, bum-paddle? But I cannot tell you hundreds of other things because they are so minor, so trivial, that only the two of us would ever get it.

And that is a *good* thing. Because most of the memories that made me giggle and smile are strange and personal things that would require tons of backstory to explain. The adventures we had, for the most part, were small and personal victories that would have us giggling for days, and the rest of the world would wonder just what was so damn funny about it. Sometimes, these adventures and moments should be personal, a special unspoken and undefined connection between two people that *should not* be translatable to the outside world. That is what makes a relationship unique. If anyone could understand the secret language of longtime partners, then that relationship loses just a smidgen of that which makes it special.

But as said, just because I can't think of many more, does not mean there aren't any more. Read on.

5

Food!

Yup, it's my favourite dish. In that regard, I have a shrine dedicated to Jughead Jones. (The happy-go-lucky burger-enthusiast of the comic books, not of the mopey emo biker-kid of the *Riverdale* series. Which is brilliant, by the way.) Anyone with that commitment to food is worthy of respect. To be honest, I've never met a carbohydrate I did not like. Especially if said carb comes in the form of an amber liquid fortified with malt and hops. But a man needs protein as well, and while I love my steaks (well-aged, well-hung, and as rare as an honest politician), there is one thing I love even more than a hunk of dead cow, and that is crustaceans. I think I may have had enough prawns once in my life, but I cannot be sure. Is it my all-time favourite thing to eat? Nope. That honour belongs to the German delicacy known as 'mett', but more on that later. Point being that if you give me a mountain of prawns with a hunk of fresh bread, I'll happily eat myself comatose.

Andrea is the same.

Except for one small thing: while refined and of superior taste, and would never say no to a prawn, she would always prefer lobster. But as anyone knows, a lobster is not exactly the cheapest meal one can have, so one needs to compromise. And in Andrea's language, that means a langoustine. And let's be honest, it's a damn fine piece of *nephropidae* to use as pre-nap Sunday lunch!

Yes, I know I said Andrea was Jewish, but she wasn't orthodox. Thank heavens. Which meant we could have bacon and cheese on our hamburgers.

But I digress.

January 13th is our date-aversary, the day we made it official and became an item. Always looking for an excuse to indulge in good grub, it's obvious that to celebrate another year where we did not kill each other, we would have an expansive — and expensive — meal. In 2012, that meal was to be a pot full of langoustines. What could be better, right? Seafood, champagne, and a hot summer Friday night.

It was our six-year anniversary.

And again, like that Friday night six years before, I was shitting myself. You know what's coming, don't you?

I was pooping my man-panties for several reasons. The first is that Andrea was a *Thoroughly Modern Millie*. Women's lib, feminist, does not believe in any of the saccharine-sweet bullshit of the trivialities of 'getting married'. "I love you, why the hell do you want to get a government involved?" was her opinion on the sacrosanct act of marriage. Secondly, I was as broke as an earthworm, and had no ring to offer her. And thirdly, if she said no, I'd be devastated. One just does not recover from a blow like that.

Man, you shoulda seen it!

Imagine this perfect dinner table, set for two: Fine China crockery, the good silverware. Crisp white linen napkins in hand-turned hardwood rings, fresh flowers on the table, candlelight. I showered and shaved, dressed up nicely, and Andrea wore this stunning emerald-coloured pleated dress (she always looked good in jewel colours) and it was one of the dozen times I saw her with make-up on. I got a nice expensive bottle of red wine and by now you know I'm talking shit, don't you?

We were outside at the patio table. I was in a stretched-out T-shirt and cut-off denim shorts (my summertime uniform), probably three days overdue for a shave. She was barefoot in cow-spot (of course) pyjama bottoms and a boob-tube. The only thing I'm not talking crap about is the candlelight, we had a citronella candle to keep the mozzies at bay.

But the food? Oh yeah! Andrea was a genius with langoustines. Boiled in salt water — that's all, but timing is *everything* — and served with a home-made aioli (I am the mayonnaise king, but that's irrelevant in this tale) and fresh bread. A bottle of champagne. Probably the real stuff. Possibly Veuve Clicquot.

We tuck into dinner, but I'm only pretending to enjoy it because there is this burning ball of nervous energy in my stomach. And so, I start prepping. Testing the waters. What the legal guys would call 'leading the witness'. Ask all the right questions in all the right ways to gauge what I think her reaction to be.

And then I found the courage to do it. I threw caution to the wind, popped down on bended knee because my knees pop when they bend, and popped the question.

Her reaction? "Are you serious?"

I assured her I was.

She said yes. She did not even hesitate. She said yes right off the bat. Boy, did we cry! And then she crapped on me: "why did you wait six bloody years before you asked, you silly, silly man!"

"For the simple reason I was scared you'd say no."

Now, of course, one needs a ring! And Andrea being Andrea, she already knew exactly what she wanted. Good thing I did not have money for a ring, she would have hated whatever I came up with. And, lucky me, she already had the diamond. It was from her mother's engagement ring, and she liked the idea of the heirloom. Frankly, so did my bank balance. She Googled and downloaded and drew and sketched until she had the exact ring she wanted in the exact setting. Now all I needed to do was find a way to pay for it. I shit thee not: I saved up for a full year before I could afford the ring, and had it custom made. On our seventh anniversary a year later, I finally presented her with the 'proper' ring.

Proper?

Because she did wear a temporary engagement ring. A toy. A piece of yellow see-though plastic with red hearts embedded in it. If memory serves, it came from a Christmas cracker. She wore that plastic ring every day for a year until my measly income could provide the ring. And she wore it with pride.

But now that we're engaged, we need to talk wedding bells, don't we?

This, Gentle Readers, is the chapter I've been looking forward to for some time. Grab a beer, this is gonna be good!

Puppies!
Laszlo & Gizi - 30 July 2011

Chapter 5 - Cold Feet.

1

As previously mentioned, apart from the unmentionable brothers, Andrea had no family in South Africa. A handful of cool cousins in Germany, but nobody here.

Me, on the other hand, if I take my entire family: uncles, aunts, cousins, nephews, nieces, the whole caboodle, we'd be, like, nine people.

Add our friends to that, and we'd have less than two dozen people on our wedding guest list.

Which begs the question, why go through all the expense of a traditional wedding? We are not conventional people, and we should therefore not have a conventional wedding. So instead of me feeling uncomfortable in a suit (the last time I wore a tie was in 1994) and Andrea spending a crapload of money on a wedding dress only to be worn once — and then blow the wad on a bar bill — why not do something exceptional with just the two of us?

We kicked some ideas around and decided on the ridiculous: We're going to Vegas, baby! What could be cooler than getting married in Las Vegas by an Elvis impersonator?

As it turns out…

I was doom-scrolling Facebook — as one does — when I saw an incredible photograph. A photo of a glass-roofed igloo-shaped hotel room, nestled in a snow-covered forest. Ideal for star-gazing. Remember I told you Andrea was an amateur astronomer? I thought she would love this!

Boy, was I right, or was I right? The Queen of Google quickly did her magic, and she found the source of the image: the Kakslauttanen Arctic Resort in Finland. Go look it up. Who would *not* want to go there?

The idea was mooted to have a winter wonderland wedding. It may be passé in Europe or North America, but as a child of Africa, snow is as alien to me as a cricket game is to a native New Yorker. I'm no great fan of the cold — I'm the type to pull on a jumper when it hits 24 degrees Celsius — but the thought of having an icy wonderland wedding? Oh, hell yes! Sign me up!

2

Sometime in 2013, I was in my office, working. Or maybe just pretending to. Probably doom-scrolling.

Andrea came walking in and said one word to me.

"Svalbard."

My reaction: "Sorry, say what?"

"Svalbard."

"What do you mean, small bard?"

"No, you idiot, Svalbard. Ess-vee-aye-ell-bee-aye-are-dee."

"Who or what is a Svalbard?"

"It's where we're going to get married."

And thus sprach Zarandrea.

And boy, what a decision it turned out to be!

3

"It's an island archipelago north of Norway," she continued.

"Wait, what, you mean there's something *north* of Norway? Isn't Norway as about as north as one can go before you hit Canada on the other side?"

"It's the world's northernmost landmass," she continued. "It's deep in the arctic circle. The world's northernmost town is there. All the polar explorers set off from there when they go to the pole."

Well, so far, she wasn't really selling me on the idea. "So, why are we getting married there now? I thought we were getting married in Finland?"

"We were, but I changed my mind." She's a woman. It's her prerogative. There's a story about a bunch of friends who got together for a weekend. On the Saturday night, the men decided to stay awake and make it their mission to figure out women. Several dozen beers later, as the dawn broke, they finally got it. They figured out women! All that needed to be done now was to triumphantly announce their breakthrough to the first woman they come across. When the first wife stepped out bleary-eyed from the bedroom, she met the drunk and over-tired but victorious men, who declared to her: "Ha! Last night we stayed up, and we figured out women!" to which she replied, "yeah, you may have, but we changed our minds."

Us guys, we just cannot win against the wiles of the women. Best to submit. Remember that, my fellow brethren. Path of least resistance brings years of joy.

Anyway, to continue the story. "In March 2015, there will be a total solar eclipse over the island. What would you say to getting married under a solar eclipse?"

SOLD!

Damn, I'm getting goosies just writing this!

I'll not lie and tell you it was easy: the logistics were enormous. And if you think the logistics were enormous, you should've seen the cost! Holy mother of Elvis Presley the king of Rock, it was expensive! That traditional wedding we skipped on? We could've had like seven of them and still have money left over for pinball games. But who cares!

For the next two-odd years, this was all we could think about. Operation Svalbard. Every spare cent scrimped and saved. Clothes sourced from literally all over the globe. I've heard the north pole is quite chilly, and my Woolworths tracksuit pants may not quite cut it. Jokes aside, the balmy tip of Africa is woefully under-equipped to deal with arctic conditions. And why should it? But we still needed our kit. Andrea found us merino wool under-layers and imported them from New Zealand. Jerseys from England. Gloves from Canada. All delivered to her cousin's house in Germany, where we would set up base camp. The plan was to fly to Germany and spend two weeks there, living in the comfort of Andrea's family home. Then we'd go from there to Oslo, and then from Oslo up to Longyearbyen, the town we'd be visiting. On the way back, we'd do Oslo again, and then onto Prague for a week for our honeymoon, back to Cologne for three days to recover, and then a trek home. We'd be gone for a month. I've never been to Europe, and now, on my first go, I'm going for a whole bloody month! It's not bad. Not my record, though. I mean, when I went to America in 2002 I spent three months there, so a month-long trip is a distant second, really. Naturally, protracted overseas visits are dead easy when you have free accommodation and the only expense is beer. But we cannot forget about the purpose of our trip now, can we? To get married! And so Andrea got in contact with the priest of the multi-denominational church on the island — Leif Helgesen — and told him our plan. Leif was just too delighted to marry us. Wow! Things were falling into place like a pro-level Tetris game.

Slowly, we built things up, one by one. A bit of money comes in, we'd pay for our Dusseldorf-Oslo flight. A bit more money comes in, we'd pay for the hotel in Prague. I can tell you, we made it by the skin of our teeth. And if you've seen my teeth, you know it ain't much. But even the spiralling cost could not keep our spirits down. Because Svalbard — the island — and Longyearbyen — the town — does not look like what you think it looks like. My first flashes of imagination when Andrea said "arctic circle" was the world's easiest landscape painting: flat featureless white ground to the horizon, grey skies above.

Erm, no.

Dramatic rocky peaks stand guard across a fjord, on the shores of which is nestled a hamlet of brightly coloured homes. It's an arctic desert, and while there are dramatic snowstorms, precipitation and cloud cover is rare, which means dazzling blue skies and piercing sunlight which glistens on the snow and ice. No featureless flat land, no grey skies, but a thrilling landscape few are lucky enough to ever see. The daily webcams and weather updates and internet searches had our happiness levels redlining. It was bloody wonderful. Day by day, payment by payment, woollen jersey by woollen jersey, the dream was turning into a reality.

I think I may have blown a fuse from pure delight when all the accommodation was booked and paid for, and Andrea came with the news: she had just booked our flight tickets.

It was happening.

4

Naturally, there were obstacles. The first of which is that I needed a bloody wedding ring. And this is a mini-adventure that needs its own sub-chapter.

Those of you paying attention may have noticed I'm not a man of conventional tastes. Or, put another way: I'm as kinky as a bowl of Ramen. I make no bones about this. I'm not ashamed of it, and I've been out as a connoisseur of BDSM for two decades. Because the universe has a sense of humour, I got myself a girl who is as vanilla as ice cream. To be sure, Andrea tried. I'll give her that. She honestly tried. But she never quite 'got' it. She would humour me, but those of you who are into the restrictive arts would know that 'humouring' is not the same as 'sharing'. Which meant my kink life was confined to friends, photoshoots, and friends in photoshoots. Because I'm a man of such exquisite taste and refinement…okay, because I'm such a kinky bastard, my mind went spinning in all kinds of interesting ways when I discovered the Cartier

Love Bracelet. For the uninitiated: Cartier makes a bracelet that splits apart, using a screwdriver to secure the two halves together. The idea is the one partner screws the bracelet on the other, which means the 'bound' partner cannot remove the bracelet. I simply loved the idea of this. I remember seeing the advertisement for it in on the internet and thinking 'that would be my ultimate'. In my mind, nothing melded the concepts of 'kinky as fuck' and 'so amazingly loved' as that bracelet does. I've never seen one in real life. Cartier belonged in Paris, New York, Milan. Not in the western 'burbs of a mining town in the armpit of Africa.

In 2002, I had the privilege — or sheer dumb luck — to end up in Los Angeles on a summer's day. I was dressed like a homeless man. Cut-off denim shorts, over-sized T-shirt, hand-grown sandals. Long hair from when I still thought a ponytail on a man was cool. Let's just say I was nobody's idea of exquisite taste and refinement. People walked past me and tossed me a dime. Anyway, there I was, walking down Rodeo Drive, and there it was: a Cartier Boutique! (Insert Jesus rays breaking through the clouds and angels going 'haaahhh' here.) I just had to go in. I had to see this famous — and kinky — piece of jewellery in real life.

But I looked like a bum.

I chanced it anyway, and they opened the door for me, called me 'sir'. I told them straight off the bat that I'm not here to buy anything. Way too skint for that. But I'd love to see the Love Bracelet. And show me they did. Seeing that piece of hellishly expensive gold had my head swimming and my heart making odd gallops the way it did when I went to buy my first set of handcuffs. The dream was real: it exists in real life, not just on the internet. I asked them why they were so nice to me. I'm certainly not dressed for the occasion, and I told them I'm not going to buy anything. Their response: "This is L.A. Billionaires dress like bums and bums dress like billionaires." They cannot judge the clientele on the clothes alone. And as for being skint? "Yes, but next year you may not be, and then we want you to remember our service." I found that a profoundly wise principle to do business by. I thanked them and left the store, my mouth dry and my heart...my heart longing for people I did not know and places I've never been to. I relayed the above story to Andrea, and told her it would be a great honour for me if, instead of a traditional gold-band wedding ring, I get her a Love Bracelet instead.

"You want to buy me a Cartier Love Bracelet instead of a wedding ring?"

"Well, erm, quite. Yes."

This is when she smiled so broadly, I thought the top of her head would pop off!

More than a decade since my impromptu solitary drop-in at the Cartier store in L.A., Andrea and I made a very deliberate visit to the Cartier boutique which had subsequently opened in Johannesburg. There, with the same trembling hands and a dry mouth — but fortunately much better dressed — I bought the most expensive thing I've ever bought: a commitment. That damn bracelet cost more than my car! Literally! And it took years to pay off. But damn, it was the fulfilment of a dream. The bracelet is around my wrist as I write this. It is a smidgen too small for me, so I do not wear it often. Also, there is something sacrilegious about screwing it on and off yourself. But at times, I need it. It's the most valuable tangible link I have to my late wife.

On the inside; an engraving: "Prim & Gerry - 20 March 2015-Forever".

'Forever' is a hope any newlywed couple has. Usually, one imagines 'forever' as growing old disgracefully together: ancient, bent-over and wrinkled couples over-burdened with happy memories and toothless smiles. Often, too often, 'forever' means 'Acrimonious comments fired across a desk at the divorce lawyers'.

'Forever' for Andrea and I meant five years and nine months.

5

To see the dream coming together over the course of years is an amazing, torturous thing. The slow creep of time combined with the slow accumulation of practical necessities culminating in a reality. There came a moment — 10 September 2014. Thanks, Facebook memories — when the caboodle graduated from 'in planning' to 'it's done'. We had everything sorted. Flights, accommodation, a willing priest, all the clothes we would need, all the photographic equipment I would need to take photos of an eclipse, passports, everything. Even a Love Bracelet. Now, I could apply for my visa. Andrea, being an EU and German citizen thanks to her father, obviously would not need one. Only I would. We download all the documents from the internet, fill them out, and drive to Pretoria. I hand in all my documentation at the German consulate, and…Visa denied. We stated we are going to stay at Cousin Norb's place while in Germany. This is a problem because they cannot verify it. Hotel bookings they can verify. They would need a letter.

You gotta be kidding me.

Admittedly, this threw me a bit. I'm nervous now. What if this does not pan out, you know? It would be a financial and emotional disaster! We drive back home and phone up Norbert. Poor guy, though great effort, had to write us a letter stating that he certifies I will stay with him during all the periods that we are not in hotels. Resubmit: denied. Because Norbert used 'Gerry' on the letter, and not what my passport says. Which are two 'orrid names nobody but a mother could love. Sorry Mister Pelser, we cannot give you a visa.

You really gotta be kidding me.

Now I'm not just nervous, but anxious. How many times can you apply for a visa, and now I have to re-apply with the same letter, but under a different name? Heck, I doubt I would give me a visa under such circumstances. Back on the phone: "Sorry Norb, rewrite the letter with my gov'mint names on it, please." The letter arrives the next day, we resubmit: denied. "How will you go from the Frankfurt Airport to the house in Cologne?"

"Norb will pick us up from the airport."

"We need documentation to prove that."

I mean, really. REALLY? You gotta be fucking kidding me.

Now I'm not just anxious, but downright petrified. I can see this dream slip through my hands. I'm just about crying on the way home from the consulate. This is where Andrea's big brain and problem-solving skills steps in.

"We should get married," she says on the way back from the consulate.

"Well, isn't that what we are trying to do," I ask.

"Nope," she says. "We should get married, here. At Home Affairs. That way you are the legal spouse of an EU citizen."

Brilliance.

Sheer fucking brilliance. That same afternoon, we arrive at Home Affairs to make an appointment. Now, you need to understand, this is a government department in a third world country. It is not pretty. Purely utilitarian. It is unfriendly and intimidating. Everybody is brusque, short-tempered, and act as if they are doing you a favour by being there. The already petrified me looks at this place and feels the last dregs of hope melt out through my shoe soles. After a lot of 'sorry, can you help me...' we eventually got in the right queue, and at the end of it, a tall Afrikaans man who looks as if he has been there since Colonel Sanders was merely a lance corporal.

We tell him we want to get married. He asks us for our ID documents, and he disappears without a word. Okay, what now? Where the hell? *What* the hell? We stare at each other, feeling as if we are in some surrealist practical joke, and about ten minutes later, he reappears.

"Second or third?" he asks.

Andrea and I look at each other. "Sorry, what?"

"Second or third?"

"Uh, this is our first marriage," we stammer in mutual confusion.

"Second or third of February?"

Phew!

The following is an illustration of how practical matters rules the world: We have a domestic helper that comes in on Tuesdays and Fridays, and the dogs just love her. He was asking us to choose between a Monday and a Tuesday. We selected the third for the simple reason we would have a day-long dog-sitter for Laszlo and Laika. Next: we need an ANC. That's an 'antenuptial contract', not the South African ruling party. Fortunately, we have lawyers for pals: husband-and-wife team, Lucio and Rina. Look, be fair, okay? Even lawyers need friends. We phone them up: "We're getting married next week, we need a contract, quick, how much?!"

Among the laughter and congratulations, they gave us the ANC as a wedding gift. I mean, how nice is that? A few days later, we were in their offices, and Andrea, with her big mind, discusses everything with the lawyers, and an hour later I'm given a document to sign. I have many talents, but understanding these things isn't one of them. "What am I signing here," I ask. They respond in legalese. Andrea hushes them with the wave of a hand. "It means no matter what happens, you will always be taken care of," she tells me.

I am not too proud to tell you I cried.

The following Tuesday, with a brand new haircut and brand new shirt and brand new bright blue Converse sneakers, I join hands with my fiancée for the last time to walk up the stairs of the Home Affairs offices in Roodepoort. She is resplendent in a bright blue dress, and I am so happy I cried. Again. This is really happening!

Lucio and Rina joined us as Best Man and Maid of Honour. We step up to the podium, and the Lance Corporal Sanders guy rattles off words so fast neither of us understood them, except that the answer was 'I do'. We sign the paperwork, and an hour later, for the first time, I take the hand of my brand new wife and walk down the steps of Home Affairs: officially a married man.

Big plans for the North Pole or not, I can end it right here.

I got the girl!

6

I got the visa!

It's absolutely ridiculous. I had previously applied for a bog-standard tourist visa, accompanied by reams of paperwork. Denied, denied, denied. This time I applied for a spousal visa. The only paperwork required was the wedding certificate. They called me two days later to collect my passport, a 5-year entry Schengen visa approved.

Fancy that, all we needed for a visa to get married, was to get married!

But now it was real. The last obstacle was out of the way. I had a bad photo of me pasted in my passport that said I could go to Europe, and it was a done deal. A few weeks later, on the 4th of March, my father drove us to the airport. We strapped ourselves to an Airbus, climbed 35,000 feet into the air, and headed for Frankfurt. This is where I discovered I've insane motion sickness. I puked for nine hours straight. I was willing to go to prison for the rest of my life, but I'm going to highjack this plane and land it and walk the rest of the way. Just. Get. Me. Off. This. Aircraft! When we stepped off the plane at Frankfurt, I felt like the Pope: I fell to the ground and kissed the floor! No worries. Only six more flights to take in the next four weeks. I'll tell you, by the time we came back from honeymoon after surviving a flight between Prague and Dusseldorf, which was the last flight to have taken off in what was the biggest storm-system in a decade, I was ready to walk back to Joburg if I could not become an illegal immigrant in Germany.

Since then, I've come to hate flying. Thank God I'm not a professional sportsman. But if anyone wants to make me an international best-selling writer, go right ahead, I'll suffer through the flights for the book signings and publicity gigs. Any New York agents around? You can find my contact details on my website, www.gerrypelser.com. I'll even take a mere business class ticket for that Oprah interview, don't even need to fork out the dough for first. Anyway, tired and puked-out, we finally arrive in Germany, and it's a two-hour drive from Frankfurt to the farming village where Norb and his family live. This drive revives me. We stop at a fuel station, and I have my first German meal: a pretzel and a can of Pepsi Max. With something in my stomach and caffeine in my blood, I'm feeling on top of the world. It's good to be me. Once we're home and our suitcases taken in, I see Andrea do something I've never seen her do before: she deflates like a slashed tire. I never knew how much tension she carried in her body until she let it go. She was happy. She was home. For the first time since I've met her, she was with her family in her familial home. In no time at all, she was dressed in...cow-spot pj's, huge mug of tea in her hand.

David Attenborough voice: Behold. Here we have a rare sighting of the lesser spotted Prim, Andreas Genii, in her natural environment. With no known natural predators, the Prim can walk around in what is the absolute opposite of camouflage, and has the luxury of sleeping all fucking day when her husband just wants to go explore.

Because that's what I wanted to do! I'm in Germany! I'm in Europe! I don't want to sit around a house and...I mean, I do that at home anyway. I'm in Germany! Have I said that? I'm in Germany! Beer! Pork! Football! Andrea waves a hand at me: 'knock yourself out,' and teaches me the only line of German I can still speak: "*Ich spreche kein Deutsch. Ich bin ein Tourist aus Südafrika. Ein Bier bitte.*"

Ein bier Bitte. What more does a man need to know, right?

Armed with my new advanced German vocabulary, I set off around sunset. The village isn't very big — I'd say smaller than some of the Leviathan shopping malls we have here, but only just — and I set off in search of a pub. I'm happy! I walk the streets, and I find my first. It looks empty and sterile. White walls and a solitary drinker at the bar. No thanks. I find my second. Lots of kids with grease-ball duck's ass haircuts and loud music. Me twenty years ago? Yes, please! Me today? No thanks. I carry on, and there I find it: a traditional German gingerbread house. It has red upholstery and dark wood, a bunch of middle-aged locals around the counter. Now this is more like it! I go inside, and they look at me. Who is this guy? I say in my best German that I can't speak a word of kraut, I'm a tourist from South Africa, and I would very much like a beer.

A reply from the opposite side of the counter in the best *cor-blimey* cockney accent you can imagine: "Boy, you guys sure as hell fucked up in the World Cup, didn't ya?"

His name wasn't Michael, and he was a fugitive from the law in England. Nothing big: just on a drunken night, he got in a scuffle and hit a cop. They wanted to lock him up for that, and he skipped the country, and now he was in Germany, working construction. And he was right, we did fuck up. A few days earlier, South Africa lost by 130 runs to the Indians in the Cricket World Cup.

And that is how that night began. Not-Michael could speak English and German, and thus translated. The locals had a ball with me. They knew Norb and his father, who patronised this particular pub so much they charged him rent. They were all just too eager to get to know this guy from Joburg now marrying into the family.

As said, it's a small town.

But herewith a word on the local beer, Kölsch. I can say many great things about my German hosts, but one thing I cannot compliment is their beer. It's like sex on the beach. It's fucking close to water. Served in ridiculous 200ml glasses, this freshly pulled draught with less alcohol content than tap water is finished before you even started drinking. Which meant I drank a lot. Having grown up in the nightclubs of Johannesburg getting puke-drunk on vodka shots and Carling Black Label, this pissy little beer was literally nothing. But I enjoyed the company. And none of the locals would let me pay for my own, nor allow me to buy a round. I left that night with almost the exact number of Euro I arrived with, save for my tip to the bartender. My new friends got slightly annoyed with me. Why am I not getting tipsy? All this beer and they are all mellowed out and I'm still able to walk a line with my eyes closed. One of them looks at the bartender and they converse conspiratorially in German. Next moment, they placed a shot glass of something in front of me. I only know it is brown.

"Be careful," the guy who ordered it says to me in heavily accented broken English, "This one is the Devil's brother".

Erm, quite.

Gerry: off his ass! At the drop of a shot glass I'm motherlessly drunk.

And now I need to get home. All I know is home is 'over there somewhere'. I start walking, and the German streets are made of waterbed. Feeling like Andy Capp after a night on the pull, I explore the way home, blissfully happy, and doing my best not to sing. By sheer bloody luck, I look down an alleyway, and spot the house. Fortunately, it was rather distinctive. The house next door had a giant picture of Obelix painted on the garage door. Ah, home, where my love lies waiting for me. I walk down the alleyway and trip over a non-existent white line in the road, and I go ass over teakettle! I sit in the middle of the street, drunk as a skunk, laughing with pure joy. I get up and stumble home and upstairs.

Everyone is frantic: where's Gerry? Remember, I've no cellphone. All they know is 'I went in search of a pub.'

Andrea, angry as hell: "Where the fuck were you?" I hold up my right hand: it's bleeding as if I stuck it in a blender.

With a big-ass grin I say: "I'm drunk and I'm bleeding!" For the next fifteen minutes, I sat on the toilet seat lid, holding my arm up while Andrea picked pieces of gravel from my hand. All the while I'm babbling like an idiot as to all the nice people I've met, and how much I love Germany.

How much I love her.

The next morning, Astrid, Norb's wife, went to do the shopping. Bread, cold meats, the like. I toddled along for shits and giggles. Everyone — *everyone* — knew about the cousin from Africa.

The next time I went to the pub, Andrea went with to make sure I did not make a fool of myself again. I didn't. Nobody bought me a glass of the Devil's Brother again. I made damn sure of that.

7

The next ten days were really odd. A contradiction of wonderment at where we were, and the excitement of where we were going. For the next week or so, Andrea and I explored small portions of Germany. She'd been there, and knew where to take me. And boy, was she right. Sitting here on a Monday morning, I'm thinking of the fancy restaurants and the street eateries, I'm thinking of pub crawls in Cologne, discovering the historical treasures in Aachen. One particular memory comes up, and I'll treasure this one.

We were in Cologne, and it was bitterly cold. Or, at least, bitterly cold to my South African bones. I'm sure the locals saw it as a pleasant spring morning. Andrea and I were dressed in our winter woollies. In my case, *all* my winter woollies, and we were walking the streets, looking for a place to have breakfast. We found a little street café just off the west bank of the Rhine and sat outside. Because why not? The wind was freezing, blowing cruelly off the water, but we could sit inside anywhere, any time. This was a special trip. The waiter came along, and Andrea ordered champagne. Because why not? I have no idea how long we sat there, but it wasn't long enough. It would not have been long enough had we still sat there. Sitting across the table from my wife, staring into her big brown eyes, the wind calling from the Rhine rippling her long dark hair... it was simply one of the better moments of my life.

You know you love someone, and you know you know you love them. But now and then life gives you a moment to remind you that you do. That windy morning was one of those moments. Just how extremely lucky I am. How happy I am. That this brown-haired, brown-eyed girl with the big brain and quirky sense of humour loves me enough to marry me. How lucky can a man like me get? It does cast doubt on her taste in men though, but God, she was beautiful that morning. Her face wasn't bad either.

Side quest! Mett. Remember I mentioned earlier about our shared love of good food, and how prawns are not quite my favourite thing to eat? Well, these Germans have given me the gift of *mett*. For my non-European readers, 'mett' is — don't puke — raw freshly ground lean pork served on bread and seasoned with black pepper and onion. Basically, pig sushi. It was, and still is, my favourite thing to eat. I can eat handfuls of the stuff! If it was available in Joburg, I'd be bankrupt by now.

Sometime during the first few days in Germany, Andrea suggested we exchange wedding gifts now, rather than on our actual wedding day. The wedding day was going to be too full of activity to really enjoy and appreciate gifts. "Besides," she said, "yours is utilitarian, and you will need it on our trip to Svalbard." Fine, be logical about it then. She handed me a package, about the size of one of my own paperbacks. Inside was a hip-flask. But not a shitty little one you buy from the cigarette counter at the bottle store, but a Swig flask, made from extruded stainless steel — no leaky seams — encased in orange leather. It was — is — a very elegant little flask. Not my first flask, to be sure, but all the others are rather shitty, to be frank about it. "Wow, this is nice," I said. It was.

"Take off the leather casing," she said. Okay. I removed the flask from its casing and saw she had it engraved with a Dr Seuss quote: 'Fall in mutual weirdness and call it love'. It was apt. I wept. As is my predisposition, I'm sure you realise by now. And of course, I needed something to fill it with. No use giving a guy a fancy-schmancy and expensive-but-empty hip-flask, is there? Along with the flask came a bottle of Talisker Dark Storm single malt. Nice!

My turn. Nuh-uh. Not yet! I've a trick up my sleeve.

Eventually, it was time. The trip of a lifetime. Norb drove us to Dusseldorf airport, where we caught a plane to Oslo via Copenhagen. I've been to Copenhagen! We spent half an hour, max, between planes. But hey, I've been to Copenhagen now. Just how well-travelled am I? And side quest: during the security check, Andrea put down her gloves, and only picked one up again. This became a Taxidermy Ducks song: 'I lost a glove in Copenhagen'. It went multi-platinum in Nicaragua.

A night in Oslo, and then we took to the skies. It was happening. It was really, really happening! Andrea hated the window-seat. She wanted aisle for ease of access to the loo, but that day I insisted she take the window. This was her dream, her effort, and she needed to see it come true first. We stared in wonderment as we flew over the fjords, then into the Norwegian Sea, and as we headed steadily north, we saw our first iceberg. The iceberg was cool, as a symbol of what we were up to, but not as cool as the look on her face. You could see the unbridled joy in her expression. Almost religious awe at the trip we were undertaking. How a lifetime of hopes and dreams had culminated into this. She stared out of the window. I stared at her. I've not seen Andrea happy often, but that moment on the plane was definitely one of them.

We landed at Longyearbyen airport, and the mood was joyous! Jubilant! I did not even puke on the plane, for once. We were officially in the arctic circle. While not at the physical 90°-north, we were damn close enough to say 'North Pole' and anyone with a sympathetic brain will not challenge us on the fact.

Wow.

As expected, it's not really warm. But not exactly as cold as we feared either, the thermometer read a balmy -12. However, the beaming grin from my wife provided all the warmth I needed. Now it is check-in time, and this is where the first of 'so much more than we bargained for' began.

"Mister and Missus Pelser, you are assigned the Hilmar Nøis suite.

"Huh? Sorry, what? Suite?"

We're not rich people, we made this extremely expensive trip on the thinnest and most threadbare of shoestrings, and we most certainly did *not* book a suite. We got a room in the basement. Next to the laundry. Not a suite.

"Yes, as the wedding couple, you've been upgraded free of charge." Bonus! As said, that was the first of many. The second was when we entered our 'suite' and there was a gift basket for the wedding couple, compliments of the hotel. For the four nights we stayed in Svalbard, we were treated like royalty.

8

Let's address a secondary matter: we were in Svalbard to witness a total solar eclipse *as well*! All this lovey-dovey wedding things, we forgot the second billing: Mother Nature's most dramatic event. We literally flew half-way around the world — and spent more money than we could reasonably admit to with a straight face — to see this thing.

And now it's bloody cloudy?

Yup, sad to say, Gentle Reader, that the weather was just not holding up. It wasn't densely packed like a German winter, but there were enough clouds in the sky to make eclipse watching a damp squib.

But no matter. We were in Svalbard! A trip so outstanding, not even Andrea dared spend it in bed. However, there was some admin to take care of first. We needed to go see the priest. Leif Helgeson is a tall man with a mop of curly hair and an incredible disposition. The type of guy who would not say no to a pint or two of beer. I liked the guy. I don't believe in God, as I believe I said, but Andrea still had a smidgen of religiosity running through her veins, and she really wanted to get married in a church. I had no problem with this. I was scared that I'd burst into flames the minute I put a toe on holy ground, but apart from that minute risk, I was okay with giving my wife a church wedding. But before officiating our wedding, he wanted to talk to us. Fair enough. The usual 'are you sure' questions were asked and once he was satisfied, he asked us for the marriage licence.

Uh, say what?

No marriage without a marriage license. He could not legally marry us. There it goes... Fortunately, just so we could get a visa, we stood in front of a fast-talking dinosaur six weeks earlier who 'nowpronounceyouhusbandandwife,thankyounext!'. We were married. Legally. Already. Thank the heavens I did not believe in!

"Oh, that's different," he said. "Now I can give you a ceremony and bless your union."

I cried. Again. Mostly with relief.

The days carried on, and the weather did not break. It was cloudy and relatively warm. We ate. We drank. We bonked. We explored. It was magical. We had a champagne tasting in the basement of a hotel. We were told the basement is not air conditioned, and the temperature remains constant all year round. It was cold enough in that basement to see your breath. Bottle after bottle was popped, and we had champers with strawberries and savouries and chocolate. We visited the international seed vault, said to be nuclear-bomb resistant. We had dinner of bidos — a Sami hunters stew — in a replica of the original hut that Willem Barentsz and his men built when they accidentally discovered the island while trying to find a northern passage to China in 1596. We bought a shitload of souvenirs. Longyearbyen only has two roads. Neither of them named. We saw a tin mug at the hotel souvenir shop which had the tagline 'Where the streets have no name' and promptly bought it for my brother, a rabid U2 fan.

The night before the eclipse we sat in the hotel room — sorry, suite — and bullshitted each other that it was okay. We were here to get married.

The eclipse was only a draw card, not the main event. We may even have believed it.

The morning of the 20th of March arrived. *The* day. I was up before Andrea, as I always was, and with legs that did not quite feel like mine, I walked over to the window, and peeked through the curtains.

"And," she asked from the bed. Even her usual pre-tea morning grogginess had been replaced by excitement.

Joyously I threw open the curtains, revealing a clear and cloudless sky — The eclipse was on!

Gentle Reader, I am here to tell you that the best day of my life has already happened. No, there is no use in trying to convince me otherwise with hypothetical what-ifs. Because I can tell you, no matter what happens in the future — Date Miss Universe, win the Nobel Prize for literature, win the lottery twice, dinner with Stephen King, Stephen Fry, Kate Winslet, and Cate Blanchett, all on the same day — no matter what, nothing, *nothing*, will ever come close to the day I married my darling wife.

And I'm okay with that.

The feeling I had when the ice-blue sky pierced my eyes that Friday morning is one of the more amazing things I've ever felt. "Put us on a tune," Andrea asked in her best South African English, and I did just that. I found the iPad, and I played U2's *Where the Streets Have No Name*. It was perfect. It is such a joyous and upbeat song. Larry's enthusiastic drums, Adam's irresistible base, Edge's mystifying guitar, and Bono singing that he wants to feel sunlight on his face, and when he goes there, he wants to go with you... the lyrics, the music, it was perfect.

You will not be surprised if I tell you it was one of several times I cried that day.

We went down to breakfast, and obviously, there was electricity in the air. Everybody was buzzing. It was one hell of a day. A once in a lifetime event not just for Andrea and I, but for literally everyone there. We found a place, and grabbed stuff from the buffet (which included, I dare say, whale).

And then: more magic. For some reason, everybody knew. We did not advertise it. It wasn't about us and our trip. Hundreds of people around the world came to watch the eclipse. We were just two of many. That we were getting married was nothing to these people, so we did not make a song and dance about it. Yet, everybody knew.

We received wedding gifts from so many people that day, that it is a miracle we did not have to pay for excess luggage. One of which was a plaque. Quite a simple little thing, really. Just a piece of screen-printed tin with the name of the town and the GPS coordinates on it, festooned with ribbons. That one came from some big fancy doctor-scientist-astrologer somebody and his wife. They had no business with us. We were nothing to them. Just this odd couple from South Africa. How they knew we were getting married is beyond me. That they gave us a gift, made me cry. That plaque is right next to me on my bookshelf. Ribbons till attached.

But there was no time to cry and stuff our faces for too long: the reason 99.5% of people were there was happening soon!

We geared up in several hundred layers of clothing, and we were all bussed out to a spot on a frozen fjord. The excitement was enough to send sparks through my fingers. Or maybe that was just the static electricity from all the wool I was wearing. Remember I said previously it had been -12, and that was quite balmy? Without the cloud blanket, the cold could come inside and sit on your favourite chair. The mercury dropped to a stunning minus twenty-eight degrees Celsius — minus eighteen-and-a-bit for my American pals — that day on the fjord. And if the wind kicked up, it plummeted to minus forty. And minus forty is minus forty in both Celsius *and* American! It is more than six years later now, and I can almost feel my toes thawing out.

I can also tell you that a Swig hip-flask filled with Talisker, and buried six inches deep in arctic ice to chill, makes for the most delicious tipple I've ever had.

Which brings me to the wedding gift I got for Andrea.

"Sweetie," I said.

"Yes, my love?"

"I want to give you your wedding gift now."

"Now?"

"Yes. Now."

From my camera bag I took out an envelope. Inside, was a single piece of A5-sized glossy paper.

"What's this," she asked.

"Read it."

STAR CERTIFICATE

The star with coordinates
RA: 9h8m52.3s DEC: +51°36m17.0s
Was successfully entered into the star-naming registry

PRIM

Under a solar eclipse, on this our wedding day
Carrying my heart, a star is named.
To show my love overflowing to the brim
Shining down on all of us – forever –
Is a star called 'Prim'

Date: 20/03/2015

Registry Number
75610-1949-1434079

It was her turn to weep, just like I am weeping now, writing this. What do you give the girl who has everything? Especially if you cannot afford a Mercedes SLK? What do you give a girl who already had her own diamond for an engagement ring?

Yes, Gentle Reader, I bought her a star. The star described above is in the constellation Ursa Major, and has the Bayer designation of *f Ursae Majoris.* If you are in the northern hemisphere, you can look up at the night sky, and see that there's a pinprick of light in the constellation of the Great Bear, which carries the name of my wife.

Please forgive the cheesy poetry. But I felt it then; I still feel it now.

Did I get a snog or what!

But there's no time for that, Mother Nature was getting ready.

"Contact!" someone yelled, declaring the first time the moon touched the solar disc. Soon, a chorus echoed in: "Contact!" "Contact!" "Contact!" "Contact!"

Game on!

Through foiled eclipse glasses, and my camera with a rented 600mm zoom lens we watched as the moon gradually but persistently obscured the sun. Every minute that passed was a minute closer to totality. It was akin to watching a flower bloom or a butterfly unfurl its wings for the first time. A slow and joyous and miraculous vision. The light dimmed, there was a sliver of sun left which exploded with a single beam of light astronomers call 'the diamond ring', and a split second later it was dark. Day had turned to night, and we were staring at the moon and the sun in an intimate embrace, a dark disc in the sky, the violent corona visible. I doubt there is anything more spectacular in nature than that show.

We hugged, we cried, we kissed. We came, we saw, we did it! We were victorious in our quest to come half-way across the world and stand on the frozen sea to watch an eclipse.

All too soon, the magnificence of totality was over, and the moon moved, revealing a diamond ring on the opposite side. Now it was the wind-down.

"Mister and Missus Pelser, Mister and Missus Pelser, your taxi has arrived," the PA system blared, and sure as heck, there it was! Travel Quest — the travel agents — as a wedding gift, organised us a taxi to take us from the eclipse site to the hotel, and from the hotel to the church, and back from the church to the hotel again. And the taxi service? "You're the people getting married?" Yes. "Then this is for you." A bottle of champagne. Treated like royalty, I tell you!

The taxi rushed us to the hotel, we undressed our minus-fuck-you clothes, and got into our wedding garb. No suits, no ties, not poufy big white dresses. Just an elegant red dress for Andrea, and chinos and a red wool jumper for me. Then: off to the church.

9

They raised the flag for us. They only raise it on special occasions, but that day, they raised it for us. The Norwegian flag was blowing proudly in the sky half-lit by a still-ongoing eclipse. Leif met us in his traditional garb and led us inside.

Two more people awaited us: the church deacon, and the organist. That was it. Five people were present when Andrea and I got married. Priest, deacon, organist, and the bridal couple themselves. As a professional photographer: we did not even have a cameraman at our wedding to take happy snaps. The organist used my Nikon to take a few blurry photos, and that was good enough. No need for a million photos when you have a memory like this, is there?

Leif was beaming with happiness. As was Andrea. As was I. We stood at the front of the empty church, and Leif rang the bells, letting the world's northernmost town know that while most of them were still staring at the sun, Prim and Gerry were getting married. Yes, yes, I cried, okay!?

I cannot remember half of what he said. But I know this: I've attended a lot of weddings in my life, both as guest and photographer, and I've never heard a wedding sermon like that. It was beautiful and eloquent, and I could not believe Andrea and I were at the receiving end of such a beautiful ceremony. I do remember one thing though, and I'm going to paraphrase here, but the gist of it is correct.

"Look around you," he said. "It is paradise. Outside, an eclipse is happening. Around us, incredible and striking beauty. It is a vision to behold, an experience to cherish. This is marriage. It is paradise. Incredible and striking in its beauty. But do not be fooled, because in this paradise, violent snowstorms can kick up at any minute, laying waste to the town, knocking out the heat and electricity. The only way to survive these storms are when we take care of each other. This is marriage. It is a fairy tale, but even in fairy tales — especially in fairy tales — storms will come. Storms that may threaten your very existence. But if you take care of each other, you may weather the storm and return to paradise, even when the storms are each other."

I can proudly say we took that sermon to heart. Leif's words were prophetic. It was a striking and beautiful marriage. And yes, as mentioned earlier, we had our storms. Serious ones. And yes, once or twice, those storms were each other. But we survived them. All of them.

Except one.

10

Leif asked if I had a ring, I replied "sort of," and got the Cartier bracelet from my pocket. My hands were shaking so much it took me three attempts to screw it on her wrist.

"I now pronounce you husband and wife," he said, and I kissed my beautiful bride. For better or for worse. In profit and in loss. In sickness and in health. Till death do us part. I do. I did.

We exited the church as newlyweds for the second time in six weeks, just as the eclipse finished and the show was over. I believe there were only two people on the planet, ever, who can say they got married under a total solar eclipse in the north pole. How damn cool is that!

The taxi took us back to the hotel, and there we had our wedding lunch: hamburgers and chips. I shit thee not. Now, whether it was the occasion and the mood or the actual food, I'll never know, but it was hands-down the best damn burger I've had in my life. To such an extent that Andrea and I had ceremonial burgers and chips for our anniversary lunch ever since.

Yelp review: The bar at the Radisson Blu in Longyearbyen: Five stars for their burgers. Highly recommend.

That night, we had our wedding dinner. Just the two of us. While the tour group was partying it up, the newlyweds went to one hell of a fancy restaurant, The Huset. Now I've been in a few great eateries in my life (but still like Hooters), and I am willing to bet my bald spot the only reason The Huset does not have a Michelin Star is because the judges never went there. It is, admittedly, rather inaccessible. But man, what a menu!

We arrive, and the Maître d' asks us, "Are you the wedding couple?" We assure him we are. "Welcome, I hope you enjoy your stay, and when you are done with your meal, please feel free to have a few drinks at the bar."

Cool!

We take our seats, and it is perfect. Just perfect. Opulence squared. Genuine silver cutlery. Cut lead-glass stemware. And the most gorgeous woman on the planet to share it with. Andrea had pre-booked the set menu with accompanying wine-pairing.

Now look, I have to admit, I'm not a wino. With the exception of the sparkly variety, I am no fan of fermented grape juice. Like Tom Hanks in *Big*, I just don't get it.

Andrea: *Sniff* Hmm…A chardonnay. *Sniff* Slightly wooded. *Sniff* Aroma of raisins, coffee, mineral water, and over-ripe lettuce and a delightful bouffe of bean fart. *Sip* Gentle on the tongue with immediate flavours of lavender fabric softener and vanilla, and an aftertaste of habanero and cabernet. Delightful! *Sip* Wait, what's this? *Sip* One of the grape-pickers was pregnant! *Sip* It's a girl!

Me: *Sniff* Smells like wine. *Sip* Tastes like wine. *Sip* Waiter, can I have a beer please!

Wine does not impress me much. I like the ritual of champers — or sparkling wine — but I cannot tell the difference between cheap fizzy plonk and vintage Dom Perignon. Yes, I've had vintage Dom Perignon. Tastes like expensive fizzy plonk. So, I was not too fussed about the accompanying wine-paring. However, the sparkle in Andrea's eye was something to behold. So, I indulge her. Why not? I'm so ridiculously in love it's not even funny. If this lady wants a wine-pairing, she can have it.

Now, for those of you who have ever done a set menu with wine-pairing, you will know you get a thimble-full of wine per course. If a fly were to fall into your glass, there won't be enough Jesus-juice in there for it to get damp, let alone drown.

Yeah, not the case. The waiter pours her the standard insulting wine-pairing measure, looks around to make sure no one is watching, and pours her a solid glug! Well now! And this was to be repeated on our second dish. But not the third. He just left the bottle on the table for us to help ourselves. Admittedly, the bar bill was starting to make us nervous. But no worry: Because we were the wedding couple, the wine-bill was on the house. Wow! We only paid for the food.

When desert comes — and more wine — the waiter reiterates what the Maître d' said: "Please have a drink at the bar after your meal." Well, fuck me, we're already tingly in the knees and foggy in the brain and we have three half-bottles of wine to take along with us to the hotel, what do these guys want? Spontaneous cirrhosis?

But y'know, why not? I'm fed up with wine I don't like. I can do with a whisky at this point, let the evening wind down easily. So, we pay the bill and go to the bar. There are a few odd patrons in the corners. An upright piano with a young lady behind it. I go to the bar and order us a final night cap, when the lady behind the piano asks, "have you had your first dance yet?"

It was all a set-up! They planned the entire thing!

We said no, we've not danced yet, and she starts playing, and sings with the voice of an angel. Song choice? Sinatra's *Fly Me to the Moon*. That was the first dance we had as husband and wife. How utterly apt. Second dance was something Norwegian, and the final song was Hoagy Carmichael's *Skylark*. Yes, I cried, dammit! For our first anniversary, which traditionally is 'paper', Andrea got me a poster of the digital wave-form of *Skylark*. It is hanging in a frame above my bed. I told you this woman is amazing.

But all too soon it was over, and as we put on our jackets, the patrons in the bar all got up, and started putting chairs away. They were not patrons, but staff. They kept the empty bar open just for us! Here is a couple who came to our icy island to get married, and we're gonna make sure they have a memorable one!

Job done. As said: royalty!

Just then a guy came running in. "Have you guys seen the northern lights yet," he asked breathlessly. Obviously, he came running just for us.

"No," we said in unison, and ran outside.

We missed it.

Which is a good thing. I think if I saw the northern lights as well that day my brain would have exploded.

And that, Gentle Reader, is how Andrea and I had a literal fairy tale of a wedding in the shadow of the moon in a magical land called Svalbard.

11

Insert the story about a fabulous honeymoon in Prague here. Stories of seafood at Zdenek Oyster Bar, smoked porter, Charles Bridge, Prague Castle, and Strahov Monastery. Stories of string quartets and street buskers. Oh, and I can definitely tell you about the two of us, lying on a king-sized bed in the Buddah Bar hotel, highly in love and on honeymoon, following the live score on espncricinfo.com on the iPad. Dale Steyn had twelve runs to defend in the last over in the semi-finals against New Zealand. I mean, despite the ultimate wedding story, there *was* still a Cricket World Cup going on…We lost. Fuck.

But those stories would be superfluous. Prague was not even the cherry on top. It was that little sprig of mint on the side of the plate.

I was married to the love of my life. This short, fat, balding guy with bad teeth (but a great ass) managed to get the girl, and marry her. Y'know, I never saw that coming. Took me long enough. I was forty when I tied the knot.

And the interesting end result: we had two wedding anniversaries. 3rd February, the legal one, and 20th March, what we termed the emotional one. We often forgot the first anniversary. Who wants to remember Home Affairs and a guywhotalkstoofast anyway?

A few months later we bought a house. A beautiful one with a double garage for me to do photoshoots in and a large garden for the dogs to play in and a pool for us to swim in (and a big stinkwood tree to drop its leaves into the pool every autumn). We had found our forever home. This was the house we were going to live in until we kick the bucket.

Which brings me to the next part of the book. The part I do not want to write, but have to. Stay strong, Gentle Reader, I need you to.

Ready? Let's go.

Andrea at the Oslo Viking Museum
17 March 2015

Part Two:
ON DEATH.

Prim, Leif & me
Svalbard, 20 March 2015

Chapter 6 - Keeping Abreast.

1

For four years, we lived the boring and mundane — yet terrific — lives of the married couple. Days turned into weeks, weeks into months, months into seasons, seasons into years.

We had some great times, like when we went back to Germany for a European Christmas in 2016, and celebrated the coming of 2017 in a street party on a snowy street in Austria. Also, the second-best day in my life: 30 May 2018. The day I published my first novel. Andrea was right there beside me, sharing my victory. We had some terrible times, like when our house started giving problems and Andrea's work dried up and cash flow along with it. Like when we did not win *another* Cricket World Cup in 2019. It was life, and just as we know it. Ups and downs, feasts and famines. Just an utterly unremarkable four-year period called life. Covid was becoming newsworthy and worrisome, but apart from that, life is life. *Na-na na na-na.*

On Sunday, the 9th of February 2020, I was in the lounge, watching telly. It was the final of the Under 19 Cricket World Cup, India was playing Bangladesh. (Bangladesh won. South Africa ended up a miserable eighth.) Andrea and I were supposed to go out somewhere, and then I would have to go visit my mother at the frail care centre. It was her seventieth birthday. Andrea was in the bedroom at the opposite side of the house, taking a shower.

"*Gerrraaayyyyy!*" came the loud and annoyed call from the other side of the house. Oh fuck…What did I do now?

"Coming!" I call back.

"Come, quickly!"

"Yes, fuck, gimme a chance here. I'm on my way, dammit!"

I enter the bedroom, and Andrea was standing there, buck naked, dripping wet, and as pale as skimmed milk, eyes as large as cricket balls. "Yes, Sweetie?"

"Is this a lump," she asks, pointing to her right breast.

I see nothing. Smooth as a baby's bum, just like it always was. I put my hand where she points and…

Oh. Fuck.

It was immediate. There was no doubt. I did not 'wonder if'. There was no 'hmm, could be, I dunno'. What I felt there under my cupped hand felt like a handful of Lego blocks under her skin. Hard, and almost 'crunchy'. I felt my stomach plummet. I'm no doctor. I cannot say that it's cancer or sunburn or an ingrown toenail that migrated north, but whatever it was, it was not normal.

Some days I still feel that odd crunchy feeling in the palm of my right hand. It is probably imprinted there forever. And it should be. It is a definitive moment of my life.

I nod and tell her that yes, that's a lump. No ifs, no buts, just a certainty that there is something in that right boob of hers that should definitely not be there.

You want to see action mode? This is action mode. Fuck the fact that it is Sunday, Andrea finds her gynaecologist's number — odd, yes, I know, but Andrea had a great relationship with her — and tells her. This is where Dr Sumayya Ibrahim springs into action. Weekend or no, she pulls her strings, and we get a call a few minutes later: Andrea was booked for a mammogram first thing the next morning at the Donald Gordon Medical Centre with Dr Russell Seider. Thank you, Dr Ibrahim!

I did not visit my mother for her birthday that day.

The next morning, Monday the 10th, I take Andrea to the Donny Gordon. Thanks to Covid, I'm not allowed to go in with her. This, as you may imagine, is rather distressing.

I park the car in a shady spot, and wait. And wait. And wait. And if I may be just a smidgen selfish here, even though in the greater scheme of things, it means nothing? While I'm waiting for my wife, my biggest client calls me: they do not need my services anymore. A huge chunk of my income just flew out of the window. Thanks to Covid, it was the first of many. By the time springtime came six months later, I did not have a single client left. Which was a disaster from a monetary perspective, but the free time that opened up was a blessing. I needed all the free time I could get.

Eventually Andrea emerges from the doors, visibly rattled. Yup, Dr Seider confirmed there was something there. Just exactly what, he does not know yet, but he did a biopsy and is sending a sample away for testing. Nothing to do now but wait for the results.

Tuesday, nothing.

Wednesday morning Dr Seider calls. Anxiously, we put the phone on speaker, and he tells us the bad news. Andrea has tested positive for triple negative breast cancer.

Wait, negative? That is good, right? When you test negative in a medical context, it's a good sign? Right? Wrong! I'm not going to report the education we got in the subsequent weeks and months, but dammit, I never knew breast cancer was so damn complicated. If memory serves, there are three predominant types of breast cancers: either oestrogen, progesterone, or the HER2 hormone are the principal causes of boob carnage. When you test negative for all three of these causes, they put you into the 'triple negative' category. Which means something else is causing your cancer. About 15% of breast cancers are triple negative, and because it is 'something else', and not one of the chief causes, treating it is challenging.

To this day, we do not know what caused it. Andrea never even touched a cigarette, let alone smoked. Neither of us did. She hated the sun, so it wasn't the African sun that gets the blame for so many cancers. We did genetic tests and there were no genetic markers causing it. With all the doctors and tests, the cancer just came. No cause, no rhyme, no reason. A literal case of shit happening. All we knew is that my wife has just been diagnosed with cancer. That terrible C-word that sparks fear in the hearts of all.

Dr Seider mulls it over and says, "You know what, you need the best. I'm going to refer you to Carol-Ann Benn."

2

This is where I sing the praises of one Dr Carol-Ann Benn.

Professor Doctor Carol-Ann Benn, or just 'Carol' (She's seemingly nobody's 'Prof' or 'Doc'), is an extraordinary woman who runs the Breast Care Centre of Excellence at the Milpark Hospital in Joburg. She started this endeavour in 2000 and is one of only three breast care centres outside the USA that has accreditation with the National Accreditation Program for Breast Centres. She is also the first to implement imaging to obtain core biopsies before surgical excisions, a development which saved countless unnecessary surgeries. Quite a big deal. But an even bigger deal is that in 2005 she established the Helen Joseph Breast Care Clinic. A government facility where she treats countless women who do not have access to medical insurance or private healthcare. Whether her patients are at her private rooms at Milpark or at the state-funded facilities at Helen Joseph, they all get the same Carol. And that is good.

No, that's bloody brilliant.

She is a blue-eyed blonde with a wicked sense of humour and no sense of self-import. You immediately get that this is a person who is absolutely in love with what she does. A big buzz-word in the world right now is '*ikagi*'. A mythical concept where what you are good at, what you love, what the world needs, and what you can get paid for intersects. Reaching *ikagi* is not for us mere mortals, but within twelve seconds of chatting, you get the sense that Carol has not just reached *ikagi*, but she has built her castle there, and she invites anyone along who wants to come. From pink surgery scrubs to glittered T-shirts, from trying to hide her braces to having a Star Wars themed consulting room, from dropping F-bombs to calling you on the phone just to hear how it is going (Which she did several times after Andrea died), Carol is not a doctor. She's a fucking *mensch*.

She is the type of person who gives reluctant superheroes their capes, and this is why this book is partly dedicated to her.

When Seider said: 'you need the best', he could only have spoken about Carol-Ann Benn.

He did allude though, that getting in with Carol is like trying to join the mafia. As one can imagine with such an extremely competent individual, demand is high. One simply does not walk into her consulting rooms. There's only so many hours in a day, and with surgery — she is an oncological surgeon, after all — consultations, lecturing, and being a wife and mother, Carol does not exactly have a lot of openings.

Carol, however, disproves this scarcity of resource. She prides herself that she will see a patient within forty-eight hours of diagnosis, whatever it takes. She consults seven days a week, sometimes late into the night. I can vouch for that. The first time we saw Carol that Wednesday evening was after eleven at night.

One can only conclude her golfing handicap sucks.

They say first impressions last. Let me tell you my first impression of Dr Benn: Andrea and I were in her consulting rooms, both of us obviously rattled and shit scared of this brand-new diagnosis which literally changed everything in an instant. It was late at night. I've no idea how late, but way beyond any reasonable person's expectation of when a doctor should consult. We were not alone. Several other people were also waiting their turn, and we had come in last. It was obviously going to be a long sit. Andrea and I amused ourselves by browsing home improvement magazines and dreaming dreams of what we'll do 'one day', both of us hoping, but neither of us saying, that there would indeed be a 'one day' one day.

Out pops Carol from of one of her consulting rooms, replete in pink scrubs. She addresses the patients and their partners in the waiting area: "You know, the oncological surgeon is going the way of the dinosaur." She then tells us for the next ninety seconds that medicine has advanced to the extent that in the future, oncological surgery would be a thing of the past. In effect, rendering her career obsolete. And I got the feeling it's an obsolescence she would love to see. She impressed the pants off me.

When it was our turn (I want to add in 'finally' here, but play fair: it may have been an hour to midnight, but it was the same bloody day, not 'we have a spot for you in October' in the dentistry-style of consultation bookings), she proceeded to impress the pants off Andrea as well. Carol is the literal eye of the storm. Where our lives were bedlam and tumult, Carol was as calm and chill as if we were discussing what to have for dinner. I cannot speak for my late wife but, screw the oncological treatment: the sheer psychological impact Carol had on me was immense. She was an irresistible force of calm in the chaos our lives had become in the last four days.

We had arrived rattled and scared and confused. We left cool and calm and collected, and with a game plan.

A game plan which ran faster than Usain Bolt chased by an angry Rottweiler. Carol rolled up her sleeves, cracked her knuckles, and got to work. No rest for the righteous, there's work to be done. Monday: Scans, mammograms, and biopsies. Tuesday: an agonising wait. Wednesday: Diagnosis and Carol. Thursday: already talking chemo. Friday: PET Scan. Saturday: A-Ha. Sunday: More imaging.

Wait, what?

3

As previously mentioned, Andrea and I grew up in the most awesome of eras: the '80s. And we were both in love with the music from then, if not exactly the fashions. Let's face it, fashion is cyclical, and everything comes back, but if '80s fashion ever makes a comeback, the human race is truly down the tubes. But the music? Damn, it was fine!

I was more of an alternative rocker, and Andrea more into mainstream pop, but we agreed that the '80s is just the best thing to ever happen to music since Woodstock. And one of the few bands where pop and rock (if not quite alternative rock) intersected, is the Norwegian trio of Morten Harket, Mags Furuholmen and Paul Waaktar-Savoy. Collectively known as A-Ha.

Stop giggling and rolling your eyes at my music taste! Go listen to the instrumentals on *The Sun Always Shines on TV* and tell me it's bad. I dare you. So, when we heard A-Ha was coming to town, we dearly wanted to go, but, alas, money was tight, so we had no chance of going. We did not have the luxury of concert tickets. In fact, we were in such a financial slump at the time I had to sell my car and Andrea had to cancel her life insurance policy just so we could survive a few months until her next project kicked off. Yes, you read that right... four months before she was diagnosed with cancer, she cancelled her life insurance. It's enough to make you weep — if there were not so many other things to weep about.

However, as shall become clear in the tome ahead, many good — and even great — people do exist, and a friend of mine who lives in Scotland gifted me two golden circle tickets to see A-Ha. This was *months* before diagnosis.

Naturally, Andrea was rattled by this whole cancer thing. That Thursday evening in Carol's consulting rooms, Andrea asked her: "I know this seems so trivial in the greater scheme of things, but we've got tickets to a show on Saturday. Can we still go?"

Answer: Abso-fucking-lutely.

This is how Saturday 15 February 2020 was our last 'good' day. And it was a hell of a show! For a guy who can get senior citizen's discount at the movies, ol' Morten has the voice like a mountain. Damn, has he aged well.

We had a ball!

Until they played *Hunting High and Low*. Copyright does not allow me to reprint lyrics without either getting my ass sued, or going through a laborious and expensive process of seeking permission, but the words to that song were just too damn apt. So I sang to her. I drew her in, and whisper-sang the words in her ear, promising that there is no end to the places I'll go to find her again.

The reality of what was happening overwhelmed us. For six days she was a strong woman and took to her brand-new cancer diagnosis with grace and a certain academic detachment, almost as if she was told she would need to have impacted wisdom teeth removed. But on that Sunny Saturday evening at Mark's Park sport grounds, surrounded by several thousand middle-aged people re-living their teenage years, the gravitas of what was happening hit, and she wept. In the fifteen years we'd been together at that stage, I've not seen her weep like that. Not even when her mother died. I've never seen this strong and capable woman just break down. That day I did. And it scared me shitless.

Today I look back at that A-Ha show as the last great day we had. The last great day *I* had. Everything unravelled from then on. I have one of the precious few photos of Andrea and me together from that day. She's all in sunshine-yellow, I'm wearing my Svalbard T-shirt, and we are smiling. We are happy. Whatever came after can be erased from memory for a moment just by looking at that photo.

As a photographer, I have a philosophy of not taking many photos. Life through a lens is a life observed, not a life lived. 'Making memories' is not on my value-list as a photographer. As strange as it may sound, I'm happy there aren't many photos of her, of us, around. It makes the ones which *are* around just that much more special.

4

We called it 'Sideshow Boob'. With the greatest apologies to Matt Groening and The Simpsons, the breast cancer debacle needed a name. And to be fair, the entire thing was a bloody sideshow. As in 'a minor or diverting incident or issue, especially one which distracts attention from something more important.' (Oxford Languages). It was most certainly a distracting issue that took attention from more important things, such as living life, but yeah, not really minor, is it? And if you are a Simpson's fan, you will know that the guest character of Sideshow Bob is not a nice guy.

Sideshow Boob seemed perfect.

We embraced The Simpsons theme, and Andrea got yellow everything: a lever arch file, pencil, pen, notebook — she even got a yellow shirt! Yours truly did the artwork. With a set of felt-tip pens, I drew out a Simpsons-esque character with a breast for a head and a nipple for the nose. This was the title page of her file that contained diagnoses, test results, scans, bills, you name it. She was determined to ridicule and shame this cancer into submission.

And eat it into submission. As said, we're foodies, as the Wüsthof knives and Le Creuset pots and boatload of recipe books and cupboard full of odd ingredients will attest to. This is how we discovered what we termed 'boob soup'. I swear to God, despite the cancer, neither of us had ever been this healthy!

Garlic, onions, carrots, celery, tomatoes, spinach, a fuck-ton of cauliflower and broccoli, and seasoned with turmeric. Cook it up and blend it up, and it comes out looking like baby poop. Looks disgusting, but it's actually surprisingly tasty! Especially when served with a hearty grind of black pepper. This is what we lived on. I'd cook up a massive pot of this stuff once a week, and we'd have at least one bowl a day. Andrea was of the opinion that if she was going to survive this thing and not let the chemo get the better of her, her body would need all the help it could get.

I still have a jar of boob soup in my freezer, been there since the second week of December, seven months old now. I just cannot get myself to chuck that bottle of soup away. It is the last meal I cooked for her.

5

Speaking of chemo, this is where I need to sing the praises of the second doctor to whom this book is dedicated, Dr Ronwyn van Eeden at the Medical Oncology Centre of Rosebank. Or, as Andrea and I called it, 'The Rosebank Oncology Centre of Rosebank'. You have to have a sense of humour about these things.

The first thing one notices about Ronwyn is that she looks like she's not even out of high school yet, let alone a highly experienced medical practitioner and oncologist. To be fair, Ronwyn does not have a Star Wars themed consulting room, and therefore comes in at second place behind Carol, but she is also just too fucking great to put into words. With infinite patience, she outlined and explained to us what the chemo regiment would be, what the treatment plan entails. To wit: a shitload of highly toxic substances will be slammed into Andrea's body on a weekly basis. This should shrink the tumour, which would allow Carol to cut it out. After the surgery — which I learned was called a lumpectomy — Andrea would then get several rounds of radiation therapy, and then, before Christmas, if all goes well, Andrea would be cancer free. Yeah, it would be a hell of a journey, but stats have shown that tripe-negative breast cancer has a 90% five-year survival rate, so the prognosis is good.

I would like to doff my hat to Ronwyn in having the spine to be straight-up and honest with us when the prognosis turned out not to be good.

To aid the chemo infusions, Ronwyn recommended Andrea get a port inserted. A permeable silicone thingamabob that gets implanted under the skin in the chest wall and connected to a major vein. This means that instead of a nurse trying to find a suitable vein to stick an IV needle into every week, the port is always available. This was one of the better things we've done. Dear reader, if you are ever in this situation: trust me, get a port!

Side quest: I have a photography pal, Jean, who also sews. What does literally *everybody* need during Covid? Answer: a mask. So I ordered some masks from Jean. A cow-spot one for Andrea. And a yellow one. For Felicity Watermeyer.

Thanks to Covid, again, I was not allowed to go into the chemo clinic with Andrea, and there was no way she was going in there without moral support. Felicity, the Stuffed Petite Baby Hippo, became my champion and gave Andrea someone to hug and to hold and cry into during the times she needed to hug and hold and cry.

Every Friday as we left for chemo, we had Andrea's go-bag. The yellow Sideshow Boob file, a yellow lunch-baggie with a juice, some cheese, nuts, and a sandwich, and 'Licity, masked in yellow. Just in case, you know, Covid spreads to stuffed animals. We would not want her infected, would we?

6

A psychologist told us it is better for Andrea to shave her head, than watch the gradual but persistent alopecia that would leave her chemo-bald. Frankly, it made sense. It was the day before her first chemo session. It was time. It was the last time I saw my wife with hair. The long and luxurious dark hair that I fell in love with had to go. She showered, and afterwards, she sat on the edge of the tub. Using kitchen scissors, I cut her hair. First in long and rough snips to get rid of the bulk of it, and then cleaning her scalp with hair clippers.

It was the most intense and imitate thing I had ever done for my wife at that point.

I had to be the strong husband here. The rock upon which she could base her battle.

But that night, the rock had feet of dry sand. Standing in the bath, and watching Andrea's hair fall into tub with every crude movement of my right hand, rolled me. I made sure I kept a lock. I still have it.

She was a much stronger person than me. I cried. She shrugged it off, asked what's for dinner, and if I want to watch some telly.

A few weeks later, my feet of dry sand showed itself again. I'm not proud of this, but... I'm a mild man. I've only 'lost it' three times in my life and regretted two of the three. The other: some bastard locked Lazslo in a room when he was supposed to be dog-sitting, so the asshole deserved what was coming to him. I'm not an angry or temperamental man. Grumpy, yes, but losing my temper is not something that I do. However, one night in April, I got overwhelmed by what was happening to my wife. I poured myself a whisky, went to sit outside, and had myself a good cry. Which turned into an ugly cry. Which turned into anger. I was sobbing with unadulterated sadness and unbridled anger. The only way to end it was to break something, and I smashed my whisky glass against the paving. This was a terrible moment of weakness, and Andrea lost her cool with me. Point one, she needed me to be strong, and point two, we have dogs. We cannot have puppies run around on the paving and grass cutting their feet. Ashamed and embarrassed, I got a flashlight from the kitchen cabinet and searched for and picked up every sliver of glass I could find. I still have the remains of that glass, in a tin along with a lock of her hair. I was planning on giving it to Andrea to ceremoniously toss into the trash once she was cured.

I'm clueless as to what to do with it now.

7

As happenstance would have it, Andrea's first chemo was the first Tuesday after the President of SA locked up the country for Covid.

It was a terrible time. I can say — and have said — many bad things about the South African government (and governments in general), but the heavy-handed approach to their Covid policing in the early days stroked terror into the hearts of ordinary citizens, and made my already dim view of politicians even darker.

A man named Petrus Miggels was beaten to death by over-zealous police officers taking their job of enforcing Draconian governmental Covid laws a bit too seriously. South Africa had turned into a quasi-police-state, and the news headlines daily saw cases of people harassed, beaten, jailed, and killed for the crime of simply being outside. The general populous was more afraid of the military and the police than they were of the impending pandemic.

This was the backdrop of how Andrea entered her battle against cancer.

Naturally, Andrea was petrified of Covid. If she were to get it, with a chemo-compromised immune system, it would be tickets. I made a printout with a photo of Andrea and her newly-shaved head, and a general 'to whom it may concern' letter which we could put up against a car window and show the officer of the law who we were and why we were out on the roads when the country was in lockdown.

Driving to your first ever chemo is scary enough. Driving to your first ever chemo in eerily deserted streets with the odd police / military roadblock seemed like a scene from a dystopian TV series. Mad Max, maybe. I used Google Maps to plot a back-roads route to the chemo clinic and back. Good thing too. Often, I would see the feared uniformed men patrolling the major thoroughfares. Often, I would read reports of harassment at the hands of these patrols.

I kept both these sightings and reports secret from Andrea. She did not need that on her plate as well.

So began her ordeal of chemo. Chemotherapy is nobody's idea of a picnic, and if you have been through this and came out the other side, kudos to you. I saw what it did to my wife, and it was not pretty. And if I may, I also saw what it did to me. She was the one with cancer and having to go through it, but I was the one observing it being done to the person I love and value above all else in the world. I could not have been more upset if someone kicked my dog.

I never knew cancer was so damn *busy*! Ah, an infusion once a week, a few days of feeling crap, life goes on… Ha! As if. It was, at least for us, an almost constant cacophony of activity and noise, hardly any rest.

Speaking of rest, I have to say that I was sleeping in the spare bedroom by now. We moved a spare mattress into my office, and this was my lodgings. Andrea needed her space, both physically and emotionally. Fortunately, she had the luxury of having the main bedroom to herself. We installed an air con to help with the hot flushes and cold spells, and blackout curtains to keep the piercing winter sun from the north-facing bedroom. It means she could rest and fight this battle without having to concern herself about me and my comfort. She could close the door and just be herself and do what she needed to do. And it meant I could do what I needed to do without bothering her. Which was mostly taking care of the household.

Which is where I need to sing the praises of one more lady whom I cannot live without: Sarah Nyathi. Sarah is our maid. Or, as I prefer to call her, my domestic goddess. Sarah has been working for us twice a week for over a decade, and we took her with us whenever we moved house. Sarah mopped floors and washed dishes and ironed clothes while I was busy with everything else. I will be quite honest about it: without Sarah, I would have fallen to part like a teenage girl at a Bieber concert. An extra pair of hands twice a week on the home front was worth its weight in gold. No matter where I find myself, if at all practically possible (that is, not emigrate to Svalbard) I'm taking Sarah with me.

But for heaven's sake, do not ask me what I was actually doing! I do not know. I cannot sit here and tell you, oh, I did this and did that and then... I cannot tell you what my days were filled with. Only that they were overflowing with a million tiny things. I became relieved that I did not have any clients left, because heck knows I would not have been able to deliver. I did three — yes, count them, three — commercial shoots during the entirety of 2020, and I've not had a single creative one. I simply did not have the time. At the end of each day, I would collapse into my bed, asleep before my head even hit the pillow, only to do it all again tomorrow. Whatever 'it' was. I can tell you that supporting a cancer patient is a full-time job. It is an incredible privilege that I could be that person for Andrea. I am so grateful that I did not have a regular nine-to-five office job. Not only did it mean I had the spare time to look after a sick person, but it also meant that I could spend every available second in the company of my wife. Even if she was sleeping in another room with the door closed and the air con on.

8

She was initially scheduled for twenty-five chemo infusions.

I used my graphic design skills and drew up a graphic: a girl holding twenty-five balloons, all of them blue, except number twenty-five, which was pink. After every chemo, she would come home and with a pencil, cross out a balloon, 'popping' it. One balloon at a time, we had a visual reference of progress.

Several infusions in, they did a progress scan, and proclaimed the tumour had shrunk. Victory! It was working! The report gave the exact dimensions, and this gave me a brilliant idea: I delved into my art-school heritage, and I made two to-scale boxes. The first with the original dimensions when she first got diagnosed, and the second with the new dimensions. I know the tumour is odd-shaped, and a geometrical right-angled box is not accurate in the slightest, but being able to see the difference between 'diagnosis' measurements and 'now' was a very encouraging visual aid. We displayed those boxes proudly on the shelf next to the chemo-balloons. We were moving in the right direction.

A month or two later, the process repeated itself. Another test, another measurement, and another, significantly smaller box joined the previous two on the shelf. The tumour had shrunk by 81%.

If this was not the most encouraging news we've ever heard, I do not know what was. The horror-show of the chemo was paying dividends. The endless bowls of boob soup had a purpose, after all. We could carry on. Nothing gives you motivation for the final push more than the knowledge that 80% of the battle had already been won.

On Monday the 10th of August, she told me she 'did not feel well'. Now, this is a crisis. You have cancer, you are on nine tons of medication, fuck knows what toxins are in your body attacking a tumour, hoping to kill it before it kills you: you are *supposed* not to feel well. So, if you do not feel well on top of not feeling well, well, this is something to write home about.

We phone Dr Ronwyn van Eeden, and she tells us to come in. She prods and pokes and looks concerned and tells us to go for a scan. We go, and you know how this ends: It was back. Almost overnight, with about eight or nine balloons left to pop, it had grown from 81% of its original size to larger than its original size. Sideshow Boob was back, and this time he meant business. Nobody could explain how or why, only that it is. And it needs to come out. *Now.*

Fuck.

You want to see activity? *This* is activity.

Tuesday we are back at Carol-Ann Benn, and we schedule lumpectomy surgery for two days' time, on Thursday. After Carol, we walk across the waiting room to the reconstructive surgeon, who would cobble her right breast back together after Carol removed the lump. He would then also reduce the size of the left breast so that Andrea would be symmetrical and not lop-sided. He informed us she would sadly lose the nipple. This is okay, lose the nipple, just get this damn thing out! After the reconstructive surgeon, we go back across the waiting room to meet with the radiation specialist who would do intra-operative radiation on the cancer-site during surgery. All this in one day, and if memory serves, it took about five hours to get all these things organised and consulted and scheduled.

And they were honest: Andrea is in no shape for surgery. She is far from healthy. Surgery is a risk, but they cannot *not* operate. There is a chance — tiny, but still noteworthy — that she would not come out the other side.

Which meant on Wednesday we call up Lucio and Rina, our lawyer buddies. In another flurry of activity, legal documentation gets sorted. Wills being the obvious one, but also what was to happen to Kerron, her business partner, should she shuffle off? I never have, nor do I think I ever will, signed so many legal documents on the line that reads 'witness' in a single day. Then it is packing and a million-and-three small things to take care of before tomorrow.

Thursday morning breaks, surgery day. I'm busy packing and taking care of Andrea and taking care of the dogs and and and when my phone rings. It is my father.

Overnight, my mother had died of Covid.

9

There's no point in writing a memoir like this if you ain't gonna be honest. So let me be honest. For the last dozen years or so, there's been no love lost between my mother and I. She used a phrase on me once, and I've since learned it was one of her stock phrases she often used, and I'll now use it on her: I loved her, but I did not like her.

I'm not going to re-hash my mother and her multitude of sins here. That would be unfair to her. Let's just say she was the founder and CEO of the Gaslight Guilt Trip Travel Agency. We drifted apart when I was in my mid-twenties, and by the time I was in my mid-forties I saw her maybe twice a year: on her birthday and Christmas.

And if I did not like my mother, Andrea loathed her. I remember one day my mother was particularly full of ire, and Andrea chirped her: "I do not care how you talk to your son, but nobody speaks that way to my husband." Well now! Andrea had such an amount of disrespect for my mother that she did not allow the old bird into the house. And I daresay it was warranted.

But your mother is still your mother. Dislike or fondness, respect or disrespect, I am still her son. When my father told me she had finally shuffled off, I was heavily conflicted.

And so was Andrea. When her mother died, she had told me it knocked her for a loop. Despite their troubled relationship, when Missus H died, Andrea had a melt-down. She told me that even though there is a fair amount of justifiable resentment towards my mother, I'll still take a knock when she dies. She then assured me she would be there for me when it happened. She has had the experience of having a parent die, twice, and she would give me the emotional comfort I needed. Just like I had for her in 2006. I still remember the wide-eyed apology from Andrea that Thursday morning when she said, "I know I said I'll be there for you when your mother dies, but I can't. I just can't." And who can blame her? She had much bigger issues to worry about than her mother-in-law, whom she could not stand.

And so did I. Right now, there was something happening I could actually do something about. I had to get my wife to hospital for what was essentially emergency cancer surgery. Surgery that had a tiny probability of her not coming out the other end. As you may imagine, this scared me witless. And if it scared her, she did not show it. She had a *laissez-faire* attitude about the entire thing. *Que sera sera.*

Remember, this is during the height of Covid. I could not escort Andrea into the Hospital. Best I could do was to drop her off at the entrance of Milpark Hospital, hug her, kiss her, tell her that I love her, and watch her go in.

This, to me, is the worst thing Covid had done. Despite the countless people who had died — including my own mum — the ultimate insult was that it separated people who really needed each other. I sat in the parking lot and cried. I cried for myself and the crap situation I was in, and I cried for my father who now needed to sort out my mother's logistics, but most of all I cried for my wife.

If it was traumatic for me to kiss her goodbye at the steps of the hospital, how much more so was it for *her*? How much of that *laissez-faire* attitude was real, and how much of it was mask? Just how lonely did she feel dragging her suitcase behind her, going in for surgery she knew she was not well enough to undergo, and there was no one there to hold her hand and tell her it's going to be okay? No one to squeeze her hand and make shitty jokes to try to make her feel better? Can you imagine that loneliness? I can't, and I've got a fucking great imagination.

I composed myself and drove home, and on the way there was a single tear for my mother. I even remember the traffic light where a tear rolled down my cheek. But that was all.

I arrived home to the panicked distress of two very overwhelmed dogs. I told you: dogs know. Laszlo knew his mother was sick, and he gave her extra special — and extra gentle — love and attention over the previous few months. They were very distressed when they saw Andrea leaving with a suitcase that morning, and when I returned home without her, the doggies were visibly upset. And upset by me being upset.

But the gift just kept on giving: a power failure. Which is euphemistically termed 'load shedding' in South Africa. Because the national electricity provider cannot supply enough power, they systematically switch off blocks of the country to save energy. I arrived home to a silent house. These power failures are scheduled to last four hours. However, more often than not, once the power gets turned back on, the system overloads and the sub-stations trip, which means several more hours of darkness. And because the power goes, the pumping stations at the municipal water supply do not work, so the taps run dry as well.

I arrived back to this and did the only thing that I could: I waited. I could not even go to the frail care centre where my mother lived and died to help my father because the friendly neighbourhood pandemic would not allow me through the gates.

I stared at the TV — we have a battery-powered inverter for just these occasions — but not seeing a thing. At one in the afternoon Andrea called: she was going in. She would phone me as soon as she was out.

Two days prior, they told us that the surgery would be about four hours. Two hours or so for the lumpectomy, and then two hours or so for reconstruction. As someone who had more than his fair share of surgeries — thirty-five-odd and counting — I know nothing is ever as long as they say. Take that four and add an hour each end and you'd end up with six. One plus six equals seven, so I did not expect to hear from Andrea until at least seven that night.

Just after three, I get a call from Carol: job done! In fact, job *well* done. She got the entire tumour, the margins are clear, it's clean as a whistle, and by all means a success. The reconstructive guy is now doing some boob-work, and that should be that.

That was when I realised I've not breathed since about nine that morning. The relief was absolutely palpable! Okay, cool! Two more hours, maybe three, she should be out by five or six.

Five comes, nothing. Six comes, nothing. Seven? I phone the ward. "She's still in theatre." Wait, what? I phone Carol. Carol gently and patiently tells me that sometimes unexpected things happen, and surgery takes longer, but that everything is fine. I believe her. At least, my brain does. My anxiety levels ignore her like a stop sign rusting away on a desert floor.

Eight o'clock comes and the inverter runs out of juice, leaving the TV a blind eye in a dark room.

There I sit, alone in the dark, my mother died earlier that morning, my wife is in for oncological surgery and should have been out hours ago, and I cannot even take a shower or make myself something to eat.

It was, at that stage, quite simply the worst and most frightening moment of my life. I hugged my knees and rocked back and forth and cried like a four-year-old who dropped his ice cream on the gravel. I am glad there was nobody around to see me. It was the low point of my life. I had never felt so lonely, or so scared.

At nine I phone the ward again. Nothing. "Still in surgery." Now I'm beyond frightened. I'm outright panicking. I'm on the verge of puking.

Nine fifteen my phone rings with Andrea's caller ID. I answer with wooden fingers which do not quite want to hold the phone. A tiny voice asks a tentative, "Hello?"

"Hey, my love, I'm out of theatre." Thank the good Lord! Hearing her exhausted and raspy and drugged-out phone-sex voice on the other side of the line was manna from heaven.

She was in surgery for eight hours. There was 'an issue' with the intra-operative radiation, but all's well. So well, the reconstructive guy even managed to save her nipples!

I would not see her for another three days.

INTERLUDE

Full disclosure your honour, for the sake of transparency and honesty.

After I finished writing the above, I had a bit of a breakdown. South Africa is having an identity crisis with looting and riots in the streets, and Covid numbers skyrocketing. The mood of the country is not a great one. The diametric opposite of what it was in 1994 and again in 2010 when us South Africans felt we could do anything. The net result of this is that everybody's staying home, and everybody is bummed. The government, trying not to over-burden the healthcare system, banned all liquor sales, both at liquor stores and at bars and restaurants.

I finished the above nine subchapters at about three in the afternoon, and when I wrote 'I would not see her for three days', I had myself a panic attack. I had every intention of finishing up the chapter before treating myself to a dinner of leftovers and alcohol-free beer.

But since Andrea died, I've not felt her loss as acutely and profoundly as I did yesterday after those last lines. I did not cry. I did not need to. I did not feel sadness — which has been a constant undercurrent in my life anyway — but by God, I felt alone.

I have great friends. I will never deny that. But friends share time and space. A spouse shares a life. There is simply no friend who could fill the void I felt yesterday.

And now it is a chilly Thursday morning in the heart of winter, and so I carry on.

10

I did not mind that I would not see her for three days. Quite the contrary, I loved it!

For the first time in six months, I had nothing to worry about. My wife is cancer free! They got it all! They even kept her nipples. It's over! Thank fuck it is over! There is still a road to walk ahead, yes, we knew that. But it was a practical road with an end in sight. Not this 'what if' constant worry. Tumour is out, clear margins.

Happy days are here again!

And guess what? For the next three days, she wasn't home, and I would not need to do a million daily things to support her in her journey. I could do what I wanted!

So I slept, played with the dogs, started a new manuscript, ordered deliciously unhealthy heart-attack take-away food, just had myself a jolly good R&R. I knew when I fetched her from the hospital, I'd have a very sick person to take care of.

But for those three nights of quasi-bachelorhood? Let's just say I needed the rest.

Getting her from hospital was a victory. She was pale and gaunt, a drainage pipe coming from her right breast. You could see she had been through a war. But so what!? She was coming home, and Sideshow Boob wasn't. I will take the next several months and nurse my wife back to health, love her back to life. And when it's all over, we'd go to Germany. For a month! And heck, why not even Svalbard? I'm ready to go renew my vows. Life is a reason to celebrate.

Y'know, I think that may have been the last day I felt *good*.

And if you think I felt good, you should've seen the dogs! Lazslo went apeshit. Laika went into a happy-yap barking spree which only calmed down four days later. I took Andrea to bed, made her a cup of tea, brought her favourite hippo, drew the curtains, and just let her be. No more chemo. No more anxiety about the surgery still some indeterminable date in the future. Now it was just healing. And wound care. I'll admit the only reason I did not study medicine is because I get woozy around blood and gore. I mean, I have the doctor's handwriting down pat. If I could handle blood, I could be a medical surgeon. Well, that and lack of brains. The fact is, I cannot stand injuries and blood and puss and all that. Those who can: are you alright? Do you need a hug?

But this is where I rolled up my sleeves, got myself the rubber gloves, and played nurse-nurse to Andrea's not insubstantial cuts. I got so good at it, that near the end, doing a dressing change only took me an hour, and it left me exhausted and Andrea irritable and grumpy. But she healed up pretty darn nicely I dare say.

And as a red-blooded hetero-normative cis-gender male? Those new re-shaped boobs looked mighty fine! But don't take my word for it. Even Andrea loved them! "I always wanted nice perky boobs, it only took breast cancer to give them to me." Ah, the future's so bright, I gotta wear a welder's helmet!

The only hurdle ahead was radiation. She would get zapped to make sure the tumour site is well and truly dead. A pain in the ass, yes, but hey, kill that motherfucker!

This is an important bit: if you know about radiation treatment, you know you are not allowed to miss. You can bomb the crap out of the tumour site, but any stray ammunition can damage the vital organs you may just need in the long run. In order to make sure they get the radiation in the right place, and only the right place, they need to map out *precisely* where it needs to go. And they do this by giving you tattoos. Cool, huh? To know where to put the tats, they have to do it with x-rays. Put you on a table, shove some radiation through you to see your insides, and then put tiny pinprick tattoos on your torso to show where to aim.

Why is this important? Because the day they x-rayed Andrea to mark the radiation site, the x-rays showed her body was clear.

Andrea and me at A-Ha
15 February 2020

Chapter 7 - The Hemingway Moments.

1

Radiation is no joke. Truth be told, many say — and I have observed — that radiation is more unpleasant than chemo. Radiation is no fucking picnic. The only silver lining is treatments do not take long. Chemo? Takes forever. A chemo infusion takes up an entire bloody day. But radiation? Skip on over to the Donny Gordon after work, get buzzed, go home, have dinner, carry on. No mess, no fuss.

This became our routine. Andrea was working again, her hair was growing back into a cute as hell short fuzz, and we made plans to emigrate. She'd had enough of South Africa. The nature of her vocation allowed her to grab a laptop and set up anywhere on the planet. Her EU passport meant she could go to Europe on the next plane out with no mess or fuss, and because I was a spouse of an EU citizen, I could get automatic residency. And because Norb and Astrid loved their cousin, their door in Germany was open.

The plan was such: she would move to Germany in January 2021 to set things up and sort logistical matters from that end, and then in May the dogs and I would come over, and we would start a new chapter of our lives in Europe. She had been given a new lease on life, and she was planning to use it. As for me? I'd follow her anywhere. I don't care where I lay my head, as long as it is next to her. Even if we were sleeping in separate rooms. Besides, that autobahn with no speed limit? Well, I'm no petrolhead, but I won't say no to making enough money to buy an Alfa Romeo Giulia and have it scream down the highway at half the speed of sound. My career would probably flourish in Europe with the type of photography I do. Sign me the hell up!

As I write this, it is July. I am still in Johannesburg, and will probably be for the foreseeable future. I do not have a career to speak of and have no rights to enter Europe. Thanks to Covid, not even as a tourist. The coveted Alfa Giulia? A downloaded .png file on my computer. Not a single aspect of that dream came to fruition.

Cancer, chemo, major surgery, it does not leave one the picture of health in its immediate aftermath. And while Andrea was getting her strength back, she was by no means healthy. Dark black circles around her eyes made her look like Uncle Fester, and that's not me being unkind for the sake of hyperbole. She really was that pale, that moon-faced, and had those deep dark black circles around her eyes. Yet she carried on working; both on work-work, and making arrangements for our emigration.

September is our birthday month. I'm on the 5th (shared with Freddie Mercury, Johann Bach, and Rose McGowan. I got Freddie's bad teeth, but alas, not his voice), and Andrea on the 22nd (shared with Nick Cave, Billie Piper, and my own fictional Leigh McCabe). Between wound care, healing, and getting herself shoved into an industrial-sized microwave, I cannot say we had the merriest and best of birthdays. But we had birthdays! And that is the important thing. We had birthdays — Almost certainly with a ton of prawns and/or langoustines!

And the Indian Premier League was on. We could watch cricket again! Heck, even Andrea's favourite team, the Mumbai Indians, won the tournament. (My favourite team, the Royal Challengers Bangalore, ended up in a semi-respectable fourth position). All's well with the world.

But something was rotten in the state of Nevada Drive, Northcliff. We were both aware that radiation is a nasty business, but *this* nasty? Somewhere around the end of October, she started complaining about stomach pains, which seemed to steadily get worse. She took a lot of pain meds, but the pain did not subside. I started getting worried. She said she was probably just full of shit.

Literally. It had happened twice before. Where Andrea's colon just got compacted with crap. A good laxative and an hour on the loo would void her bowels and the stomach pain went away. Laxatives were bought, hours were spent on the loo, but the pain did not go anywhere.

And along with the increasing pain came increasing weakness. She was permanently exhausted. At times so much so that she had to hold on to the wall in the hallway to keep upright.

I wanted to take her to hospital, but she was resolutely against it. "What are they going to do? X-ray me, give me a laxative, and send me home?" To be fair, it has happened exactly that way twice before.

On the early evening of Thursday, November 12th 2020, we went for radiation. She could barely walk. I remained in the car — yup, Covid protocols again — and waited. When she emerged, clinging to the hand-rails at the entrance in a death grip and sweat on her brow, I knew that something was wrong.

She fell into the passenger seat and for the one and only time in our entire relationship, I went against Andrea's wishes.

"You can scream at me when we get home and divorce me when you get better, but right now, I'm taking you to hospital, and no amount of logic or pleading will stop me."

I expected a fight. A denial. She just nodded and whispered, "Okay".

Not even five minutes later we were at the doors of the casualty unit at Milpark. I saw her go in, and I got relegated back to the car again. I think I spent more time waiting in a car in 2020 than I did collectively between 1974 and 2019. I knew the radio presenters so well I felt like I could invite them over for dinner. It was an excruciatingly long wait. An occasional WhatsApp from Andrea. 'Seeing a doctor now' and 'Going for tests' and 'Still waiting'.

I can only tell you of my experience because it's the only point of view I have. But I can imagine — and probably write myself into another breakdown — what it must've been like for her. In pain, confused, being sent for test after test with no support system with her, when she expected to be home watching telly with a doggie on her lap while her hubby prepares a late dinner. God, it must've been terrifying.

2

I belong to several writers' groups on Facebook. I hate to say it, but the trash-to-treasure ratio of these groups — indeed, any group — is dishearteningly low. For every person who can add value and provide valuable insight and knowledge, there are two hundred idiots who never even read a book who now think they are the next Dan Brown.

Or Hemingway.

To wit: I was on a Facebook writers' group one day and some dope who cannot spell his own name without looking at his ID card asked a question: "How do I get to write like Hemingway?"

Questions like that should be shot, taken outside, and shot again. I may as well ask: "How do I get to sing like Pavarotti" or "How do I get to dance like Fred Astaire" or "How do I get to paint like Claude Monet." Answer: you don't. And if you even have to ask the question, you lack even the intellectual capacity to sit in the same time zone as Hemingway, let alone write like him. But that was just me being grumpy.

I decided to take the question at face value. How *does* one get to write like Hemingway?

Billy Shakespeare takes the mantle of the greatest writer in the English language, although personally, I cannot understand a word he says, not even 'the'. But second place, I think, is a street-brawl away between Dickens and Hemingway, with Conan Doyle coming in at fourth. (All you poncey academics screaming sacrilege and throwing Chaucer and Milton and Elliot in my face: go jump in your pretentious lake.)

I've read Hemingway and Dickens, and I can tell you, both of them are as dense as my attempts at cake. My expectation of Dickens was great, but my experience was akin to if I wanted three months of unrewarding hard labour, I'd ask my wife if she wanted chores done around the house.

Hemingway, however… Man, that man can take you on journeys. Yes, he is dense, his dialogue stilted, and his imagery about as cinematic as a blown TV, but the *feeling*?! Ye gods! There is no way you cannot read Uncle Ernest without getting enthralled and taken on journeys. From war zones to fishing to love to loss, nobody writes like Hemingway. Not because he has great and memorable characters or because he has the visual eye of an impressionist painter — which he has neither of — but because Hemingway makes you *feel*!

The only reason Hemingway can make you *feel* what he is writing is because *he* felt it. Whether it is a story about a geriatric fart going fishing (The Old Man and the Sea) or about a young man's search for love and beauty in wartime Europe (A Farewell to Arms), Hemingway makes you feel for one simple reason: he was there.

A central adage in writing is *write about what you know*. This is not the end all and be all, because imagination plays a huge role — face it, Gene Roddenberry had never done any interplanetary travel — but no matter how fertile the imagination and how proper the research, when it comes to things that really matter, no one can ever write with any authority or authenticity if they had not had first-hand experience of the subject.

And this is why Hemingway writes like Hemingway: he knows, man, he *knows*. He knows because he has been there. Hemingway was a bad ass mother who saw front line war action as an ambulance driver in Italy in World War One, was a wartime journalist for the Spanish Civil War, and was at the Normandy landings. Then he got bad ass…

The point is, if you want to write like Hemingway, you needed to have lived like Hemingway. No cosseted and isolated comfortable suburban life will ever lead to the heights of Hemingway.

I know I'll never achieve Ernestian accolades, but on that Thursday night, I had my first ever 'Hemingway experience'.

My phone pinged. A Whatsapp message.

Please come. It's back.

3

I had to mask up and sanitise and sign waivers, but they allowed me in to see her. She was lying in a corner bed, secluded from everybody else, an IV drip in her foot because she did not have veins left in her arms for the needle. She looked at me with those big, beautiful brown eyes, and I held her hand. She squeezed my hand, I squeezed back, and a tear rolled down her cheek. I kissed it away.

"Please tell me everything is going to be alright," she asked in a whisper.

"Everything is going to be just fine," I lied.

I sat there and held her hand. We did not speak much. We had nothing to say, really. We were both shocked and surprised.

We were waiting for the results of a Covid test. She was to be admitted, but they needed to know if she was going to be in isolation, or if she could go into the general ward. Way past midnight, the test results came in, she was negative. I kissed her goodbye, and they rolled her away. I drove home and fell into bed around one, and cried myself to sleep.

Five hours later, my second Hemingway moment arrived.

Just after six a.m. on Friday, the 13th of November, she called. I answered the phone, and there was no hello back. Just a shocked and totally deadpan reply: "I've got six months."

This has been, and always will be, the biggest jolt of my life. "What?"

Now the shocked and deadpan voice cried. "Ronwyn was just here. It's back. It's everywhere. I've got six months!"

You read it often in romance novels and thrillers: 'I grew cold'. I wrote it a time or two myself. That Friday morning, I felt it. I literally felt how my blood drained from my face and my body-temperature dropped several degrees. It almost felt as if my body somehow shrank, my skin contracted.

My love. My poor, poor love. It was just not right.

4

The cancer had indeed spread *everywhere*. It ended up in her lungs, her sternum, her spine, her kidneys, her lymphatic system, and, most notably, her liver.

Why or how this happened, nobody knows. Remember I said earlier that when she had the tattoos done to mark the radiation site that it was clear? Prezactly! About a month prior, she had been x-rayed, and there was nothing! Nothing! She was clear. And now it was 'everywhere'. Both Drs Carol Benn and Ronwyn van Eeden commented that they had never seen anything like this. Where did it come from? Why? There was zero indication that Andrea had any form of cancer in her, let alone totally overcome. It remains a mystery to this day.

There was nothing they could do for her. Chemo would be an expensive and uncomfortable joke. The best you can do: Go home, live your life, enjoy the last few months with your family and friends. Sounds like the plot of a bad Christmas movie.

So that is what we did. I took her home and made her favourite meal and bought an expensive bottle of champagne, and celebrated her life.

5

One of the first people she called was her business partner, Kerron.

Kerron: What a guy! A typical chest-thumping tall-and-broad Alpha male with (what he thinks is) a wizardly beard. Always up for a party when the occasion calls for it, and always up to speak to the captains of industry and world leaders if the occasion calls for it. Well-travelled, well-educated, a foodie like the rest of us, and even part-owner of a brewery in Dullstroom (which, believe it or not, I've not been to!). Let's just say that if the day breaks, Kerron fixes it and then asks what's next on the agenda. I have a lot of time for this guy.

The relationship between him and Andrea was of such a nature that if I did not know better, I would have thought they'd had an affair. You should see the WhatsApp exchanges! The only time I've seen insults, snide remarks, and bickering between two people at this level was between Al and Peg Bundy. Often, when Kerron came to our house for a work catch-up session, I would sit in my office while the two of them were at the dining room table, and I'd just eavesdrop on their banter. It was like something from a well-scripted Blackadder episode! And oh, Kerron is also a cricket lover, and would shoot Jonny Bairstow on sight if he ever met him in real life.

I'll never forget when Andrea was asked: "So, are you retired now?" and she replied in cricketing terms: "No. I'm retired hurt." Kerron and I both knew what that meant. She packed away the Dell laptop, never to be used for work purposes again, and started the slow but deliberate handover of the company to Kerron. I'm happy to say that Kerron is swamped with work and Andrea's legacy of Sidus Consulting lives on. She created a business from scratch, convinced her old boss to come work for her, made him full partner, and now he is the owner-slash-director of a consultancy which does financial and infrastructure consulting all over the world.

Remember when I said Andrea cancelled her life insurance four months before they diagnosed her? The only 'inheritance' I have received was a business insurance pay-out so that Kerron could buy Andrea's shares from me so that I did not end up a fifty percent partner in a business I have no business businessing in. Take my advice, folks, get life insurance. Losing your spouse is bad enough. Losing your spouse and your income — and with it your home — is no fucking joke. If you have a spouse and (especially) a child, and you are not insured, put down this book, and run to the phone. You will not live forever, and it will be the greatest gift you can give them.

While Andrea wound down her business and handed it over to Kerron, she got to work on another project: me.

She has always accused me of being an under-achiever. I, sadly, cannot contradict her. I'm always a day late and a dollar short. Throughout our relationship, she has accused me of not believing in myself, of not living up to my potential, of not putting my talents to good use. *Mea culpa.* I've not done what I could.

"I've got six months. I'm going to fix that. I'm going to make sure that after I kick the bucket, you have a career!"

See why I love this woman?

She called it 'Brand Gerry' and she started out carving a career for me. What I should wear on public gatherings to establish a recognisable 'image' (This turns out to be an idealistic mix between Daniel Craig and Mags from A-Ha — the contemporary one, not the '80s one. Yeah, she had high hopes for me!). What I should put on my blogs. She did a severe editing job on my galleries on my websites, and then downloaded three dozen images from the internet as inspiration: "You need these types of images in your portfolio, lets organise the models and the makeup artists and do it!" As for my new as yet unpublished follow-up novel? She jumped in there as well and we set a publication date. "I'm gonna check out around April, May. I wanna be there for you when you publish Giulia!"

Death had lit a fire under her ass: she was dead set (pun intended) on getting me sorted by the time they carry her away feet-first.

Oh, she was not above using her illness and looming death as a marketing trick. "Play the sympathy card, my love! Milk my illness and death for your benefit! People love a good sob story! Shit, if I have to die, you may as well profit from it." Gotta love it!

We were both so busy carving a new life for me, we did not have time to think about death and what all of that meant.

Which may have been the very idea in the first place.

Somewhere in this muddled timeline, she was in hospital for something, and I sat by her side, and asked her the essentialist question: "Are you scared?"

She shook her head. "No, I'm not scared. I was never scared of death. But I am pissed off."

"How so?"

"Is this it," she asked. "Is this fucking it? I have had so much shit in my life: abuse, rape, losing my parents, my own brother using me as a punching bag, financial issues, illness, all this shit, and now I have to *die*? I'm pissed off at God for giving me a miserable life and then a premature death."

If I believed in God, I would have been pretty pissed off at him, too. Sometimes, I wish I believed in a God. It's hard being pissed off at nothing.

6

The fourth woman whose praises I have to sing: Sister Mel Griggs. I get this call from nowhere one day. "Hi, this is Mel Griggs, from Discovery. I'm your palliative nurse."

"Huh, sorry, what? I think you have the wrong number…"

It wasn't the wrong number. It was an extremely welcome addition to our lives for the next few weeks. I did not know how much I needed someone like Mel until she showed up on my doorstep. Mel works for Andrea's medical aid scheme, and she was assigned to do the palliative care and duties during the final weeks and days.

It takes a special person to make the end of life your career, to deal with death on literally a daily basis. Mel is such a special person. She was a pillar of strength for me during the last days. Without her, I'd be a puddle on the bedroom floor.

Because the cancer was in Andrea's lungs (as well), she needed oxygen. I just get a call: "Oxygen delivery is here!" I opened the gate, and there was a guy rolling out an oxygen machine (which, for some reason — or maybe, logically — reeked of stale cigarettes) as well as a big oxygen tank.

Where did this come from? Mel. She organised the whole thing.

We hooked Andrea up to the oxygen machine, and that will forever be the sound of the death-watch to me. The asthmatic rhythmical wheeze of the oxygen machine as it *brr-paaah*'d its way to filling Andrea's lungs with life-giving air. For the next three weeks, that sound became a constant background noise. I remember lying in bed next to Andrea — I was kinda, sorta, back in the main bedroom now — reading a book, and listening to that loud and emphysemic wheeze of the machine and thinking how grateful I am for that annoying and stinking machine. As long as that machine is making its noise, it meant my wife is still alive.

But before I get to the Marvellous Mel, I have to get to Ernest Hemingway. Again.

7

They said six months. Three weeks in, the shit hit the fan. Not gradually, not gently, but out of nowhere. Blood? You want blood? God, I've never seen so much blood in my life. She was literally haemorrhaging from every orifice. One day I was in my office, doing whatever it was I was doing, and she sent me a Whatsapp. A selfie. She had stuffed tampons into her nostrils to try to stem the blood flow. Blood was coming from her mouth. Her face and chest were caked with it. Below it, a simple caption: 'Help'. She could not speak or call for help due to all the blood, so she sent me a message.

On Tuesday, the 8th of December, I took Andrea to the Rosebank Oncology Centre of Rosebank for an emergency appointment with Ronwyn. Mercifully, the haemorrhaging had stopped. For a bit.

I got her showered and into clean clothes. She was so swollen she could not fit into any of her pants, and she went to the clinic in old and over-washed pyjama bottoms where the elastic had deteriorated into nothingness. It was the only thing that would fit.

We were in Ronwyn's office, and the usually jovial and positive Ronwyn was everything but. Andrea asked Ronwyn straight: "How sick am I?"

Ronwyn replied: "You are terminal. But you knew that. What we are going to do now is devise a way to make you live as long as possible, but unless you land under a bus on the way home, your cancer will be the cause of your death."

Nothing we did not know.

Ronwyn excused herself to speak to the pharmacist, and this is where something unspoken happened between Ronwyn and I. She wanted me to follow. She never said, "Gerry, come with me," but I knew I had to. I excused myself under the pretence of needing to go to the bathroom. I met Ronwyn in another consulting room, and she closed the door.

I'm trying to be the comic, and in my best put-on Yankee Texas oil-magnate accent ask her, "Okay doc, give it to me straight."

Ronwyn looks at me and says the words I will never forget: "Andrea is very, very terminal." She actually said, "very, very."

With my heart hammering slowly in my ears, I ask: "How terminal?" Remember, at this stage, three weeks prior, Ronwyn had declared 'six months.'

"A week, maybe two. But she will not live to see Christmas." I nodded. I cannot say I was surprised at that prognosis. I had seen the steep accelerating decline in my wife. "Should I —"

"How did this happen," I interjected. "Carol got everything out. When we did the scan for the radiation, she was clean."

Ronwyn looked at me and said some truly honest words. "We don't know. She's dying of cancer of the short straw."

I'll never forget those words: 'cancer of the short straw.' Because that's all it was. Sheer bad fucking luck.

She asked the next logical question, and I answered: "No, I will," Then, a breath later: "What happens now?"

"Now you just take care of your wife. And yourself. Mel will sort everything else out."

With that, we left the room, and Ronwyn 'returned from the pharmacy' and I 'came back from the bathroom', and amazingly, I kept my composure. Andrea never suspected a thing. Yes, we lied to her, but I think you will agree that, ultimately, it was better that way.

On the way home, however, Andrea picked up on *something*. "You seem angry," she said. And then I realised, *yes, I am, I am angry*. I admitted I was. And then *she* lost her temper with me. "Well, excuse me! I'm the one fucking dying here. What right do you have to be angry!?"

And I lost my temper with her. What a time, right?

"I'm fucking pissed off because my wife is dying, and I cannot cry with my best friend about it. And my best friend is dying, and I cannot cry with my wife about it. I need to be strong for both of them. I'm losing the two most important people in my life at the exact same time and I cannot say a word about it because I'm supposed to be fucking strong for both of them!"

"I never thought of it that way," she said in a small voice. I pulled over. It was not the first time we wept that day.

At home, I got her comfortable in bed and made her a cup of tea. I got Felicity to sit with her, and Laszlo was on the bed next to her, Laika on the floor.

"Sweetie," I began.

"Yes?"

"I have something to tell you."

"Yes?" with suspicion.

I started crying. Violently. "You're dying!" I managed to squeeze out between sobs.

She rolled her eyes at me. "Yes, I know!"

I shook my head. "No, you do not know," I sobbed. "I did not go to the bathroom. Ronwyn did not go to the pharmacy. We had a meeting outside her office." Then I repeated Ronwyn's words verbatim. "You have a week. Maybe two. But you will not live to see Christmas."

This was the first time I experienced the power of pure emotion. How this unstoppable wave of pure unadulterated feeling can just consume one. I did not cry, I did not weep, I wailed. I held onto my wife as tightly as I dared, and wailed.

That was my Hemingway moment. Not even the moment she died, as mind-numbingly terrible as it was, was as bad as having to look my wife in the eye and proclaim her death sentence to her.

When I got married in 2015, I knew that my wedding day would be the best day of my life, and nothing would ever top that, and I'm okay with that. When I told Andrea she would be dead before Christmas, I knew it would be the worst day of my life. Nothing would ever top that, either.

And believe me, I'm more than okay with that.

8

The following day, the Wednesday, Kerron came to say goodbye. On Thursday, my father came. During this time, we arranged for her body to be donated to science. She never liked the idea of a grave or cremation. It was all pointless to her. 'Let them use what they can use, burn the rest,' was her attitude. With the cancer that was 'everywhere', organ donation was no longer an option. I called up Wits Medical School, and they sent through the necessary forms for her to sign. How bizarre that must be. We were slightly wrong on the organ donation though. Apparently, the corneas would still be viable. She signed the donation form for that, too. Trying desperately for a silver lining to cling to, I told her: "You have just given somebody the gift of sight," and that was the last time I saw her smile. She was pleased. And then she disappeared slowly into the fog that would claim her.

On Friday evening, I went to bed next to Andrea. "Oh, you're sleeping here tonight," she asked, in a final moment of lucidity. By this time, she was not quite herself. "You're not sleeping in your room?"

"And miss an opportunity to sleep next to my wife," I replied. "As if." I kissed her good night for the last time, and then, somehow, I fell asleep holding onto her.

And woke up the next morning to something that looked like Andrea, but wasn't.

9

On Saturday morning, the 12th of December 2020, all the legal requirements of 'life' were still present, but that was it. There was nothing there. I called everyone to come. My brother came to say goodbye, but she did not recognise him. Theresa, her best friend from school, came, as did Kerron and my father. I think she might — might — have recognised my dad, but I have my doubts if she knew Kerron and Theresa. A saw recognition in her eyes when she saw me, and she had an instinctive 'feel' for the dogs. But what was on the bed that December morning was largely vegetative as far as intellectual capacity was concerned.

Sister Mel came along and hooked Andrea up to a painkiller and muscle relaxant.

It was time.

With the help of a palliative nurse, Mel and Theresa washed Andrea, put her in her favourite washed-out yellow Homer Simpson T-shirt, cow-spot PJ pants (of course), and put fresh bedding on the bed. Felicity was on the bed with her, as was Laszlo, who gave his mother gentle kisses on her arm, and Laika nestled into the crook of her mother's knee. Theresa held one hand. My father stroked her leg, and I held the other hand. I looked into her eyes and repeated over and over again: "You are loved, you are loved, you are loved." I was determined that the last words the conscious mind my wife hears would be the assurance that she is loved. Because she was. She is.

At two minutes past twelve, on a sunny summer's Saturday afternoon, Sister Mel declared Andrea 'Prim' Heidgen dead.

She is survived by her husband, two doggies, and a Stuffed Petite Baby

Hippo named Felicity, and countless others who cared for her. She died in her own house, in her own bed, surrounded by those whom she loved and cared for, and cricket on the telly.

She was forty-four years old.

Andrea - Prim - Heidgen
22 Sep 1974 - 12 Dec 2020

Eclipse watching
Longyearbyen - 20 March 2015

Part Three:
ON LIFE.

The day after Andrea died, I started keeping an online/Facebook diary of sorts. I titled it the same as the title of this book: *Chronicles of a Reluctant Widower*. I never intended to publish it as a collective, but many people — from my best friends to complete strangers — have encouraged me to do so after they said it really helped them through their tough times of bereavement.

Death has been with us since the beginning of time, but Covid has made bereavement a daily visitor to many, and if my words can help, then I'm happy.

What follows in this section is me going through my diary and combining a more-or-less chronological reportage of events combined with present-tense thoughts and observations. Writing these thoughts and observations down has been the healthiest thing I've ever done in my life. I really hope it can help someone else too.

However, because of the odd present/past tense nature of this section, it may not read as coherently as one would like.

Please forgive me for this.

Prim & Felicity & Covid Masks
6 April 2020

Chapter 8 - The First Step.

1

I had lived with the knowledge that there was to come a day when I would need to face life without my wife by my side.

As long as that cursed oxygen factory shook and rattled in the corner, that day would be kept at bay. At about ten-to-twelve, Sister Mel looked over at me and asked me if she could turn off the oxygen machine. I nodded. What else could I do? All that machine was doing was delaying the inevitable. It was not fair to anyone, least of all Andrea. Mel flicked the switch, and the mechanical rattling wheeze grew still.

The day had come.

Andrea was dead within minutes of the machine falling silent.

It was the second-worst moment of my life next to telling her a mere four days prior. I had never seen a dead body before, and my initiation was that of my own wife. I held her still-warm hand and wept. I do not know how much longer we were all in that silent room with her, but after a while — two minutes, an hour — I asked everyone if I could have the room.

The dogs could stay.

I closed the door, wept, and said my goodbyes. I kissed her, and gave her one last look, told her I love her, turned my back, and walked away.

That's when Sister Mel sprang into action and did all the things I would not know how to do. I owe an entire chapter to what this woman did for me that day.

I delegated Kerron to make us sandwiches. My dad got beers from the fridge. Theresa sat with her head in her hands. One question circled in my head: What now? What now? What the hell do I do now?

The step between life and death had been taken, and now I had to take my first step in a new life. A life without my love. My wife. My best friend. My breadwinner. My champion. My part-time employer. My everything.

When Michaela — *slinky* — died, her mother told me it is like 'a blunt amputation', and with this I concur totally. This absolute blunt feeling of painful loss. Nothing can ever bring it back. There is no prosthesis that will even give the illusion of completeness again. I sat with my beer and my chicken mayo sandwich and wondered how on God's green earth I am going to cope. I am still wondering that.

Lucio and Rina came along, helped with practical matters, bought me sweeties, helped me remember our farcical, wonderful, wedding day at Home Affairs.

Sometime in the middle of the afternoon, the funeral director came to take her away. They asked me if I wanted to say goodbye. I shook my head. I said my goodbyes. They took her body away, and I did not see it go. I have no regrets about that. I quite like my last memory of my wife lying peacefully on her own bed. I did not want the last memory of her to be zipped up in a body bag and taken away on a stretcher. The way my last memory of her sits in my mind is perfect.

Later that evening, a bunch of my buddies came along. Juan, Martin, and Christo. They brought booze and ordered food. I poured a shot of vodka for my recently departed wife, and they stayed with me to make sure I didn't go off the rails. An unenviable job. The evening did not last long, though. I said 'thank you, but no thank you' and kicked them out, shutting the door behind them, standing alone for the first time in a silent house.

I did not think I would sleep that night, but I passed out and slept like a rock. Even though the mind was a screaming mess, the body had been stretched to breaking point, and I was taken by sleep as soon as my head hit the pillow.

On Sunday morning, I woke and let the dogs out. I finally understood that Skeeter Davis song: Why does the sun go on shining? This absolute surrealism of normality. The birds are singing, the pool is blue, the lawn is green, the dogs are doing their morning ablutions… same as it ever was. How? How can it all just be just so damn fucking normal?!

Don't they know the world ended?!

But the sun was not shining that Sunday morning. It was raining. And it suited my disposition perfectly. I don't think I could have coped with a sunshiny-happy summer's day right then. I did not have the strength to survive glorious weather.

The house was so big, so odd, so quiet. No bedroom door to close to keep the noise out while she was sleeping. No tea to make. No need to pee quietly against the rim of the bowl. I could aim straight for the water and piss noisily. Her quick-dial button on the home screen of my phone. Half a box of dry white still in the fridge. It was just all so damn odd.

I was — understandably — extremely distressed, and I forced myself to sit down and 'take stock'. To pull myself towards myself.

That is when I gave myself four rules to live by for the short-term future.

- **There are no rules.** There is no 'right way' or 'wrong way' to grieve. Anyone who says there is, can go jump in the lake. What you are feeling and experiencing is true. Do not think you have to follow a certain path, or the classic Kubler-Ross way of anger, denial, etc. Everything you feel is true.

- **Be kind to yourself.** It is very easy to relegate yourself to a third-class citizen after the one you dedicated your life to died. You are not. You are still as worthy as always. You are hurting. Be kind to yourself.

- **Do not let her die over and over again - once was enough.** Do not reprise Andrea's death scene over and over in your head. This is not kind to you, and it isn't kind to her. She died once. Do not allow your mind to sabotage itself and let your loved one die repeatedly.

- **Call for help.** You cannot do this alone, no matter how strong you think you are. With the help of others, you will survive. Alone, you will falter.

I called for help. Hard and often. I'd like to give myself that credit. But I'll give the help even more credit: they often came without being called.

2

I want to tell you about something I loathed. The phrase 'Sorry for your loss'. I hated it. I really did. It is such a trite cliché. Can't you come up with something more original? Even, "Sorry, that sucks," is better than, "Sorry for your loss." But now I get it. What I am feeling is an enormous, bloody, monstrous and looming *loss*. A part of me has been ripped away, a vital part, and its absence is nothing but that: a simple-yet-overwhelming loss. 'Sorry for your loss' may be trite and clichéd, but it is heart-breaking in its accuracy.

I have to sing several praises here.

Social media is a cesspit. Twitter is downright toxic. Facebook is slightly better. Social media is a way for society to hold up a mirror to itself to show it just what an ugly humanity we are. However, the friends I made on Facebook showed themselves for who *they* really are, too. There is still some humanity left in humanity. A friend ordered me chicken wings and beer via a delivery service. Nice, huh? Well, consider this: said friend lives in fucking Norway! Pals sent food and beer and care packages. Some people I've never even met in real life, yet there would be a knock at my gate with someone dropping off something so that the brand-new widower would not need to worry about grub. Pals took me to Hooters and stuffed me so full of chicken wings I looked like Obelix's fat friend. I got offers to stay in guest houses and holiday homes from down the road to Cape Town to Idaho to Switzerland so I could 'gather myself' — offers Covid prevented me from taking. They made sure I was never lonely unless I wanted to be. Pals of mine — Chris and Sue — live in Idaho, and they have a lake house they are renovating. Chris asked me, "Can you wield a hammer?" I said yes. "Can you hold a paint brush?" I said yes. Then he said to come over during their summer, and, "I'll put you to work!" It was one of the better offers I received in my life, and if not for this fucking pandemic, I'd be in Idaho right now learning to install ceiling boards instead of freezing my ass off in suburban Joburg feeling sorry for myself.

The first week or two was a whirlwind of activity. By far the bulk of it arrived with the truest and most honest of intentions. But tell the truth and shame the devil: there were also a few rubberneckers who enjoyed the *schadenfreude* at Gerry's Drama TM. Yeah, fuck those guys.

But a pal who I need to mention specifically here is one whom I last saw in 1999, and from her lips came the wisest words I've ever heard regarding bereavement. This is a lady named Jasmin di Bres, or as we know her, 'Jazzy Baby'. I've known Jasmin since I was nineteen. She's a year older than me. We have vastly different value systems and objectives in life, but we clicked since day one. We were such opposites that we could never attract, not in the romantic sense, but she was a true pal, even if she drank and smoked and did weed and drugs and all kinds of shit I was never into. She met a guy — Dion, his name — and got married, emigrated to Holland, and got herself a kid. I've not seen her in over twenty years. We kept sporadic touch via Facebook, but not much. She lived her life, I had mine.

Four years ago, Dion had died of cancer, leaving her a widow with a child. I only found out a year later.

That Sunday, I get a Facebook Messenger call from Jasmin, all the way from her little village in Holland.

This is her wisdom, which I'll never forget.

"Buddy," she began. "I've been there. A spouse with cancer? I've been there. The hell of chemo? I've been there. The news that they are going to die? I've been there. Those last picnic-filled days? I've been there. Holding his hand while he died? I've been there. I have *no* idea what you are going through."

I could have hugged her. Jasmin understood that no matter what we may have in common, every experience is unique. She did not pretend to know what I was going through, even though we had walked incredibly similar paths. You can show people photographs, but you can never take them where you live. Your journey is your own. My journey was just beginning.

Thanks, Jazzy Baby.

3

The Monday after Andrea died — less than forty-eight hours later — the gearbox on her car conked out…When life kicks you, it makes damn sure you are down first. Its laughable in its ridiculousness.

I got new glasses. I had to go before the year ran out, lest my insurance benefits expire. How odd to go to the optometrist two days after your wife died, and he asks you, "So, where's Ands?" and you have to say, "She's dead." Then he looks at you with shock and a wide-eyed stare and asks, "When?" and you reply, "Saturday".

Yeah, it's odd.

And then on the way back, the car decides its had enough of its gearbox… Oi!

I found I could handle daylight hours. As long as the sun hung in the sky, I was fine. I could somehow deal with it. The worst times, though, was sundown. It is the time the day winds down, work is done, and interaction begins. Normal conversations about 'What's for dinner' and 'will you go buy me a bottle of wine' and 'how was your day' and 'what do you watch on telly tonight?'. While we literally lived with each other twenty-four-seven for the better part of a decade, daylight hours were working hours. Her office was right next to mine, but daylight conversations were mostly work and practical issues. Sunset conversations were personal. This is when it hit the hardest. The silence of twilight mocked and bullied me.

Once it was full dark, though, it was better. I could handle the darkness. After dinner, I could face life again. Down the hallway, towards the main bedroom, a prison gate would slam shut, sealing the route. When darkness came, I was fine, but I could not cross a specific grout-line in the hallway tiles. Beyond that line lay something I could not face while the stars shone. By day, that gate would disappear, and I could access the main bedroom quite easily, but at night? No way.

The television remained blank for months. I never switched in on. Not even for cricket. I devoured books. Re-read Frankl's *Man's Search for Meaning* twice. I still haven't found any. And so, with every day that passed, I moved a day further away from the day my wife died, and a day closer to my uncertain and empty future.

More praise-singing, this time to two hairy Hungarians: Laszlo and Laika. I swear, if not for those two loud and hairy crazy dogs, I'd not be here. They gave me reason to carry on, to live. To get up, to shower, to go to the shops. They had lost their mother. Laszlo was very attached to his mum, and her death left him devastated. Whenever Andrea was out of the house — visiting a friend, at a doctor's appointment, on a business trip — Laszlo and Laika would wait for her at the front door. Heck knows why; we never use the front door. We come in from the garage through the kitchen. But those two mutts would lie by the door and wait for her and then go off like a happy furry hand grenade when she came home. Dogs know. They were on the bed with her when she died. Neither of them had lain by the front door waiting since.

They are good puppies, they keep their dad sane. It was their birthday week last week. Laszlo is ten and Laika nine. They are in good health, but they are not young anymore, and only have a life expectancy of twelve to sixteen years. I try not to think about the fact that there will come a day when I would need to say goodbye to my pups as well.

Heck–excuse me while I go play with them!

4

What I'm about to say you've heard a million times: Its only when someone dies that you realise what matters in life. All the little things you thought were so important end up meaning squat.

And the stuff buried away in a box for later? Those are the things which mean a lot.

Now I'm alone. My life, my love, my world has gone. It's a vast empty space filled with… holy crap, was this girl a hoarder! Andrea could collect junk like it was nobody's business. The sheer amount of 'stuff' that we have — no, that *she* had, and I now sit with — is mind boggling. Even a brand-new Philips air-fryer we've never even used, still sealed in its box. That one I donated to my father, who may have figured it out by now.

And the truth is that you do not own stuff. Stuff owns you.

Look, I like nice things. *Everybody* does. Even people who claim 'I'm not materialistic' have a thing they like. But, because of (lack of) insurance reasons, I am facing a very stark reality that I may have to pack my bags and dogs and go live someplace else. And take what with me — exactly — when I move? The three metric tons of crap and dust-catchers?

Material things mean very little. Not quite nothing, but little. You need tools to survive. But you most certainly do not need trinkets. A few quality kitchen knives, and a handful of pots and pans and skillets which you can trust. Sturdy crockery and nice glasses. A comfortable chair to sit in, a table to write on, and a mattress that is just right. Good sheets and perfect pillows. A handful of good books, meaningful books. A small box of the sentimental stuff. A refrigerator to keep the beer cold. A reliable car. A camera and a computer to carve out a career.

But the rest? What am I supposed to do with the chipped crockery, the drawer-full of mismatched measuring spoons and blunt cheese cutters, the washed-through bedding, and the curtains we've been keeping in a suitcase for 'one day'? All the little 'oh, that's cute!' dust-catchers sitting on a shelf that does what, exactly? The hundred-odd paperbacks that are almost universally forgotten the moment they are done. Do I really need that dog-eared copy of Jeremy Clarkson's rants I picked up at a flea-market for ten bucks? The nine million ball-point pens that's all over the place but never around when you need one? Mouldy six-pack cooler-boxes that were used once and never again? Just… you know, random crap. (Let me think about the Clarkson rants for a minute, okay? It's a troublesome question!)

Truth is that this rather substantive collection of random crap is weighing me down. The useless things we've kept simply because we did not know what else to do with them. I want to own a handful of good quality stuff that will make my life easier and more comfortable, not stuff I did not even know I've had which makes my life more cluttered.

Do you know what I find the most valuable?

The art.

The paintings and drawings and photographs from everywhere. There is enormous value in visual art for me. Art makes life more beautiful, and I need beauty. I need comfort. I need utility. And I now understand why Dumbledore only wanted woollen socks for Christmas.

Everything else… well, who needs it?

As the weeks and months rolled by, and I got a bit of money here and there, I framed things. There are now several things hanging on the walls which Andrea and I kept 'to frame one day'. For about half those things, 'one day' had arrived. We should have done so sooner. Having beautiful things to look at makes a hellish life easier to handle. I hope Andrea is pleased with the framing of the polar bear etching she bought in Svalbard, which is now hanging in the lounge.

It should have been there five years ago.

There are still a few boxes I need to take care of. It's a highly emotional experience. But every now and then I'll tackle one, and I'll be a step closer to sorting out the crap. And then, sorting out the non-crap. Prioritising material goods so that should I need to leave my house, I only have what is necessary, and none of what is weighing me down.

Which brings me to jewellery. I'm male. I know nothing about gems. I don't even wear a watch. But Andrea had a fair amount of it. I collected it all — with the notable exception of a Cartier Love Bracelet — took it to a jeweller and exchanged the gold and silver for cash. I used that money to help fund a doggie rescue centre. It's what she would have wanted. Rings and chains in the jewellery box mean nothing. But happy doggies? That means everything.

5

I never knew dying of cancer — and dying in general — was such a damn busy activity! Always off somewhere. Doctors, hospitals, chemo clinics, radiation clinics… All day, every day, you just have to go, go, go!

I was so damn busy in the months leading up to her death that I have totally worn out my poor middle-aged body. But I was so emotionally and psychologically engaged with what was going on with the most important person in my life, that I did not even notice Gerry's body shouting, "For shit's sake, STAHP!!"

A week after she died, I stopped. And the fatigue set in. Not necessarily sleepy, per se, but come ha'pa'nine at night, my head hits the pillow, and that's me, out for the count. However, during daytime, I was functional. It's not like I was sitting around stifling yawns and looking forward to my afternoon nap.

It's not a sleepy tired. It's a 'put the body down and allow it to recover' tired. A 'stare at the horizon for a week' tired. So tired that I did not even have the capacity to deal with my emotional turmoil. "I'll mourn later. Please, just let me rest."

It is now seven months since she died as I write this. I don't think I've even begun to rest. The practical matters of dealing with death, no matter how well-organised, still find a daily entry into my life. Just yesterday I had to deal with a debt collector who, for some Godforsaken reason, cannot understand that Andrea is dead, and no, you cannot speak to her, no matter how important it is. I actually got so sarcastic with someone who, one day, insisted on talking to my dead wife, that I said I can organise a medium for them. How difficult is it to understand someone kicked the bucket and therefore cannot come to the phone? I guess if these people were any smarter, they would not be working a call centre (A joke I'm allowed to make, I spent eighteen months working in one!).

6

The yin and the yang.

In my conservative Afrikaner upbringing, the yin-yang symbol was regarded as evil and satanic; best be avoided. (Well, truth be told, in my conservative Afrikaner upbringing, *everything* was satanic, including *Christmas with Boney M*... wait, they may have a point with that one!)

But the Yin-Yang symbol — and its cousins, the 'peace' sign and the pentagram — had a hatred and disgust reserved for the devil himself. Why? Because the yin and the yang symbolise the balance of opposites: in all evil there is some good, in all good there is some evil.

What blasphemy! There is no evil in good! There is no good in evil! The stuffed-shirt, black-suited religious leaders would have an aneurism at the very thought that someone could find redeeming factors in evil, and totally explode at the thought of finding something bad to say about the sacred.

Luckily, I shrugged off that idiotic and dogmatic ideology years ago. As did I shrug off the childish ideologies of Eastern mysticism — in which I dabbled purely to piss off the fundamentalists.

But since Andrea's death, I've found myself caught up in the wisdom of the yin-yang. The balance, the eternal offset of opposites.

There will never be a happy moment in my life without a pang of regret and a hollowness to it. There will never be heartbreak and weeping without a pleasant memory to take the edge off. Germany can never win a FIFA World Cup without me crying a tear for my wife. And South Africa can just never win a Cricket World Cup, period. (Hang on while I try to find some good in that... nope. This is where my analogy breaks down.)

The up and the down. The left and the right. The joy and the sorrow. The light and the dark.

I've had close on fifteen years where my life was illuminated by her light. Now it is my turn to sit in the dark.

And this, too, is a gift.

7

Amazingly, the Wednesday and Thursday after she died, I was fine. Life actually felt 'normal'. As did most of Friday. Went to the shops, worked on getting *Defining Giulia* ready for publication, played with the dogs. Life has this harrowing habit of carrying on, and it carried on, and I was okay.

But I've not put up the Christmas tree yet. We've been a tad busy trying to figure out how to die — and the practicalities thereof — to concern ourselves with a tree.

This is where I need to tell you about Andrea's obsession with Christmas trees that bordered on the fanatical. Her annual mission was to build the best Christmas tree she could. We have two storage containers — each large enough to store a giraffe — which are chock-full of Christmas decorations in every conceivable colour. We have *three* different trees. Three! Each year, she would choose a colour-scheme, and over the course of two days she would put up the Christmas tree, arranging and re-arranging and re-re-arranging every bauble until the tree was just perfect. Andrea's trees got legendary status in our small family. Each year it was a case of "What is Andrea going to do this time," and every year she out-did herself. I'll tell you my fave tree of hers: It was right at the beginning of our relationship. Maybe our second or third Christmas. Not a single tasteful glass bauble or kitsch decoration in sight. Nope: Andrea spent the GDP of a small central-Asian country and decorated the tree with colour-coded Lindt Lindor chocolate balls. You get why it is my favourite tree now, don't you? Sadly, she never repeated that performance.

She did not have time to put up the tree for Christmas 2020. She wanted to, but she just ran out of time.

If there was one thing I could do to honour the memory of my wife, it was to put up a tree. She would have wanted it.

The Saturday after she died, at about five in the evening, I put on some Christmas songs, purely to remind me of the happier times of my youth (Even — especially — the Boney M Christmas album). In my miserable childhood, December holidays were beacons of light punctuated by horrid Christmas songs, but even today those 'orrible songs make me feel good.

I fetched the Christmas-goods storage boxes, got out the stuff, and there it was: the chainsaw to the gut. It knocked me flat on my ass. Bawled my eyes out for half-an-hour. The illusion of 'normal' shattered by a bloody Christmas bauble.

I invited Theresa — Andrea's best buddy from school who was with us when she died — to come over the next day to help set up the tree. If I'm gonna get hit, I may as well have company to diffuse the blow.

She came, and for a few hours she put up the tree while I pretended to help. My hands were shaking too badly to do anything productive. Thanks to Theresa, I had a tree up for Christmas 2020, a tenuous connection to my wife, even if it was only for a week or two.

Side quest: I'm an insanely private person. Three-quarters of what I'm writing here — and wrote on Facebook before I formalised it into book form — I did not want to. I fear becoming *that* guy. You know, the one who only has one song to sing, and now he is becoming insufferable. However, many people told me they find value in my bereavement writings, so I carried on, and I'm carrying on. If you find me insufferable, buy me a beer, come visit me and we can talk about cricket!

Which is exactly what people do not want to talk about. My fucking wife died, and it hurts like hell. That chainsaw to the gut? Its real. It hurts. It is not just 'sad', grief has a physical and visceral pain to it. Sometimes the chainsaw is just a stab-wound, other times it is running at full speed, spreading pieces of me all over the wall. I preferred my own company for a long time after Andrea died, for the simple reason that even with the best of intentions, when company arrived, they flicked the switch on the chainsaw and set it running. I do not blame anyone. I know it's human nature and they had the best of intentions, but the constant fawning and 'poor you' reactions only made it worse. You know what helped for the chainsaw? The illusion of normality. Let's complain about the cricket and eat heart-attack food and drink beer. With my buddy for an hour or two, life is bearable. Hell, I can even have a good ol' belly-laugh and not even fake it. When we part, I got the whole damn day to deal with the chainsaw. I did not want to deal with it while in the company of friends as well.

8

Seven months ago, I had the terrible privilege of holding my wife's hand as she fought her final battle with cancer, and lost. It was abso-fucking-lutely harrowing. It's not a sight I wish for anyone to see, nor an experience I would wish for anyone to undergo.

Yet, I'm happy I was there. I'm so glad I could comfort her even as the brain lost its cohesiveness, and I'm doubting if it was still my wife on the bed. I can live the rest of my life knowing I was there for her. I never let her down, never let her go, never let her fall.

But crap, what about me? Fifteen years of memories are gone, missing. When I think of Andrea, all I see are the final moments playing out again and again, like a movie on loop. My brain simply refuses to summon anything else. If I try to force myself to find another memory of her, all I come up with is Andrea at chemo, at radiation, in hospital, but nothing before. Cancer has consumed my memories, erased fourteen years that we had before cancer defined our lives.

I go through her stuff, as one does, and I find a love-letter I wrote to her many moons ago. And in it I listed all the great memories, the great times, the fun we've had. The mischief we got up to.

And suddenly, just like that, my wife was no longer a cancer patient with pasty skin and dark eyes and chemo-hair. She was *Andrea* again. She was a voluptuous, vivacious woman with whom I danced in the streets of Austria during a snowy New Year's eve where we drank champagne straight from the bottle. She was the woman with whom I danced as Billy Joel himself serenaded us. A woman with whom I excitedly got new puppies with a decade ago. A woman who shared a third of my life and most of my adulthood with me.

That letter reminded me not of what cancer made us, but what we were before. The people who loved each other and got married on a frozen fjord under a solar eclipse in the north pole.

Without that letter, my wife would still be dying several times a day. Now, she's alive and well and kicking my butt and telling me to get my life together!

Write more letters. Not instant messages. Not emails. Just honest to God old-fashioned letters. You never know when they may come in handy.

9

This one I titled 'The Fringe People'.

You have your 'core' group of people. Those people that you can call up whenever, and they will answer your call for help and/or talk crap. Or they will just randomly pitch up at your place and drink your beer. The good friends you've had for a while who are just part of life. As reliable as a Cortina engine. (Get off it, Toyota people, you know those damn Fords run forever!)

Then you have 'group two'. They are not far removed, but they are not the homies you hang with regularly, either. You call them up to find out how they are doing, and sometimes you get a call from them. They look after you. They looked after me. I hope I sometimes look after them.

But then there are the less celebrated 'fringe people'. People you know because you were once at the same party, or you were at a presentation or workshop together and somehow got along. People whose phone numbers you don't even have, but you see them around on Facebook and you may bump into them at the next [thing].

I came to realise those 'fringe people' are bloody awesome. Not because the other two groups are not, but because one does not expect the fringers to actually care. But they do. And they somehow provide a tertiary grieving service I did not even know I needed.

Cases in point: some woman I met exactly once in a bondage club years ago is part of my Facebook friends — but I would not have recognised her if she bit me in the leg at the corner shop — and she offered to bring me chicken pie and malva pudding. Which she did. And she brought me hot, home-cooked meals twice more. Why? We're not 'friends'. We don't 'hang out'. I tied her to a pole in a fetish club twenty years ago and never saw her in real life again. Yet, she bought me chicken pie and malva pudding.

Or let me tell you about Ami-Raine. She is just some rando redhead model I met during a photographic open day once. Quite by accident, she ended up as the original cover girl of 'Discovering Leigh', but again, we're not mates. Met her two or three times at photography open days, but that's about that. She sent me a care package from across town. With, get this: dog treats. (And a snarky note stating the treats were not for me...)

Or Tuesday Houston, an artist from Cape Town whom I've never met. Heck, I do not even know how we ended up being Facebook buddies! I love her work, though. Beautiful and whimsical, featuring a lot of octopus tentacles and suckers. I had coveted a Tuesday original for many years. She sent me one of her artworks when she heard Andrea was sick. Her work of octopus tentacles holding up lanterns entitled 'For the Dark Days' now hangs on my wall. I still leak at the eyeballs sometimes when I look at it.

Or Natalie (AKA 'Murf'), an alternative model with more tattoos than skin and a brain the size of Djibouti. I've met her face-to-face three times in my life, and did one awkward shoot with her. Ding-dong: care package!

And I can continue this list for many pages, but the point is that the biggest surprise in this entire sordid affair, is the fringers, and how they just deliver. Sometimes without even knowing it. Many of these fringers got promoted to 'group two' now.

Social media is a cesspit. And yes, it is. But fuck me, without the peeps I met mostly on Facebook, 95% of my support would not exist.

Hey, Zuck, your platform actually has a purpose! Imagine that.

10

22 December 2020 – Day 10

Ten days in, and I can confirm the most common emotion is 'weird'.

It's not 'denial', but just a peculiar oddness to life. Denial is 'why?' My overwhelming feeling is 'how?'

How can my wife be dead? It's not right!

I have the 'why' down pat. She had cancer, it was fatal, and she died with me holding her hand. I'm quite clear on the 'why'.

But this damn 'How can it be?' keeps tripping me up and make me want to hurl. The chainsaw to the gut demands a spew every now and then.

Also, I've discovered there is a notable difference between 'heartbreak' and 'sadness'.

Heartbreak is an all-consuming thing that kicks me in the belly whenever it wants to, and it hurts like all hell. I can't stop it, I can't predict it. It sneaks up on me like a practical joker and smashes me to pieces, leaving me a mess on the floor tiles, wondering how I am ever going to get back up again.

But sadness…it's not what I expected it to be. It doesn't 'hurt' the way heartbreak does. However, it's omnipresent. The heartache is rare but intense, whereas the sadness is a low-octane constant companion which fills every single nook and crack I did not even know I had. And just remains, wondering if I'll ever get rid of it.

I wonder if I want to.

It was true when it was fresh, and it is true now: there's no 'lonely' feeling. I'm alone, but not lonely. Empty, yes. A big, aching, and gaping void, but loneliness is surprisingly absent.

And I think I know why. Because I am so well taken care of by my friends and fringers. But none of them can ever fill the hole Andrea left. I miss my wife, not a random person to eat chicken wings with. I have many of those, and I love and value all of them. But the void can only be filled by one person, and she's not here anymore, and I think my mind has made a certain peace with that. No use feeling lonely when the person who can take the loneliness away is lying on a slab in a medical school ten kilometres to the east of me. The absolute finality of it all has insulated me for loneliness. Does that make sense?

If it does, please tell me, because I'm not even making sense to myself.

11

23 December 2020 – Day 11

Two days before Christmas I was stuck in a 900-hour long power outage. And when I say 'stuck' I mean stuck! My driveway gate would not open! I could not leave my own yard. Not even to buy a new battery for the damn driveway gate.

Thus, I was forced to 'deal with shit'.

There is only so much reading and napping a guy can do in a day, and there are a lot of practical things to sort out, so I headed out into the cupboards and…

Damn, this was a lot harder than I thought!

I mentioned Andrea was a *lot* of a hoarder. She's got crap from God knows when or where, still in boxes, sealed and unpacked, from the first time we moved in together. She moved this stuff with her for fifteen years without even opening a box.

I'm the opposite. I like simplicity and a lack of clutter. If it does not have a function, it goes. Sentimentality only gets you so far.

Or so I thought…

The bulk of the stuff was easy to trash. While technically 'hers', it's like the warehouse in *Raiders of the Lost Ark* in there: hasn't been seen by human eyes in centuries. It's easy to throw away what you did not even know you had.

But that other slice of the pie… shoo. That was tough. A sealed packet of about two hundred business cards. That was really tough to chuck. But what else am I going to do with it? Put them in a box and move it with me for the rest of my life? There will come a time when I will get rid of them, so why not hurry up the process? I've got a lot — and I mean a lot — of her stuff that I want to keep. Some decorative, some sentimental, and some even downright useful, like the half-dozen Lamy pens! There is no usefulness or aesthetic value to a business card. Especially not two hundred of them.

But throwing them away felt like I was tearing off a piece of my own skin.

Sometimes making the right decisions hurts like hell.

Hell…

I've been complaining a lot during 2020. And with reason, I think. I had an insane number of things go bad.

When teenagers complain they can't go visit their pals and *this is the worst year ever, man*, I want to take out my 5-iron and practice my short game on their shins. Not that I play golf, but I digress.

The point is for some of us this has been hell. Multiple close deaths, personal injuries, illnesses (and not just 'a bad cold'). Even our geyser burst and rendered an entire room of the house useless. Talk about insult to injury.

But 'tis the season to be jolly falalala, etcetera.

And maybe I should use this opportunity to see which gifts were hidden in the box of darkness 2020 has been.

2020 has revealed to me just how much stronger I am that I've ever given myself credit for. I did not buckle. Not once. I bent a few times, but I came out on the other side "bloodied but unbowed," and that, my friends, is something this here little boy did not expect.

I've also learned just how fucking awesome people are. This I've always known. People are not the pond scum the permanently pissed off will make us out to be. But to be the first-hand recipient of that kindness of friends — and even strangers — is awesome. From a dozen frozen dinners to chicken wings all the way from Norway to a WhatsApp saying, "just checking in," and a million other people doing a million other things they do not have to…wow.

I've learned how set in destructive habits I've become, and now I have the freedom to change them.

And speaking of freedom, the greatest gift of 2020 is a terrible freedom, one that I would not wish upon anyone. But it's a gift of freedom, nonetheless. And the worst thing one can do to an incredible gift, one that cost someone their life, is to not use it. Putting this gift of freedom on the shelf along with my Peanuts collection and Morph figurine to gather dust like a trinket, would be a desecration. Yet using that gift is an act of courage.

Because I simply do not know what it means.

To everyone who is looking out for me: thank you.

To Andrea for her box of darkness: thank you.

12

24 December 2020 – Day 12

It's Christmas eve. My first Christmas without Andrea. It's midnight, and I cannot sleep. It is way past my bedtime. It is the first time since she died that I've not passed out the moment my head hit the pillow. I have been sleeping like a rock from sheer physical and mental exhaustion.

I'm tired, but for some reason I'm a-tossin' and a-turnin' tonight.

So instead of telling you just how crap my life is, I want to tell you something else.

I am honestly bowled over by the response I've had to my writing.

I've never been the guy to keep it all in. I'm the shit-talk-king of Facebook, after all. I'm known to be vocal and outspoken. I make no apology for that. But within 24 hours I stopped my moping and posted, "I'm becoming insufferable, aren't I?"

That was a catalyst message, because since then, something amazing has happened.

I've received dozens, literally dozens, of emails and DMs from people begging me not to stop my 'grief-writing', and that my Facebook utterings are helping them make sense of their own grief. This I have never expected.

And forced me to re-evaluate.

The last ten months — since her diagnosis — was not easy. It was a very 'busy' time for me. I pushed my body in ways power-lifters would be envious of, and pushed my mind in ways Kasparov would applaud. All to make life as easy and 'practical' as possible for Andrea so she could beat this thing. And when we found out that she did not, to make her last days as comfortable as possible. My life revolved around her.

And suddenly, she was gone! And that 'gone' has left a void in me. A great, big, stomach-churning void that even a man like Hemingway would battle to put into words.

Point being: all I want in my life right now is some peace. Her death has forced me to re-evaluate Gerry. Who am I? What am I? What do I want? I've defined myself so long as being 'Andrea's husband' (and fiancée and boyfriend) that the newfound bachelor Gerry is totally unknown.

I wrote in my Moleskine journal that I do not want much out of life right now. In dealing with all the noise and clutter, I've come to the conclusion that I want quiet, I want comfort, I want function.

And by God, I want beauty!

Life is ugly, if I can have some beauty… A sweet, quiet, comfortable beauty; a small space filled with the bare minimum required for me to eat sleep and create in comfort. That's all I want.

Sounds great, doesn't it?

Then the sucker punch came: "So, Gerry, what are you going to *do* with that nice quiet comfortable place which has all that is necessary for you to create in?"

Well, I've not thought of that, have I?

My writing over the last dozen days has given meaning to many people. I've written things which they told me they could never express. And somehow, that has more meaning than almost anything else I've ever done in life. When a total stranger DM's me and says: "Thank you for writing what you did today, it helped me make sense of my own heartache," it makes a man re-evaluate what he wants from life.

I'm not an altruist. I'm certainly no do-gooder goody-two-shoes who just wants to go out and take care of the old people and puppies and babies. I'm a grumpy git who metaphorically yells at kids to get the hell off my lawn. And yet, here I am with a mailbox full of people thanking me for putting into words that which they never could.

And that, my friends, is giving me a reason to question myself and my motives ever further. Maybe this is one of the shining jewels in that great box of darkness. The unexpected capacity to give a voice to those who have not had the courage or opportunity to examine their own grief.

And if that is the case, then it will be a duty and a privilege I shall take on with honour.

But those damn kids still better get off my lawn!

13

Buckle up, Gentle Reader: this is not a pleasant subchapter.

My life is an open book. I was 28 (now I'm 46) when I decided that hiding myself for the sake of society is a sure-fire way to guarantee misery. I've been out of the kink closet for almost twenty years now. (As an example — my kink has squat to do with this post. My editor would take that sentence out with a slash of a green pen: 'irrelevant exposition!!!'). I've been largely happier for it.

And I've also been vocal — if not advertising — my atheism. I was a Jesus junkie for a long time. I read my Bible and studied scripture in-depth. That's *how* I became an atheist.

But if the Abrahamic religions are true, if heaven and hell indeed does exist the way the Bible says it does, then yesterday I booked a one-way ticket to hell. If my place in the hot spot was not guaranteed by my past actions and beliefs, then yesterday was the final nail in that coffin.

I cursed God. Whatever he/she/it/them may be, I cursed it.

There are any number of really bad people on this planet who could have been taken and left the world a better place. Including me. There's fucking *scum* out there. And they roam freely and happily.

And Andrea? One of the kindest and most generous souls you would ever meet. A person who created genuine value both personally and professionally. She was a shining beacon of what humanity *should* be.

And the powers that be decided it's okay to give her a slow and painful death at forty-four?

That is an act of cowardice. And I told the gods as much. No amount of 'God works in mysterious ways' and 'the earth is not God's realm' or that pretentious line in Isaiah that 'the righteous would be taken early to spare them the wickedness of this world' would convince me otherwise. If the world is so bloody bad that we have to die to be rescued from it, then why the hell have it in the first place?

If my outburst yesterday lands me in hell, I'm going there as a political prisoner: happy in knowing I've got more morals than the unfair and sadistic and downright *cowardly* being who sent me there.

I wished I believed in God. Not for comfort, but so that my cursing did not fall into nothing. I needed God to hear just how little I think of him.

I'm not a parent, but I know any worthy parent would do whatever they can to keep their children from harm. I know that a parent would give up their own lives to save those of their children. We are children of the Lord? Then why didn't he save her from a slow and painful premature death? Either he couldn't, which does not make him worthy of worshipping, or he did not want to, which does not make him worthy of worshipping. Either way, he loses, and wins the "All-Time Greatest Bad Parent" award.

If I'm going to hell, I'm going there without an ounce of remorse.

14

25 December 2020 - Christmas Day – Day 13

I spent Christmas eve at my brother's house. It was a pleasant enough evening. But my first Christmas without her — especially seeing as it was not even two weeks in — was tough.

How tough?

God, not even I know the answer to that question.

I seem to get overwhelmed quickly these days. I enjoy seeing people, but in single-serving packets, and the evening grew too heavy for me. Especially since there was a six-year-old overactive redhead with two new puppies around. I love these peeps, but...

So, I took the Uber home (did not trust myself not to get totally fuck drunk) and then... Ooh. *Then!*

Have you ever known something, or at least thought you knew something, but then you absolutely fucking *get* it? This profound realisation of the true essence of a word or a concept? Yeah, put a pin in that, we'll get to it.

I always drew a distinction between 'thoughts' and 'feelings'. This has always been logical to me. 'Don't think about your feelings, feel them. Don't feel your thoughts, think about them.' I even wrote as much in my first novel.

So, it's well after the Christmas eve celebrations, I'm home alone, I put all the gifts we bought for each other — which we would have been handing out had she not kicked the bucket — on the table, I pour her a shot of vodka, and I get myself a beer, I take out the Christmas cracker I pilfered from my brother, (Holy run-on sentence, Batman!) and I toasted my wife, pulled the cracker, read the joke (it was awful!), put on the paper crown (it was purple) and spoke out loud about the gifts, which included a box from Amazon that arrived three days before she died and she ordered me not to open. (Sorry, editor and Gentle Reader, I could not help but have some fun with the run-on sentence. Once it started, it just kept going. Sue me.)

And then it hit me. Grief came a-riding. Thoughts: I can think about Andrea easily, without a trigger. I can make the jokes — Monty Python's 'Dead Parrot' sticks its deceased head into my conversations quite often — and I'm perfectly okay. I don't need euphemisms to soften the blow. She's dead, Jim! Dead! D-E-D Ded! And in none of those thoughts am I 'triggered' into a feeling.

Opening our gifts, this feeling came without a single thought attached, and just assaulted me. It beat me senseless. Pummelled me like Muhammad Ali would beat up a guy he caught breaking into his car. It hurt, dammit, it *hurt*!

There was absolutely no thought. Nada. Just pure empirical *feeling*, and I was powerless to it. It came, it saw, it conquered. There I was: a puddle of Gerry on the living room couch, not even crying, but making those godawful guttural noises and leaking from every orifice in the front of my face.

I caught myself: Gerry, pull yourself together, old chap! Then I thought to myself: Why? Why the actual fuck should I pull myself together? For whose sake? Mine? Hers? The neighbours who must think someone is having a stroke — or some really great sex — next door? Screw that!

To (mis) quote my fave band — James — This wave will bear my weight, so let it go!

I let go, and it was glorious. To allow myself to succumb to pure feeling, no restraints, no self-control, just surrender. I wept in all my glorious and all-encompassing agony and distress. I took my motherfucking surfboard, rode the wave of grief. But then I had to get a-hold of myself. I had to break the wave. Why?

Have you ever heard of someone dying, and then not even a month later their spouse is also in the ground at Westpark pushing up Dandelions? It happened to a cousin of mine's parents. Mum died, and ten days later, dad was gone too. My paternal grandparents as well. The time between my grandma dying and my grampa kicking it was about six weeks.

I was in genuine fear I was going to join that club. That if I do not contain this wave of pure feeling, I'm going to drown. Emotionally it was obvious bedlam and tumult, but there were physical effects that I did just not expect. Effects so strong and physically painful that I thought that if I don't calm the fuck down, I'm going to make myself a candidate for a heart-attack, a stroke, an aneurysm, or maybe the trifecta of all the above.

I caught it. But it was a bigger battle than Hemingway's old man catching his marlin. I pulled myself together, washed down two tranquillisers with a beer, and went to bed.

Bottom line: Grief, my friends, comes at you without warning. And no matter how big it is, when it gets there, it's bigger. You cannot fight it. You cannot deny it. The best you can do is ride the current and hope it spits you out on shore again.

15

Still 25 December 2020 - Still Christmas – Still Day 13

On Christmas day I had a pleasant lunch of not nearly enough prawns with my father. I did mention I love prawns, right? Just making sure. This is a matter of great import, my love for garlic-butter crustaceans.

My least fave time of day arrived: sunset, the hour of the ghost, and in my confused and jumbled mind, a new 'purpose' slowly started to form. And funnily enough, it had nothing to do with my *Chronicles* I've been writing, which gained so much positive feedback.

No, I've been 'studying'. Instead of chillin' on a hot Christmas day's evening with a good book or a movie…I've hit the books. I'm learning.

Life had indeed become strange, and was becoming even stranger…

16

26 December 2020 – Day 14

Boxing day. Out of nowhere I got a bee in my bonnet, and I cleaned the fridges. (Yes, fridges, plural. We each brought one with us into the relationship. I inherited mine from my grandma who got it before I was born, which means it's at least 47 years old, and still going! They don't make 'em like that no more.)

I spoke a lot about 'emptiness' in my previous entries. It was the one thing I did not expect: this empty void. An abyss which is following me around. Maybe I should read Sartre.

That emptiness has never been so sufficiently symbolised as by a refrigerator. All *her* stuff is gone. Things I'd never use. For example: Her half a box of dry white. And: we have three packets of sealed whey powder in the freezer. All of them expired. Why? Frozen jars of Boob Soup. Now, both fridges are eerily empty.

'Before', sometimes both refrigerators combined would not be enough for us. Now I think I cannot fill up half of one, and that includes a three-day supply of beer, a fortnight's worth of frozen meals, and a tub of ice cream.

I am not a clutterer. Not quite anally neat, but I like a place for everything, and everything in its place — even if that place is in the corner of the bookshelf in the foyer. But seeing the fridge so empty is haunting. And knowing it will never fill up much more, scares me. We always had yoghurt, eggs, and milk in the fridge. Now I have no reason to buy any of these; they are no longer the staples Andrea lived on. I no longer have to keep a watchful eye on the milk level for Andrea's tea.

There is a ghost in the fridge where the milk used to be.

An empty fridge, a freshly made and unslept-in bed in the master bedroom. Those are the things that terrify.

17

27 December 2020 – Day 15

I often wondered if I should continue with publishing my *Chronicles* on Facebook. It felt like my song has been sung, and the time has come to put down this particular pen and take up the others I am so familiar with. Fiction and photography; my two great earthly loves. No one wants to hear Gerry whine.

Then I get this message via Facebook Messenger from somebody I've never met, who is not even on my friends list: "Helping others work through their grief is the biggest legacy you can give your wife".

Sucker punch in the gut, right there. And then this one: "I love reading your recent writings. I'm so happy you are sharing."

Two unsolicited messages from total strangers on the same day.

And about a dozen others in the same line in the weeks since Andrea died. So many people, so many of whom I've never met, not even on FB, contacted me and/or commented on my writing, and told me how much my writing touched their lives. I've been humiliated often, but this is the first time I've been humbled.

Well, the second. The first time was to see just how much people can, and do, care for me, (and by extension, others). That was amazing. The second was the responses to my writing. It is truly... I cannot think of a word for it; and that's a problem, because I'm the alleged writer here!

But it's wow. It is overwhelming. And as the fifteen-day mark passes, and the novelty of being a recent widower loses its lustre, I'm wondering about the value I can still add: has my song been sung, as asked earlier.

Then this afternoon a pal of mine (Who freely admits he doesn't read my long-winded stuff, but he reads these!) told me I should put it up on a blog. And my initial response, after again being flummoxed by such a response was, "Why?"

Then I learn of a friend who had a recent bereavement. Shit. It hurts. Ask me, I know. But the problem is, if you "ask me", all these things I'm writing will just fall away in Facebook's timeline until they do not exist anymore. Obscurity calls as certain as oblivion.

I now have a responsibility. My journey is still very fresh, but I'm out of the starting blocks. Others are just settling in. And if I can help one — just one — person deal with this shit, this pain, this hurt, then isn't that reason enough to carry on? To be honest with myself, and my newfound audience?

This is why I'm writing this book. To honour Andrea's legacy, to help others. And if by chance I can make enough money to keep my house in doing so, then why the heck not? But mostly because I've come to realise I have a responsibility now. Most may roll their eyes and say, "Dammit, Gerry, stop your long-winded whining," but for the few who hold on to my stories as it gives them hope and insight, I'm here for you. And more: I'm here for me.

So, where am I? I'm good! I am relaxed, tummy is full, I'm doing my stuff... I'm aces! But I'm not fooled. Not for one bit. It may not come tonight, or tomorrow, or before the new year, but it will come. And it will take me like an over-zealous lock-forward spreading a diminutive scrum half like a pint of Marmite and put me out of the game for a while.

Am I ready for it? *HA!* Of course I'm not ready for it. No one can be ready for it.

But I can acknowledge it.

I can welcome it when it comes, and I can sit with it. Allow it to hurt, to burn, to etch my soul. Avoidance is impossible and trying to drown it in substances would be to deny it. But that is just not an authentic experience. And authenticity is my 'thing'. To deeply feel that crucible of grief upon the soul hurts like a mother, but is more valuable than rubies.

18

28 December 2020 - Day 16

"The Unexpected Chronicles of Leigh & Mikey."

This one caught me off guard, and shows one just how powerful the subconscious actually is.

The ghosts of Andrea are ever present. In every corner, in every chair, in a Netflix program, in a cooking pot.

The worst day was the Sunday after she died. I went to sit at my dining room table, and her ghost was there with me. That was just one ghost too many, so I moved the table. Which left the dining room/foyer area of the house empty.

But not for long! I bought myself a new drawing table, and I put that in the empty space, along with an old desk and a bookshelf I had in storage. I had made my first little 'my space' since we've moved in together. I put down a table runner and a pen holder and lamp and a this and a that, and I stood back and called it good.

And then it struck me: This is *exactly* the way my fictional Leigh McCabe would have set the space up, except she would have had the addition of an ashtray. But the point is, Leigh would have made that corner of the desk look pretty *and* functional, all the things she'd need, none of what she would not.

I've done the same.

And, once the desk was to my liking, I hit the books for a study-session and did exactly what I imagined the fictional Mikey Marais would have done in such a space.

All these years I thought I've thumb-sucked the 'mannerisms' of my characters. As it turns out, it was just aspects of me that never got room to manifest. It was quite enjoyable to see that, and a lot of fun to live in that space.

In that little three-by-four corner of the house, I feel as if I'm living in one of my own works of fiction, and that is downright awesome.

It's a place with no ghosts, and a hint of a meaningful future.

19

29 December 2020 – Day 16

I made my very first 'non-school' friend at eighteen, when I met this scrawny string-bean of a girl named Barbara in art college. Three days after Christmas, she came for a visit; the first time we saw each other face-to-face in twenty years, if not more. And we just picked up where we left off.

What was weird is that she stayed for about six hours, sitting at the dining room table, talking crap about, well, everything. And there was no wife to worry about. No "Hey sweetie, are we too loud for you?" No "Excuse me, I need to organise some dinner for Andrea." No consideration for my ailing wife to take into account.

That was the yang in the yin (or is it the other way round?). That spark of something dark that otherwise was a brilliant evening. This terrible freedom I now have: to get pals over and talk crap all night long. The freedom is wonderful. The reason, terrible.

It takes some getting used to.

And then I wake up and I hear the Prezzident made some arbitrary lock-down regulations again, and I wanted to write a soap-box rant about how...

But I thought that actually, no, while I *want* to throw my toys, I do not *need* to have a rant. An arbitrary Covid lock-down would be a good opportunity for me to catch myself; to do a stock take, and to figure out just what the hell happened the last ten months.

I've played a supporting role my entire life. Before Andrea, I was Ria Pelser's son, a forced supporting role in the drama of my mother. Then I became Andrea Heidgen's partner, a happy and eager supporting role in the capacity of my wife's life. But now those roles have ended, and I'm thrust into the starring role of my life. And I have no cooking clue what to do with myself!

And a wee bit of lock-down may just be what the doctor ordered — even if the anarchist in me rebels against it. And seeing Barbara for the first time in twenty years was one hell of a way to enter a period of solitary confinement.

Que sera.

19

30 December 2020 – Day 18

Since being overcome by pure *feeling* on Christmas day, I've been surprised by just how okay I was. I wasn't falling apart, I was enjoying the company of friends, I was working on new things, I was just, well, me! The casual observer would've looked at me and thought, "Wow, this guy got over it quick!"

But there was — and still is — this constant sliver of sadness in me. As omnipresent as a mythical merciful god. It's not big, but it's sharp. Like the thin little cut of a scalpel blade. And while it is thin, it is long, and grows longer by the day. Soon, it will cleave the entire being in two.

My psychologist gave me encouraging words: "The worst thing that can ever happen to you, has already happened, and you're still standing," a sentiment I wrote about earlier. Indeed, the worst thing that has ever happened to me has already happened. Everything else can suck, but surely it can't be worse?

She's right though: I survived! I held my wife at the end of a ten-month journey and saw her die as I gazed into her eyes. And I'm still here. I survived! I'm a winner. Not only do I win the grand prize, I also get to take home the 'Recently Bereaved' board game and season tickets for the show!

But what if my psychologist and I are wrong? Because every day that thin little sliver of sadness grows longer, and there will come a day when that sliver divides the mind and soul, and I fear that will be the worst day of my life: the day the shock and awe of it all fades into the mundane, and all that will be left is the blunt finality of it all. That day I will have to face. And, somehow, work through it.

A few days before New Year's, Andrea visited me in a dream for the first time. Details of dreams fade, but feelings remain. It was a happy dream. I dreaded the 'Andrea dreams' for the demons they may bring, but it was just so damn cool to see her. I could not wait to dream of her more often.

Sadly, it was the only 'good dream' I've had of her. Every time I dreamed of her since, it was highly distressing. I cannot use the euphemism of 'visited me in my dreams' in all the subsequent times she haunted my sleep. The dream demons of death are all too real, and leave me both physically and mentally exhausted.

20

31 December 2020 – Day 19

On the morning of the last day of the year, I had a very pleasant and unexpected call from Rita, my friend Michaela's (slinky's) mother.

But what was so refreshing, so amazing, is that in the short conversation, Rita and I spoke briefly about Andrea, and briefly about *slinky*, and I have found the old adage is true: 'sorrow shared is divided, happiness shared is multiplied'.

In the three weeks since Andrea died, I've tried to make sense of it all. And I know it's a futile attempt because sense is not there to be made. Yet, one is hard-wired to make sense of it, ain't it?

But in the absence of sense, there can still be 'meaning'. I've got my disagreements with Frankl, but he makes a very valid point when he says (and I paraphrase) that sorrow without meaning is an opportunity wasted.

I've been touched by death many times. I've carried many coffins to their graves. This year alone my mother, godfather, and wife, died within four months of each other, and Jesus, that's a heavy load.

But in slinky's suicide, I've found a meaning, as those who have read *Defining Giulia* would attest to. And (I hope!) it's not a selfish meaning, but one that might impart some sort of meaning to others.

I thought *Giulia* was my 'Dark Tower', my magnum opus which can never be surpassed.

As the old year shuffled off and we drew a nice and neat line under it and hope for the best for the next solar rotation ahead, I'm not so sure.

I have the duty and responsibility to use my capacities to make something Andrea and slinky both would be proud of. And then to share it with the world, and maybe, just maybe, make it a slightly better place.

As for 2020? Most of us made it! Too many have not. We had high hopes for 2021, little were we to know about Delta variants and even more crap. For me, personally, nothing could have been worse than 2020, but I am well aware that I'm in a relatively small minority in this, with 2021 bringing even more heartache and bullshit. But on the last day of 2020, it was just about for everyone 'the worst year ever'.

For some of us 'the worst year ever' has been nothing but getting caught up in the *zeitgeist* because you could not hang with your crowd.

For some of us, 'the worst year ever' left our souls in the aftermath of a Viking plunder.

There is this arbitrary marker at a full revolution of the earth around the sun that Julius Caesar decided is the new year, and we are glad for it. Even me. Symbolism is good for humanity: even your very name is a symbol on which to hang your identity upon.

On the cusp of an arbitrary notation that advances a calendar one year, I usually do not wish my friends and my family 'peace'.

'Peace' is defined as an absence of war, and war is an *action*. The opposite of war also needs to be an action, not merely the *absence* of one.

I wish for everyone a great action which is the opposite of war. How you define that, is up to you.

On the last day of 2020, my 'opposite of war' action was a book and a beer, and to wake up in the new year, one which I hoped everyone survived. A child's dream, but a worthy one.

*Merode Castle Market
Germany – Christmas 2016*

Chapter 9 – 2021. (... and beyond?)

1

1 January 2021 – Day 20

'All is quiet on New Year's Day.'

I went to bed at ha'pa'nine, just as usual, woke up at sparrow's fart, just as usual, and "nothing changes on New Year's Day". (Bono, please don't sue me!)

Same same.

I made no resolutions for myself this year. No "I'm going to go out and get this!" No goals or...

Four years ago, on this very day, I found myself at a ski resort in Austria, quite by chance. A little holiday town analogous to the seaside holiday villages of my childhood — except for sea, see Alps, and instead of sunburn, see frostbite — but the rest... 'tis pretty much the same. Young drunk kids having fun and middle-aged drunk adults pretending to.

How I ended up there is literally coincidence and chance. Andrea wanted to show me a European Christmas, and so she planned for us to visit her cousins in Germany over Christmas 2016. They were just too happy to have us, but told us we would need to go home before New Year's day, because they had already booked a chalet in Austria for their winter skiing holiday. Fair enough. They called back not even an hour later: "We have an extra bedroom in the chalet in Austria. Do you want to come along?" Well, if you insist... And that is how this guy from Joburg got his ass unexpectedly in a ski resort in Austria. Now, if you ever met me, you would know that I'm not friends with anything that involves physical activity. I hate physical exertion, and more than that, I'm clumsy and uncoordinated and unbalanced. I went skiing once in the Lesotho mountains, and it was by sheer luck I did not end up with my face imprinted in a tree. I've no desire to check out like Sonny Bono. I'd happily go to Austria with you, but you ain't strappin' no planks to my feet and then sending me downhill in the snow. I've got better ways to die, and I like all my limbs whole, and preferably attached to my torso.

Norbert and the rest of the happy German family had hit the piste, and Andrea was sleeping off a hangover. Admittedly, New Year's in Austria was quite the party!

So, New Year's Day 2017, and I've got nothing to do. By some minor miracle, the local convenience store was open, and I bought myself a little bottle of Stroh 80. Yeah, *that* one. And it being Austria, it was ridiculously cheap, even at tourist mark-up prices.

For the remainder of the day, at minus screw-you degrees outside, so cold my beer froze in the glass, I sat outside on the balcony in the New Year's Day Alpine sun, and had myself lots of beer and even more Stroh rum.

I was happy.

New Year's Day four years later? I was sad. How life just rolls you like a pair of dice and whatever side you come up on, you come up on.

I never even *thought* of ever going to a ski resort in Austria. It happened simply because my wife wanted to visit her cousins in Germany for Christmas. They, in turn, wanted to go skiing, so they asked us to tag along. Hey, bonus! What a *jol*!

I never even *thought* of being widowed at forty-six. Maybe in a car crash or a wood-chipper accident, but never this way! It happened by chance because Andrea drew the short straw of cancers.

We did not plan any of these great and terrible events. Or even considered. And this is life: make a plan and hear God laugh.

Thus, on the Friday morning of the 1st of January 2021, there were no resolutions. No goals. No nothing. The universe is playing dice, and where I end up on come another solar rotation further, is where I come up on.

But I had a theme for the year ahead: Recalibrate.

It will have to happen anyway, so I may as well plan for it. Or, at least, prepare for it. And where I'll sit on New Year's Day 2022, I do not know, nor do I particularly care.

The only thing I care about is the health and wellbeing of those I care about, and if I can come out with a full complement of people on the other side, it will be a win.

2

2 January 2021 – Day 21

In my youth, the first and second of January meant a day spent at my uncle Koos's house (The one who looks a bit like Billy Joel. My uncle, not the house.) He had a pool! Usually with a watermelon floating in it. The pool cleaner would be taken out and the skimming net suspended on two patio chairs across the pool for a makeshift volleyball net, and us cousins would bump a ball in the harsh African summer sun, getting blisters burned and our hair bleached, and loving every second of it.

There would be a *braai* (A barbecue for my international friends) and tons of meat and salad, not to mention sweet snacks galore! And, of course, the mandatory game of backyard cricket, which my late Uncle Jimmy (who never looked like anybody but himself) would win blindfolded. We would play until the ball went into the impermeable ivy — cricket-ball Narnia — or across the backyard fence, instantly transformed into a dog toy for the Boxer who lived next door.

They were my favourite days of the year.

This is in stark contrast to how I spent New Year's Day 2021, where (apart from an agreeable 90-minute drop-in from a buddy) I spent the day alone.

A rough count tells me about half the people who were at the heydays of those New Year's Days are now pushing up dandelions. Three of the four cousins got married and moved on with their lives, my uncle sold the house, and these great days of celebration dissolved into literal nothing.

And now with Andrea gone, even our solitary New Year's Day with traditional cream-soda-float breakfasts was a barren day. I had nothing to do, and all day to do it in.

At about ten, I got a bee in my bonnet and cleaned out the bookshelves.

So many dead trees in one space! Holy crap! Among these, AC Grayling's *The Meaning of Things*, which I've never read. But I'm interested because I had been searching for 'meaning' for the previous three weeks. Three weeks already? Only?

But the title struck me: *The* 'Meaning' *of Things*, but I have become concerned with the *meaninglessness* of things. Note: things.

In our combined ninety years on this earth, we collected a lot of crap. Keywords: 'lot' and 'crap'. Random things, trinkets, dust-catchers. Why do we have this? I mean, as in really, this is a useless plastic thing that came from a Christmas cracker sometime in the last decade. Many of these accumulated on the bookshelf I was trying to clean. Chuck 'em!

But then it went one further, and my thoughts turned to blasphemy and sacrilege: books. There is nothing as valuable in the world as a book.

Bullshit.

A book, as a physical object, does not have any intrinsic value (obvious exceptions such as rare and signed editions notwithstanding). It is just a ream of paper with ink on it. The value of a book lies in the stories they tell, the information they give, the entertainment they provide. In the age of the internet and a myriad of places where the sum of human publication is available for a small fee, and carry-able in the palm of your hand, why the hell do I have all these tattered second-hand paperbacks which I'll never read again? And if I do want to delve back into them: Kindle is the answer.

I got rid of more than half our/her/my book collection. The rest are some books that I still want to read (why buy on Kindle what you already have, right?), some sentimental ones, some very informative reference volumes, and… uh, that's it!

I was ruthless. Nothing was spared. Even Harry Potter and Stephen King went into the 'donate' pile.

It was painful, but liberating!

I then understood a literal meaning of 'enlightenment': to make life lighter. And you cannot make life any lighter if you don't get rid of the heavy load you are carrying. Especially the heavy load of meaningless things. In a physical sense, my bookshelf is lighter by more than half this morning, and only the books with 'meaning' remain.

And I felt great! It was the best I've felt since Andrea died, and God knows how long before.

This leads me to the question: what else is sitting in this house of mine (or more accurately, the bank's) that I'll just chuck into a box come moving day, or won't even notice if it goes missing? How much meaninglessness am I carrying with me?

'Meaning' anchors one in life. 'Meaningless' just moors you at the dock and makes exploration more difficult; if not downright impossible.

So, anyone want to offer me a good price on the complete Harry Potter?

3

3 January 2021 – Day 22

What is interesting about value systems is how they change and adapt. The last time I went scuba diving was 23 November 2009. (Thanks, logbook!) And then, just like that, I had enough. It was nice, but I had my fill. I enjoyed the water, but the 'effort' got to me. Get up, kit up, throw up… it took way too much effort and energy for something that should have been relaxing.

My last scuba dive was a cage-less shark dive. I was never so scared as I was then. (In hindsight, compared to what I've experienced the last ten months, those sharks were just calamari!)

I had no interest in diving again. Life changed and moved on. I've got thirty-three logged dives in four different countries and two different oceans, and that is more than enough for me to declare that I have had 'The Scuba Experience'.

And now, 4,058 days after my last dive (Thanks, Excel!), out of the blue, I have the urge again. Just to float weightlessly in the water, drifting with the current. Complete silence, nobody to call your name, no ringing phones, no marketing reports, no word-count targets, no wives slowly and painfully dying of cancer… just complete isolation in a weight-less silence.

If I sell enough books, I'll reward myself with a diving trip. Maybe the ocean can wash away the sadness. If not, it can hide the tears.

4

7 January 2021 – Day 26

Jesus, it creeps up on you, hey. At the three-week mark, I've been okay for a while. A long while. So much so that I've wondered if I'm doing 'grieving' wrong. I mean, I should be a puddle on the kitchen floor, right? Falling apart like a sandwich in a swimming pool. Yet I'm upright and doing my stuff and sorting admin and prepping for *Defining Giulia*'s launch and and and… Pretty darned functional.

Too functional, for what I expected. A constant undercurrent of sadness, yes, but so what? I mean, is this it? Is this all there is to it?

HA!! In the afternoon of the first Monday of the new year, I started feeling weird. Do not ask me *how* weird, just weird. Like 'something is off.' And I tell myself: "Your bloody wife died, Gerry. The light has gone out of your life. Of course something is off!" And then I reply to myself: "Yes, but she's been dead this morning too, and I've not felt this way then. Or yesterday. Or New Year's Day…"

But something was throwing me off-balance all evening. A constant 'nagging' sensation that there is something brewing just out of sight. And then, just as I am prepping to go to bed: BAM! Breakdown. Massive amounts of energy moved, and this metric ton of emotion just hit me.

It's not even ugly crying. It's not blubbering boo-hoo. It's taking ugly crying and running it through Spinal Tap's amp and turning it up to *eleven*. Loss of all faculty. Muscle control a memory. Thought a vaguely remembered capacity. All that there is, is this violent hooting noise I never knew humans were capable of making until three weeks ago. The sheer *volume* of emotion was staggering. Look, I'd describe it if I could, but all I can say is that emotion was bigger than any amount of thought.

Then, as before, I grab hold of myself and tell myself to pull myself together. And again, as before, the question: why? Why should I? For whose sake?

This grief is a gift. Imagine having loved — and been loved — so much that you get to experience this! It's amazing. It's a gift that came with a price no one should ever pay, but pay it we do. And pay it I did. It will end by itself. Either until it fades, or until I pass out, but either way, it will end. There is no need to grab hold of it, is there? That's just me denying myself. Denying the depth of my grief. I'm not talking about a masochistic basking or a self-pitying languishing. But rather an acknowledgement of what it is. A great and terrible place to be. To accept it for what it is, to allow it to consume me with all its fire and ferocity and pain.

I'm typing this not out of self-indulgence or chasing sales (you should see the stuff I don't write!), but because I want to bring to the forefront the awe of the experience. And how unpredictable it is. And ye gods, how it hurts.

I'm petrified of that hurt. It scares me more than any orthodontist visit ever could! But why? Because getting these hurt-attacks — these unexpected breakdowns — tests the depth of the soul and displays vividly the quality and quantity of love we've experienced.

I don't mind the hurt at all.

What I'm shit scared of is the unpredictability…The sucker punch. All the unpredictability of it does is magnify the uncertainty of the future. One I've never imagined, yet need to deal with. Right now, in the present.

I've wept like a person who has lost more than I've ever gained. But that's not true, is it? Because what I've gained from my fifteen years with her…that loss is enormous, but my gains are a tiny sliver more than the loss. I need to acknowledge that and be grateful for it.

Fuck, how I miss her.

5

8 January 2021 – Day 27

Fast forward about eighteen hours later, and I'm at Andrea's laptop. It belongs to her business, and is now the rightful property of Kerron, her business partner. It contains several confidential files for big clients. This is an important piece of equipment. But I cannot give Kerron all the company things before I remove all of her personal stuff, ya dig? So, I copy her personal drive over to my machine, and out of curiosity, I go over it.

I literally laughed out loud. She kept every single piece of communication since the very beginning. Anyone remember Microsoft Messenger? Yup, all the complete logs! I spent a good hour reading our first tentative messages to each other. It's strange how I recognise the people in those conversations, but yet not. That was fifteen *years* ago! One grows and develops in strange ways as time marches on. I may not recognise or realise it, but *Gerry-then* and *Gerry-now* are two different people. This made me realise that *Gerry-now* and *Gerry-2036* will not be the same person either.

And my responsibility right now is to make sure that *Gerry-2036* looks back upon *Gerry-2021* and says: "Well done, old chap!"

And then I stumble upon it: the very first photo of me I ever sent her. A photo with my pants down, hairy butt-cheek exposed, proudly displaying my impressive 4x4 accident bruise!

It was meant to be, I tell ya!

6

8 January 2021 – Day 27

It's been just on a month, and one of the more interesting things I've been doing (As distinct from things that happened *to* me) is to consciously bring a certain thought-pattern from the subconscious in the back of the mind to the forefront of conscious thought.

My goals and ambitions in life.

Andrea and I always dreamed of having a small-but-nice designer place to live in. One of those fancy-pants architectural things that no sane person could ever afford. (She had her mind set on this one apartment building in Hamburg that made my good taste drool!). But that is just one example.

Out of nowhere I'm asking myself, "What do I want?" and the answer is, "A lot less than I did a year ago." But then the more interesting follow-up question: "*Why* do I want it?"

Example: I think everyone wants to be independently wealthy. To live a life of steady income, no debt, have money for nice things. Right? I have a dream of becoming a dollar millionaire. Why? Why do I want a million bucks in my bank account? A New York Times Bestseller! Oh yeah, bring it *on*! But *why*, though? What does having a popular book (which may arguably give me the million bucks!) have to do with my hangover on a Saturday morning and my sadness on a Friday night? Would having several zeroes in my bank account ease the pain? *Any* pain? Hell no!

So, Gerry, what the hell do you want now that you've realised all the dreams and ambitions are useless? I want to create value. Simple as that. I want my life to have just a smidgen of meaning. I do not want my pain to be for nothing.

It's just too easy to go sit in my little corner and bawl and shrug and go on chasing the dream of a million dollars. What good would that do?

Which is why I'm writing again. Which is why I want to get back into my art again. Which is why I cleaned out my garage and turned it back into a photographic studio again. In the hope that something I do, something I create, may make someone feel something authentic. That way, my life and my pain become justified.

Which means I can't write or draw because there is just way too much admin to sort out! Holy crap, dying is busy business!

* * *

Present tense update: Looking back on the above on a chilly winter's day six months after I wrote it, I can say with absolute certainty that the 'why' question has not been answered. I am still at a loss for meaning and purpose. Only a strong desire and hope that my writing may touch the lives of those who need it. And so far, I'm the one needing it.

And I'm still not through the admin. Even several months after she died, I'm still stuck with some administrative stuff that needs to be sorted out.

It never fucking ends.

7

8 January 2021 – Day 27 part II

The days had not been kind to me. The universe held up a mirror, and I saw a few things I did not like.

Back-story: life has never really been kind. From early on — *too* early on — I needed to grow a thick skin and impressive callouses. As my shrink says: "Resilience."

'Suck it up, buttercup.' I've got a skin as thick as a whale's and can withstand just about most of what life has thrown at me.

'Most.'

But those times I cannot… jeepers. Now *that's* kinda sucky.

I've had several discussions with pals, and they had the balls to tell me just what an asshole I've been at times. Because the personal things that are painful to them, are things that I just had rolling off my back since I was eight. To me, their pain was just another day. Why should I care about anyone else's lesser issues, right? When you've been through what I've been through… don't compare your headache to my migraine, okay? Don't complain about your stubbed toe to my amputated leg.

This is literally and figuratively a callous position. My 'resilience' is not a thing to be proud of. It's not something to hoist on a flagpole and brag to the world about it. Without it, I'd be decomposing below my own headstone, but still. It's like being proud of the fact that you have to wear a prosthetic leg: wouldn't it be nice if you did not have to wear one at all?

And so, finally something penetrated my calloused armour of resilience. I felt something as deeply as others, and it scared me shitless in how dismissive I've been towards others' pain in the past. It may not be a migraine, but a headache still hurts. Then you learn that your migraine actually pales in comparison to another's cluster headache, and don't you feel the right idiot right then? I've learned of a pal whose husband didn't just die, but committed suicide, and got her kids estranged in the same clusterfuck. I mean, shit. By comparison, I'm sitting pretty!

But there ain't a comparison, is there? No matter what it is, the worst thing that has ever happened to you is still the worst thing that has ever happened to you; whether it's having your wisdom teeth out or your entire family gassed by a mad Austrian. If you have never felt anything worse than wisdom teeth, then you will feel slightly pissed off if the guy who lost his family dismisses it.

And the reason for this public self-flagellation is not for likes or hugs or even 'told you so' responses — which would all be justified.

The reason for this self-flagellation is when you see me being a cunt, slap me up the head, okay? I'm a nice guy. I really am. But I tend to be too dismissive of others' journeys. I hope I never make that mistake again. To all those I've wronged: I'm sorry, okay, I really am.

This is yet another gift in that box of darkness Andrea has left behind.

How ironic that her death may yet make me a better person.

8

9 January 2021 – Day 28

What I've heard more than anything else in the first month is to "Take it easy on yourself", "Take care of yourself," and "Self-care is important".

You may as well try to tell a blind man what the colour green looks like.

Yes, but what does it *mean*? This 'self-care' thing? Long walks on the beach and Pina Coladas? Buying too many books you'll never read? Getting pissed on expensive peated Speysides?

Side quest: About ten, eleven years ago, I worked doing corporate design (yes, it's a thing), doing executive reports for the brass upstairs. My boss told me: "These guys are like spoiled six-year-olds. They don't want to do anything they don't have to. They don't want to read, they want to see a picture." So, I set to work, and a day later presented him with a schematic layout of how our IT infrastructure would look like once completed. It was a masterpiece. A picture tells a hundred-page report. Boss man hated it! I asked what's wrong with it. And he said to me that it's a 'wow' picture. Well, what's wrong with a picture being 'wow' then? He replied: "I don't want the brass to go *wow*. I want them to go *ah*. *Wow* impresses. *Ah* clarifies."

Back on main quest: So, what is this self-care thing? I needed to find my 'Ah' in this matter. And at last, I got it!

I put myself in the position of the third person. What if I was not me, but my own best friend? If my best mate — or Andrea, for that matter — came to me and said: "Gerry, I feel like shit, I just want to…", how would I respond? What would I tell my best buddy? What would I let her do? And for how long would I let her get away with it before I tell her she's going into victim-status, and she better go for a walk before she sinks deeper into a hole?

And then I understood the foundation of self-care. Treating yourself as if you are your own best friend. Giving yourself the space to do what you need to do, the permission to feel what you need to feel, and not allowing your own personal feelings to put you in the 'poor me' school of thought.

It was a Saturday morning, and I'd seen someone every day that week, and I was seeing someone every day the following week. But I had one open day, and it was a 'me' day. I was going to spend it however I wanted. If I ended up studying, I'd study. If I ended up drawing, I'd draw. If I ended up writing, I'd write. If I ended up cleaning out Andrea's closet, I'd be a blubbering mess. But what I did doesn't matter. There were no consequences to my actions that day. I purposed the day by just allowing me to be me, whatever that may have meant for the next 30-odd hours: I 'gained' a day by just allowing me to be me.

And that, Gentle Reader, is the basis of self-care.

8

10 January 2021 – Day 29

As anyone can imagine, the last while has been rather confusing. I think I said it before, but it may be worth repeating: The biggest emotion I'm feeling is not heartache or loneliness, but confusion.

Huh? Sorry, what?

There is, of course, this underlying feeling of surrealness, and I've felt that before when people close to me died; my grandma, for instance. And with Andrea it's all so damn surreal. We spent nights apart when she went on business trips. I'm 'used to' not having her in the house. She's in Durban or Zambia or Witbank. She's gonna come home any second… Well, no, she ain't. There is a death certificate right here on the desk next to me. The surrealism of it all I expected, and it's not that big a deal.

But this confusion? Holy crap, I did not expect that. You remember those old-fashioned electrical beaters your mom used when she baked? If she was a good mom, she'd let you lick the batter from the beaters? If she was a great mom, she would turn the machine off first? Well, I've got one of those in my head, whisking the living hell out of my brain. Nothing makes fucking sense!! I don't know what to do. I end up bored, I make lists, I do them, they seem pointless, I read, it's fun, then my mind wanders, and it's this entire bowl of badly mixed confusion.

One morning I did something strange: I locked myself in the guest loo for half an hour. Why? To see if being in a stimulus-free environment would quiet my mind. No phone, no computer, no million practical and admin things to do. Just…quiet. Peace.

You know what: It worked!

Because staring at my bathroom wall trying to calm the fuck down, I realised something: the second mourning. Remember earlier that on

Christmas Eve I finally 'got' something, realised its very essence, and we'd get back to it? Well, this is what I've been saving it for.

My wife died in our bed on 12 December. That morning I realised 'Andrea's husband' also died. 'Andrea's husband' no longer exists. Only Gerry exists now. I knew that 'Andrea's husband' became legally null and void the moment of her death, but that morning I discovered what it really meant. I had my *own* death. The 'husband' part of me died as well.

We've been together for close enough to fifteen years to call it. We've been cohabiting for over thirteen of those years. We both worked from home for the last eight years or so, and we were always in each other's company. We became a 'unit' where the whole was so much greater, fun, and more functional than its two component parts.

Cancer destroyed that unit. For more than a decade, I've defined myself through Andrea. And she, through me. It isn't quite co-dependence, but we were each other's champions. I've lost my wife, my partner, my champion.

But I've also lost an identity: my entire way of life and the way I do things is just no longer valid. The habits and rituals and obligations… poof, gone.

I'm not just mourning and missing my wife, but I'm mourning and missing *me*, too.

I first had a guilty reaction to that: "Jesus, Gerry, she's the dead one! You are still here alive and kicking," but then I showed myself kindness: No, I *am* allowed to mourn me. There were two deaths that Saturday morning. I may acknowledge the other one.

But along with the second death, came a rebirth. A great big blank canvas the world has pushed me onto and said: "Here you go, live!"

And because of my capacities and talents, I now have a responsibility — to all the people my *Chronicles* have touched, my wife, and above all, me — to make that rebirth work.

I'll let you know how that goes.

9

17 January 2021 – Day 36

I've concluded grief is a great liar. My more devout friends say that Satan is the master of lies. Ha! They don't know nothing. The greatest master of lies is this thing called crippling heartache. Because it misleads one and tricks you into believing all kinds of falsehoods you know not to be true. But like Goebbels said: "Repeat a lie often enough, and it becomes truth." Grief just keeps chiselling away at my notion of truth so much that I have come to mistrust my own knowledge.

Bastard!

There are many lies I can tell you of, but I wrote this at half-past-four on a Sunday afternoon, and I hate this time of day. Hell, I hate Sundays in general: a hangover of my childhood. (To quote *Calvin & Hobbes*: "Any day you have to take a bath and go to bed early is not a day off in my book.") Andrea and I called it the 'Sunday Night Blues'. I'd wager it's a pretty universal feeling.

So here I sit in my three-bedroom house, of which I use one, with eight Le Creuset pots of which I use two, and uncapped internet which I use up, and I am feeling so... 'Lonely' is not the right word. It's this weird frustration of absence of company. But it's not loneliness in the traditional sense, it's a longing, more than 'mere' loneliness. Andrea made sure I'm well taken care of, at least, initially. For the first six months to a year, I do not have to worry about an income. Which means I do not have the luxury of the distraction of work. The difference between what I'd do on Friday vs Saturday vs Sunday vs Monday, is none. All these days mean the same to me. It's in that sameness that the Sunday Night Blues feels alien. Move the calendar one day — or three days — along, and it would make no difference. The Sunday Night Blues occupies a Wednesday morning. But damn, this strange loneliness...

That loneliness is a lie. A big fat lie. A pork pie big enough to feed a family of four. And another porkie: the meaninglessness of life. Life seems very devoid of meaning right now. Loneliness mixed with meaninglessness is a horrid combination.

But this is the essence of this entry: to kill the lie and remind myself of the truth.

And I'm doing so, firstly, by acknowledging gratitude to the dozens of people who just crawled out of the woodwork and looked after me. From chicken wings from Norway to dog treats from Pretoria. From home-made malva pudding to frozen dinners. And a million-and-one messages asking me how I'm doing, and the promises of, "Any time, just call." Reminding myself of the fact that several good people showed up is not only more than sufficient to not just demolish the loneliness lie, but also eliminate the need to make that 'any time, just call' call. Knowing the safety-net of good people is there to catch me, is enough not to need the safety-net, if that makes sense? So, to everybody who did something for me the last seven months, and before: Thank you. Thank you for the stinky cheese, the flat Fanta orange, the photoshoots, the WhatsApp messages, the angry-yet-benevolent phone calls to tell me to get a grip, and hour-long conversations from Europe. The memories of those are worth more than the deeds themselves.

And secondly, to kill the bigger lie: the pointlessness of existence. Look, ultimately, we're not even a millisecond of existence on the 24-hour clock of the age of the universe. We are insignificant specs in all of creation. And frankly, I like it that way. But while we are but a millisecond, we are still here, aren't we? We still exist. (You, the solipsistic philosopher at the back: get out of my classroom!) And while we exist, we will always be driven by what the great psychologists have identified as our three motivating powers: The will to power (Nietzsche), the will to pleasure (Freud), and the will to meaning (Frankl). I'm in the Frankl camp — begrudgingly. I like the nihilism of Uncle Freddie a lot more than Frankl's auto-altruism. But just because I like it, does not mean it fits like my favourite glove. Because I *am* looking for meaning.

And weirdly enough, I think I may have found meaning in writing this. Because *others* are finding meaning in this. My search for meaning has become a meaning itself.

As an aside: please forgive me if I'm prone to bouts of anger or cynicism or poor-me-ness. It still hurts like lemon juice on a paper cut, only worse. But know that beneath the anger and sorry-assed face, there is a human being deeply grateful for what others have done for him. And one that aches to bring his journeys to others, so that they may find comfort.

So that *I* may find comfort.

10

20 January 2021 – Day 39

Here's a question: what is 'okay'? When someone asks you, "are you okay?" where's the cut-off point between 'yes' and 'no'? Assume a spectrum between "bliss" and "complete non-functional being blubbering in the shower unable to speak."

Because here is the thing: I'm functional! I can have reasonable and rational (or maybe not so rational) conversations with people. I can go to the guy who did my ears for my three-monthly check-up. I can catch an Uber half-way across town to collect my prescription glasses. I remember to buy lunch for the gardeners. I am fully functional.

Except, I'm not. I lack a motivation and a drive. I have a to-do-list as long as my nose-hairs from my marketing team. I could do it in a week but have not done it in a month. And I just cannot get past an hour's work before I lose the capacity in a 'what's the point?' wave of existentialist blues which both Nietzsche and Eeyore would be envious of.

I'm sad. I won't say 'morose', (As The Dead Poet's Society so eloquently put it), but I'm sad. Hell, it would be a really interesting case study for my psychologist if I weren't! But I'm sad not once (for my late wife), not twice (For 'Andrea's Husband'), but thrice. As I chicken-scratched my way through the long sleepless hours as the birds started their morning song by filling up pages of Moleskine paper with Lamy fountain pen ink, I realised that a third person died, and that was my best friend. And I came to this slow realisation six weeks in.

It was a bad day, and I needed to talk. And while literally dozens of people said I could talk anytime, (and most of them will know that yes, I did. And do), I did not want to talk to somebody else. I wanted to talk to *Andrea*.

I wanted to tell my best friend that my wife had died, and I'm really, really sad because of it. And that was a fresh and new pang of emptiness. It's both grammatically and emotionally easy to say, "Andrea, my wife and best friend," but on Sunday, when I needed her, I actually saw the differentiation: My wife, *and* my best friend. Two distinct 'entities'.

I needed my buddy on Sunday. I did not need my wife; I needed my friend. And that doubled the sense of loss instantly. And because the psyche is a bitch, suddenly I wanted to go to my wife for some cosseting because I have lost my best friend. And I wanted my best friend; to tell her my wife is no longer available, and so this vicious circle came round, and I got caught up in this maelstrom of self-perpetuating frustration and sadness.

I do not want to know what my phone bill will be this month, because I called everyone and spoke to anyone who answered the phone. Just to talk. No 'about', but just to talk. A semblance of normality.

Only days later did I claw my way out of this malicious cycle, and I felt almost human again. And only as a very stiff back woke me up at just after four did I have the clarity of mind to go sit and explore the process in my journal.

So, am I okay? No. Yes. I don't know. I honestly do not. It's a pretty damn good facsimile of functionality, but is it 'okay'? Or is the fact that I can fake functionality an indicator of just how okay I really am? A strange

Catch 22: When you can fake your own capacity to carry on, you don't actually need to fake it?

I don't know. All I know right now is that I don't know, and strangely enough, that's okay.

42

23 January 2021 – Day 42

Forty-two. The meaning of Life, The Universe, and Everything. But this is not a reference to an obscure-yet-mainstream trilogy greater than *Lord of the Rings* and *Star Wars* (but not *The Godfather*), but to something even more obscure.

A good few years ago a friend and I went to a Buddhist thingmabob where the chief bald-guy-in-charge gave a morning talk as to what being a Buddhist is all about. I was curious, so I tagged along. He said that they (obviously) believe in reincarnation, and that the 'being' gets reborn forty-two days after death.

Awfully specific, but okay. I raised my hand and asked a question: is it *linear*? I mean, is it forty-two days in the *being's* timeline, or forty-two days in the *earthly* timeline as well. Could a soul be born forty-two days after it died, but pop out in 1850 to help overthrow the Burmese monarchy? The answer was essentially, "No, don't be daft". (Amazing how people who can believe in any preposterous and unproven concept will scoff at an equally preposterous and unproven concept, but I digress). The point is: you will be re-born forty-two days after death. And hence, eternal life. (Which begs a few other questions: where do the 'new souls' come from? Is abortion just fine and dandy on day forty-one then? What happens to all the beings when the sun eats the earth in five billion years' time?)

Today is day forty-two. (And yes, I've been saving and savouring this one!). According to that monk, Andrea's being will be reborn today! Yay! Joy to the whirled! Except, I've never in my life hoped someone was as wrong as that wilfully bald monk. My biggest fear is that he is right, and somewhere some heavily pregnant woman is swearing her way through contractions to pop a sprog who used to be my wife.

A few days after the news that she was terminal toppled our lives, I asked Andrea if she's scared. "No," she replied. "I'm not scared. Pissed off, yes. Flabbergasted at the unfairness of it all. But not scared." And then she added, "But I'm shit scared of reincarnation."

She did not have a happy life. She struggled with many things. Life kicked her in the shins more than it kicks most people. She was petrified that she would need to face this life and all its failings yet again. She would rather take the Christian hell than be reincarnated back into this life.

No one should ever have to live a life that traumatic. And yet, here we are. And here I am. Forty-two days later, and it is coming ever clearer to me that if there ever was a rebirth, it is mine. And if I'm allowed my literary hat: my third birth. My natural one on day zero (or is that day forty-two?) back in 1974, the second one on an undetermined day back in the mid-to-late '00s when it became clear that with Andrea, 'this is it, this is forever after'. And now the third: my new life. New marital status, new financial status, new career (sorta), new friends, new values, new opportunities.

And while I'll embrace the silver linings of new opportunities, I'd change them all if neither of us had to experience this.

12

25 January 2021 – Day 44

So, am I okay? Actually, yes. Very okay. So okay you'd think there was nothing wrong. Except sometimes.

And these 'except sometimes' moments creep up on me.

When Andrea started her own company, three of us (Andrea, Kerron and I) had a WhatsApp group where we talked a lot of crap. Insults and weird shit and jokes and puns and genuine questions.

This morning I received a weird shit-talk mail from Kerron that would've made no sense to anyone but the three of us. I read and replied and then out of nowhere: *whammo*!

This awesome *banality-a-trios* is now a lame twosome.

It supersedes any and all thought. This absolute wave of emotion just hits, and I don't even cry. It just comes out in these uncontrollable guttural honks. If sadness is a landmine, this is a nuclear bomb. If sadness is a hole, this is the celestial void. It simply removes all thought from the brain, leaving me literally senseless apart from pure unadulterated feeling. Nothing in the universe exists except for this 'thing'.

I do not even know what 'this thing' is. Grieving? No, I'm continually grieving. And doing so while quite competently carrying on with every-day tasks. Weeping? It's so much more than a mere weeping.

It just *is*. And when it comes, it is *all* there is. It comes in unannounced, plops down on my favourite chair, stays as long as it wants, and there is Sweet Fanny Adams I can do about it except wait for it to blow itself out like a typhoon.

Then it stops, I get up, wash my face, wish I smoked so I can go have a 7-minute holiday staring at the rain, and somehow, somehow, I carry on.

And if I am really lucky, I'll be able to allow it to stay, and maybe it will shape me, hone me, refine me. It is a privilege to feel this deeply. But it's not something I'd wish on my worst enemy.

13

30 January 2021 – Day 49

Buckle up, this one's a pisser.

A few days ago I had a shoot, and it was a long, fun-filled day. The most fun I've had in literally more than a year. It would have been even more fun if we had beer, but hey, fuck the government. But I digress. (The powers that be thought it a good idea to ban alcohol in the wake of Covid). Anyway, it started at 8:00 and ended around 16:00 and then I needed to clean up so I can put my car back into the studio… erm, garage. I showered to get the sweat out of my cracks and fat folds, and then I was just bushed!

It was the most physical activity I had since I shouted at the TV during the 2019 Rugby World Cup final.

I had no energy for anything, so I plonked my ass down on the couch for some telly, and I found something to watch. I was a bit Clarksoned out, so *Grand Tour* was off the menu (a situation which shall rectify itself shortly), and I found myself something else.

Scene: twenty-something mother of two's husband leaves her, and she moves in with her parents. Back to her childhood home, to her childhood bed. (Yes, I discovered *The Marvellous Mrs. Maisel*).

And that's me, bang, done. Man down. Blubbering idiot.

'Home'. What an interesting word that is. What an *emotionally charged* word. I realised I am now 'Homeless'. Yes, I have a brick structure with fibre internet and a television and a pleasant kitchen and comfortable beds and occasional electricity and a plumbing system that mostly works, but I have a house, not a home. If I'm lucky and work well with my insurance pay-out and not blow too much on cars, hookers, and cocaine… erm, chicken wings and beer, I'll have a brick and mortar structure to sleep comfortably in until I shuffle off my mortal coil, but I don't have a 'home' anymore.

Home is a place where you are always welcome. Home is a place of comfortable familiarity, a place where there is always unconditional love and support, no matter how many pity-parties you have, and how many mistakes you make. Home is a place where there is someone to argue with about what to have for dinner. Home is a place where you get to pluck that annoyingly long, strange single hair from someone else's back every three months or so. Home is a place where someone will rub Voltaren gel into your tired over-worked thigh muscles from too many hours semi-squatting in the studio. Home is a place where *Law and Order* takes four hours to watch because you get into moralistic discussions about the case at hand. Home is a place where you need to be as quiet as possible on a Saturday morning because God knows why but you were awake at daybreak, and she will sleep until ten.

Home is a place of responsibility.

I don't have that anymore. I have an empty shell and an overwhelming amount of freedom. That empty shell is temporarily filled with two dogs, and then…?

I have a brother who is cool and my dad who is awesome and some of the most amazing pals you never could even dream of, and they all keep me sane. Except when they don't, but that's another story. But come bed-o'clock, it's just me and the pups in this empty shell and a looming emptiness disguising itself as freedom.

And it's fucking strange, man. Strange!

When we found out she was terminal, Andrea asked me to please not end up like her mother. Missus H totally lost the plot and became a really insular and cantankerous old woman who subsisted on Benson & Hedges and Sparletta Cream Soda after Andrea's father died at age forty-five. (I'm older than Andrea's father, and she died younger than him! Mindfuck!).

I replied: "No promises, but I'll try".

I speak to Andrea often, in two ways. The first is in a Peanuts-themed notebook that arrived a few days before Christmas from Amazon. In my line of work, I go through a crapload of notepaper and fountain-pen ink, and she bought me the coolest notebooks throughout the years. This was obviously a gift for me for a Christmas she would never live to see. I use this notebook now to 'talk' to her. I use other notebooks for general notes, arbitrary thoughts, journaling, whatever, but this one, and only this one, is Andrea's. I'd pour myself a cold one, go sit at my writing desk, and talk to her. Tell her about my thoughts, my day. The other way is through a candle. Yes, passé, I know, and no, I'm not one of those people who believe in spirits and new age woo-woo, nor am I the sentimental type to have an 'eternal flame' in her honour. But quite soon after her death, I found a candle gave me something to focus on. Often at bed-o'clock, I'd do the routine and turn off the lights, and the last thing to go would be 'her' candle. Before I blow it out, I'd have a little conversation. The dogs look at me as if I'm nuts, and maybe I am, but I like that little ritual. It does not happen every night, but it happens often enough.

Why though?

Because as long as I talk to her, and think of Andrea in present tense, I can bullshit myself into believing I still have a home.

14

31 January 2021 – Day 50

Is 'Fake it till you make it' a valid life strategy?

A year ago, we had it all figured out. We were looking to internationalise her company, set up the head office outside of South Africa, and leverage the ever-increasing workload into international markets. We were going to emigrate: first to Germany, and then, who knows?! Andrea was due to go in January to set things up, and I would follow in May — at the start of the European summer — and bring the dogs with me. She'll have an office and I'd have a studio, and we would settle in with her family for a while until we were both established and then we would go find our new forever home. We planned to travel through Europe often, Beer in Belgium, street cafes in Paris, seaside vacations in Dubrovnik. We'd feast on fresh food purchased from markets we'd make in our colourful Le Creuset collection, and just be happy.

And on December 12th all that came crashing down, and the entire dream is as invalid as an unused movie ticket that you never went to.

Now I'm sitting with this incredible hot potato of 'what do I do now?'

Life seems so pointless… The Le Creuset pots we collected over the years, fancy and colourful and ever so practical, are unused. Europe seems a banality, as is staying here. I have no reason to live, to carry on. It's so empty. So achingly fucking empty. Absurd. Absurd to the point that Camus as Kierkegaard would tell me to liven the hell up!

But what do I do? Really? What do I *do*?

I cannot just 'exist' in a vacuum. Suicide is not an option — albeit the only thing which makes academic and emotional sense now — so I'm here, right? I'm just… here. Now what?

Write. Draw. Photograph. Create. Why? Because it's all I know how to do, even if there is no point to any of it.

I hope a point will become clear in the future. Maybe this too will pass. But today I can go sit and write, simply because I have nothing else to do.

It will be a distraction. And maybe, it will make me happy. And maybe it will allow me to create a life Andrea would have been proud of. And maybe that's reason enough for living, and living well.

15

1 February 2021 – Day 51

I have an interesting thought: Andrea's death *cheated* me. "Well, duh," I hear you say. "It's all you've been complaining about for fucking months now. Sing a new tune, will ya!" But hear me out.

On August 13th my mother died, as I described in an earlier chapter. But because of the sheer amount of shit I had to deal with emotionally and practically, I never even gave that fact much thought. 'My mother died' had about as much emotional impact on me as 'My BMX got stolen when I was fourteen'. I got way too many things to worry about to focus on such a triviality of my mother shuffling off.

And then, things got worse. Andrea was recovering from major surgery, it's all aflutter here, I'm so busy I can't blow my nose without missing out on something important. Then, about mid-September, my father calls again: my godfather died. Well, you know, sorry to hear, but I've got bigger fish to keep from spoiling.

Only now did it hit me: wait a minute! My mother's *dead*! My godfather's *dead*! I've not mourned either of them! I've not even had a chance to *think* about my mother. Let alone my uncle. Two of the most seminal and formative figures of my life died within a couple of weeks of each other, and I've not even given them a thought. I'm so pre-occupied with this sheer crushing overwhelming loss of my wife that my own fucking mother came a far distant second, and my uncle brings up the rear, roughly a light year behind.

This is another thing Andrea's death cheated me out of: mourning my mother. And now, in some strange way, it's too late. I've already gone right through to 'acceptance' without unpacking all the other emotions that come before it. 'My mother is dead' is not an emotional impact, but merely an academic reality, much the same way that George Michael or Larry King is dead.

Sorry Mom, tough break.

And guess what: it ain't about to change, because I'm still sitting with Andrea right here. It will be a while.

16

12 February 2021 – Day 62

A year ago today was the day it all changed. On my mother's birthday; a happy reminder so I'll never forget. (Coincidentally, Andrea and I got married on my father's birthday. Seems one cannot postpone an eclipse). It was to be my mother's last birthday: Covid, Multiple Sclerosis, and sixty years of two-packs-a-day smoke inhalation finally got to her. When we scattered her ashes, we could not be sure if it was Ria Pelser or John Player Special we were pouring out of the box.

That day I felt a lump in the palm of my hand through the clear alabaster skin of my wife, and nothing was ever the same again. Not for me, but more so, never — ever — again for her.

I've discovered I'm more fuzz-brained now than I was in the first few weeks. I'm more confused and frustrated, and I was plenty confused and frustrated to start off with! My hypothesis is that in the first few weeks the shock is so overwhelming I didn't actually register it. The adrenaline that rushes through the body kept me relatively focused. But as the shock faded away and the care packages stopped arriving and the tedium of real life took hold and the admin and have-to-dos dry up, there is a lot more room for reality to stretch its legs.

As the movie said: Reality bites. The movie just never mentioned that it bites this fucking hard and this continuously.

And that reality bites to destroy.

17

13 February 2021 – Day 63

I always wanted an Astrid Table.

"What's an Astrid Table," I hear you ask?

Well, it's an interesting question.

Astrid Steffens is Andrea's cousin's wife in Germany. At fifty something, Astrid is a generous mom to two adopted boys, which is challenging, and wife to Norbert — which is even more challenging! The Steffens cabal lives in a converted barn right on the main street of what used to be a farming village, but is now this little rural suburb surrounded by farmlands on one side and a coal mine on the other, half-way between Cologne and Aachen. Its tiny, and either very peaceful or very boring, depending on your mood.

The kitchen of the Steffens' compound is on the second floor of the barn, the table seats eight comfortably and ten at a squeeze, and looks southward toward the main street. Across the street is *St Cäcilia's* church with its pinkish-orangey walls and a graveyard with weathered headstones dating back centuries. Buses and cars and pedestrians and kids on bicycles and skateboards are constantly in the street, and sitting at Astrid's table, one has a vista of all this paradoxical activity. The uber-modern German-engineered buses in stark juxtaposition against the old church that has been there for God knows how long — but construction on it began around 1550. Roughly a century before the first European set foot on the southern tip of Africa.

All this is a magnificent thing to see, and within the cosseting environment of Astrid's kitchen, one feels taken care of and comfortably at home. I've spent many a happy hour with a Lamy fountain pen and a Moleskine notebook at Astrid's table, writing and watching the world go past.

As distinct from our own dining room table that has a view of the paintwork of the lounge wall.

I always wanted an Astrid Table, and the day after Andrea died, I moved the dining room table to the lounge where I could look out of the patio door onto the garden: the lawn, the pool, the flowers, the tall wooden fence. It is peaceful (Hadedas excluded). It lacks the "activity" or "history" of the Astrid Table, but its mine. The view is the best I've ever owned. I need to enjoy it while I can, because once the estate is wound up there's a good chance I'll be out of this house.

Yesterday I bought myself a laptop. A small machine that is nothing but an electronic typewriter. I did not want a good, solid machine with a lot of muscle, because all I'm then going to do was anything except write. I don't want a machine with a HD screen powerful enough to run three instances of Photoshop simultaneously. I've got a beast of a desktop to do that with should I need to. No, I just wanted something that can run Word and enable me to write without the Lamy-induced writer's cramp.

And thusly I enter a gorgeous Saturday morning, and the sky is clear and the sun is up and I'm feeling good. I take my brand new laptop to my newly positioned dining room table with the view of the lawn and the pool and the tall wooden fence and…

Waterworks. Instantly, I was back in Germany at the Astrid Table, and the knowledge that I will never sit at that table with my wife by my side again, broke me in half.

The unexpected memory of a kitchen table half a world away took my soul and kicked into touch.

Will it ever end?

God, I hope not.

And in the meantime, I've got a table. One I know Andrea would want me to create great things on.

18

17 February 2021 - Day 67

So far, every *chronicle* I wrote had to do with my emotional reaction to my wife's death. Well, why wouldn't it be, right? It is a very emotional topic. To wit: Andrea was only the third girlfriend I've ever had. We lived in each other's spaces, both of us working from home, thus being with each other twenty-four-seven. I'd gladly say I lived in her light. We had our problems, to be sure, but mostly we were solid as the Witwatersrand mountains. And plenty in love with each other, y'know? As a pal of mine said, "We've not grown resentful of each other as so many others do."

So yeah, losing my wife to cancer has been the most stressful thing that I've ever experienced, or ever will experience. They say (who the hell are 'they', anyway?) the only thing worse than losing a spouse is losing a child, and since I do not have kids, I think I've maxed out my stress-o-meter. It is quite strange — and oddly liberating — to know that the worst thing that can ever happen to you, has already happened. Or maybe it is still present continuous tense: 'is happening'. Emotionally and psychologically, it is still rather unpleasant, old chap.

But for the first time since the whole shitshow started a wee bit more than a year ago, I felt it in my *body*. I was working on my new website, a job that desperately needs to be done, and making good headway. Happy as a lark, getting things done at a steady beat, no problems, when around 14:00 my body just shut down. Not a gradual 'I'm getting tired', but out of nowhere I was winded as if Tyson sucker-punched me with a garden spade. I went to 'lie down for a bit' and woke up more than two hours later to two agitated puppies. I played with the dogs, made dinner, pretended to watch TV — my mind too fuzzy to concentrate and I dozed through the whole experience — and then I was slap-bang passed out again before nine!

I woke up the following morning feeling like Tyson was still having fun with me all night long, and instead of just the spade, he employed the entire garden shed. Including the lawnmower. I came to realise that stress is not just in the mind, it's also in the body.

I *know* this. I have enough intellectual capacity and educational knowledge to know this as an academic fact. Any two-bit self-help book on the shelf will tell it to you. But in the melee of what is left of my sanity, I've forgotten this.

I've forgotten that my body has been on a steady journey through hell since February last year. Yeah, sure, Andrea is the one who died, her body has been through more than mine, but let's not discount the fact that for ten months I was her 24/7 caretaker and had to watch her get sicker by the day before my very eyes. And I had to do all this while living in the time of Covid, and just as Andrea's illness reached its crescendo that would send her to an early grave (or at least, the slab at Wits medical school), my mother died. And a few weeks later my godfather died. And then Andrea died. And then my father got ill and nearly died. I'm carrying a shitload, and I've been *intellectualising* it all, totally forgetting that my body was taking its punishment too.

That morning, the ol' bodywork reminded me that if you march into hell for a heavenly cause, it's not just the mind that gets tortured, the body gets burned as well. And as Churchill (I think) said: when you are going through hell, keep going!

So that's what I'm doing. I am keeping going-ing. (That's a technical term.) Feeding the body good nutrients. Supporting it as best I can without breaking it down further. Playing with dogs. Taking short leisurely walks. Allowing it to rest. Allowing it not to do what it must, but what it can.

Which is why I'm back on my website today…the sooner I can get this baby done, the sooner my mind will allow me time to hit the road to a place where there are mountains and trees and beer and I can just totally unwind.

* * *

Present tense update: Apart from two weeks spent in the Kruger Park with my father, sadly, this has not happened. Seven months later, and I'm fatter and unhealthier than ever, more tired than ever, and lusting after a time of peace more than ever.

Maybe one day I can go on a holiday without the burden of responsibility on me, where I can talk to people without the annoyance of social distancing, without the anonymity of a Covid mask. Until such a time comes, I'll keep on going.

Somehow.

19

19 February 2021 – Day 69

I had a strange day where many things happened. I am physically pooped, I think it all got too much for me and when my body went into shut-down mode, it made the mind vulnerable to new information.

And new information I got in droves!

I want to reference *The Lion King*, when Rafiki hits the young Simba over the noggin with his staff and says: "Who cares, it's in the past!" and Simba replies, "But it still hurts".

Now I get it. As in really *get* it. In a hundred years from now, who the fuck will give a crap that Andrea is dead? Or me, for that matter? Or you? It simply does not matter. We are all destined for a future where we lived in the past with forgotten names.

But it still hurts. The present still pretty much hurts like hell. So, what does it *mean*? Oh, dear me, have I been asking that question for a year now: what does it all mean, all this hurt and suffering and pain?

I had a conversation with my buddy Juan, who is arguably the most enlightened person I know (More on Juan later). I know he is enlightened because he says he isn't.

He told me that the purpose of life is simply to be experienced. That's it. Nothing more, nothing less, simply experience. Joy is an experience. So is pain. So is anything else. And one day we will all experience our own deaths and find out the answer to The Great Unknown. The meaning of life is simply 'experience'. It was the first answer in forty-six years that actually made sense to me. Some bald guy from Roodepoort working as a retail manager gave me more wisdom than a hundred people with psychology PhDs, philosophers, and clergy.

Then, at bedtime, I was reading Camus (Dangerous grounds in my state of mind, I know). He has been on my to-do list for a while. I knew more *about* his books than the books themselves.

The last words of *The Stranger* were a sucker punch: "The benign indifference of the universe."

Guess what: existence *is* indifferent.

God(s)/goddess(es), The Universe, The Is, The Nothing, whatever the fuck it is (or isn't), does not give one solitary toss about anything. Nick Cave wrote it well too (Doesn't he always?): "God does not care for your benevolence any more than he cares about the lack of it in others."

Existence is indifferent.

But Camus wrote *benevolent* indifference, and I sat uneasily with that adjective. In my experience, there isn't much benevolence going around, but quite a substantial amount of malice. Arguably intentional.

Needless to say, I did not sleep well that night. Then it hit me: Camus used 'benevolence' as the opposite of 'malicious', as distinct from intentional malice. The universe is not malicious, it simply *is*. And it is indifferent.

What science has proven is that the universe is ruled by two things: entropy and chaos. The only things we know for sure is that entropy and chaos expand and there is more of it every moment. What I saw as maliciousness, was simply entropy and chaos in action. It's not malicious, merely indifferent.

Quid: Nothing in the universe is 'out to get you'. It's not personal, it just is. And existence is completely fucking indifferent to anything in life. Hopes, dreams, disappointments, pain, achievements. Nothing matters. Literally *nothing* matters. Which is beautifully nihilistic.

The Universe actually makes sense if you let go of your need for it to be kind.

But it does not answer the 'Yes, but it still hurts' question. The present is very real, and very painful, not easily dismissed by benevolent indifference explained away by entropy. The answer of 'it's just here to be experienced' makes so much sense to me. For close on fifteen years, it was my turn to experience the unconditional love of an exceptional woman. Now it is my turn to experience being a widower. Thus, I get to experience several things in life, and in doing so find an indifferent meaning to experience.

This, at last, makes some sense to me.

For now.

20

25 February 2021 – Day 75

I started off with these things as a once-a-day thing, like a multi-vitamin for the psyche. However, between this entry and the last, a week had slipped by. Simply because there was nothing new to say. There was nothing fresh or different, no insights, no happenings, life just 'is'. I'm not getting used to things; life right now is something impossible to get used to. But I'm adjusting to it. It is the hallmark of every living organism: adaptation.

Adapt or die.

And some days, I *do* feel like dying. Not because I want to die, because I want to stop adapting. Adaptation is a painful process. I'm done growing for a bit, may I please go into my comfort zone for a while, please?

The subtitle of today's piece: what day is it, anyway? Well, it's strange how days just flow into each other. Not sure if it's Sunday or Wednesday or Whateversday. And if it even matters. I'm reminded by something Frankl wrote about in *Man's Search for Meaning*: 'Days are long, but weeks are short'. And today, on Whateversday it is, I'm staring at my computer, and a to-do list as long as my Peanuts collection, and all the energy of a Malagasy sloth to do it.

And (again) I ask myself: "What do you want? No, seriously Gerry, what do you want?" When I still had my wife, I could answer that question instantly with no thought or consideration. I knew what I wanted. I had it all figured out. Now, I just do not know. I had a novel coming out in May, and a shitload of stuff to handle before then, and while the urgency and desire to do it existed, there was no motivation for it. I mean, why? To what end? So what? Nothing matters. Then I catch myself and acknowledge that I'm still supremely sad and shaken by the whole thing.

But still, finding the energy and motivation to actually work on my website and marketing is just not there. So, what do I want to do instead? I don't know. I don't wanna go back to bed. I don't wanna go for a drive. I do not wanna visit friends. I don't wanna sit in a pub and get slaughtered on draught beer. I don't wanna watch TV. I don't wanna read. I don't wanna write. I just don't wanna nothing, like a tempestuous and tantrum-throwing toddler, I just don't wanna.

And there is no '*do* wanna' either. A limbo caught between all the things I do not want to do, and yet with no knowledge of what I do want to do.

On my PC desktop there is a photograph I took of Andrea in Germany at a Christmas market in 2016. One of the few photos I've had of her as she was extremely camera-shy. It's edited in a skeuomorphic rendition of a Polaroid photo, and the caption reads: "You've not come this far to only have come this far." My wife is smilingly berating me and encouraging me from a cluster of pixels on my desktop. It makes me want to cry, because I miss her, but also, because I fear she may be wrong. Is this how far I'll ever come?

So, should I take a Ritalin and *carpe* the fucking *diem*? Or would methylphenidate only focus the listlessness? A question for the sages.

21

6 March 2021 – Day 84

I've not written a *chronicle* for a while now, and that's because it's SNAFU: 'Situation normal, all fucked up'. Nothing changes very much.

A constant undertone of sadness and emptiness punctuated by moments of sheer terror and absolute misery.

But the last two weeks or so I've not been doing well, physically. Just a mild case of the snots. Nothing to write home about. Usually, 'the snots' would take a few days and I'll be fine. Now it's a few weeks. I need to remind myself that I had a year of living in a combat zone. Where every day was not just a fight for my life, but also Andrea's, and by extension: our future together. I'm sure the guys who actually got shot at in a war will laugh at my melodrama, and they have a right to, but this is exactly what it was: a war. One we lost. And there are no medals for bravery or a flag-draped coffin. For a year I was running on pure adrenalin.

And now the crisis is over. I'm glad it's over. And as the song says, from now on every minute of the future will be a memory of the past. And now that it's all over, bar the sheer terror of the future ahead, there's no more adrenalin to keep me going, no more 'fight or flight' instinct. Now that the mind has calmed down to misery, the body is raising a little white flag. And boy, do I feel it. I feel the absolute panic I've lived in since August 13th (when she had the lumpectomy) in every fibre of my being. My back is in spasm, my colon is cramping, my stomach is aching, my head is buzzing, my sinuses are leaking, and my muscles refuse to cooperate.

I was useless the last 2 weeks.

And guess what, I still had a book to publish. Not a tall order at all!

* * *

Present tense update: 'Defining Giulia' was published on 18 May 2021 to no great fanfare. No launch party, no champagne corks, no friends, no speeches. A few people ordered from me, I couriered the novel, and mentioned it on Facebook. The greatest thing I've ever written, and arguably ever will write, entered the world with hardly a whisper. This in itself is a tragedy. But one so trivial I've often forgotten that I've got another novel on the shelf. I see my paperback on my table and go 'oh, yeah, that's mine, I wrote that,' and it feels like I'm talking about a stale sandwich from yesterday which I forgotten to eat. Yet another thing Andrea's death had stolen from me.

22

8 March 2021 – Day 86

I'm not 'over it'. I'll never be 'over it'. At least, I hope I will not be. I don't want to ever be 'over' the fact that the greatest person I've ever known, never mind shared a life with, has died. The pain I feel is an honour. It's not masochistic, it's a symbol of just how fucking tremendous it was. No, I'm not over it, but I've come to accept it. It sucks almost as bad as your first day in orthodontic headgear, but I've made my peace with the reality that I'm a widower now and the greatest era I've ever had — or will have — is over.

Then came an unexpected ghost, and it rattled the shit out of me.

I had a photoshoot. A paid shoot for a new client: an author headshot. Pack the car, set the GPS, follow the robotic voice that illogically tells me to 'at the next roundabout to take the second exit'. Listen up, you silly tin-brain, it ain't 'Take the second exit at the roundabout', it's 'go straight at the traffic circle'. But I digress. The point is the satellite signposts in the sky tells me to take back routes I did not even know existed, but I got there. And on time, too!

Unpack, chat, take the shot, re-pack, say goodbye, and head home. I ain't in the mood for the idiotic robot voice to tell me about obscure back roads. The client lives two blocks from the main road, I can take that route and know exactly where I'm going without needing instructions from the demonic offspring between Google and Garmin.

So that's what I do: turn onto the main road and instantly Tyson hits me with that chainsaw in the gut. The last time I had driven this road was on Wednesday December 9th, three days before Andrea died, and the last time she was in a car. The time I drove her home with that terrible secret in my heart that I still needed to divulge in the gentlest way possible.

As I drove down that road, the memories of how I felt at that time came rushing: my hand on her leg, my face the best poker-face bluff of confidence ever seen on the planet earth. I need to tell her she is going to die real fucking soon, but for now I need to hold conversation as if nothing is wrong. Idle chit-chat about Meghan and Harry, plans for a Christmas I know she will never see.

On the way home after the shoot, an Andrea-like entity was next to me on the passenger seat. It looked like a bad facsimile of my wife: an Andrea-shaped thing, riddled with cancer, a fearful and malicious force of evil that would tear my wife — and everything associated with her — apart in the next three days. It was such an overwhelming force that I nearly had to pull over to regain my composure.

I'm not religious, not even spiritual. All supernatural experiences can be chalked up to ignorance and/or psychiatric conditions. The ghosts that I've seen and the gods I've experienced turned out to be mere hallucinations thanks to TLE. But often I wished there were a hereafter, that ghosts existed, and that Andrea could haunt me. I'd welcome it. Leave me messages on fridge-magnet alphabets like in that Steven King story. I miss her.

The self-created apparition of my wife going home for the last time with a body that is more cancer than Andrea, was a very unwelcome addition to my evening. I still wish she could haunt me. But I'm damn glad that whatever sat next to me was nothing more than my own insistence of memory, and not anything supernatural. Because if it was, I would finally have found something more terrifying than that final drive a mere three months ago.

And that is something I just do not even want to comprehend.

PS: Anyone know where I can get alphabet magnets for the fridge?

23

14 March 2021 – Day 92

March 12th was the three-month mark of her death. Only. Already. Feels like yesterday, a lifetime ago. It was a red-flag day for me, and on top of that, I had cabin fever galore. I had to get out, so I took myself for lunch. I packed up my book and my new prescription sunglasses and pointed my car in the general direction of Lucio's Pizzeria and had myself a lunch. It was early afternoon, and the place was almost deserted, except about three minutes before me an older couple came in, and was being seated. Just the three of us in that section of the restaurant.

They seemed happy, jovial, and I heard the man say to the waiter it is their wedding anniversary: forty years! That was a gut-punch. Because the following Saturday, the 20th, would've been — still is — our sixth wedding anniversary.

I followed my instinct: I did not think about it at all, I just approached the table and congratulated them. And told them to have a bottle of wine on me.

Not because I'm magnanimous, but because I'm envious.

That poor bastard had to put up with his wife's shit for thirty-four years longer than I had to put up with mine! And I hope he has plenty more. I will not be celebrating my wedding anniversary next weekend. I'll not have the burgers which has become our traditional anniversary feast. I'll be doing something else. (As coincidence and the universe would have it, that 'something else' is a rather unique and singular experience in my life, but that's a story for another day.) But even if it weren't a unique and singular experience waiting for me, my sixth wedding anniversary would be just a day. One I hope I won't fall apart too badly in.

But on Friday, it wasn't about me. It was about that poor old codger who had yes-dear'd his way through four decades of marriage. And that should be celebrated! Even if it is not my celebration, I could step in and have a wee bit of vicarious joy by offering them a bottle of plonk. They invited me to join them. And no, just no. That's not what it's about. It's not me wanting to make new friends or about having company for an hour. It's about an acknowledgement and salutation on whatever the hell they may or may not have been through: failures, affairs, infidelity, arguments, bankrupcies, whatever this life threw at them. However shaky and wobbly their marriage could hypothetically be, it did not matter: they fucking made it! And on that Friday afternoon, they were sitting in Lucio's celebrating the fact that through the obstacle race that is life and the tricky curves of marriage that requires finesse to navigate, they made it.

And what a privilege that is! One that would be denied to many. And you know what, you two old fogies having a pizza for lunch? Just to say, "well fucking done," have a bottle of plonk and put it on my tab, because I'll never get to have that. And that two-hundred-buck (about $13.00, for my American friends. Or about ten quid for my English ones) bottle of whatever it was (thank you for not being polite and getting some of the cheap stuff!) was me dipping a toe in the ocean of 'what might have been' that I shall now never swim in.

That bottle of wine was an act of kindness and empathy and charity and generosity.

To myself.

24

29 March 2021 – Day 107

The last week, Andrea has often come to visit me in my dreams. This is new because by the three-month anniversary, I think I've dreamed of her once.

I must admit, when it was still fresh, I was scared of her coming to visit me while I sleep, and it seems I was right to be. These dreams are the sweetest things. I can converse with her the way I would converse with anyone else. We had such a laugh last night. She said it was like a real-life *Calvin & Hobbes*. While I'm home with her, she is alive and kicking and life as we knew it just carries on. It is only when I'm with others, or step out in the world, that she's dead again. We had such a chuckle. It was so good to see her. And then, as with all dreams, one wakes up to the terror of reality.

And that's when the dream turns into a nightmare. Upon waking, it is like losing her all over again, and I take a good while — sometimes the whole bloody day — to get my bearings again.

Even so, I would not exchange these dreams for the world.

In the last week of March or so, I had a strange dream. One that, if I were a spiritual being, I would have said actually *was* Andrea, and not just my brain concocting up pleasant memories of her. And in that extraordinarily strange, intense, and very real moment, she told me she's okay, I am allowed to move on now. Whatever 'move on' may mean.

I took a step in that direction on an early autumnal Friday when my faithful and loyal — not to mention vital — domestic engineer, Sarah, came for her weekly trip to iron my clothes and clean the house. I did not even think about it. I did not hesitate. I did not second guess. I just opened up Andrea's closet doors and said to Sarah: "Take it all".

Andrea's clothes have hung undisturbed in the closet since…well, since. I always knew I had to let it go, but it was peeling back the Band-Aid one painful hair exfoliation at a time. I could not stand it anymore, and in one swift move I am still 100% uncertain of, I ripped off that massive Band-Aid, and now it's gone. All Andrea's clothes have now been donated to people who can use it. People who can find comfort, warmth, protection, and luxury in it. Because let's face it, what am I going to do with it? Yet I clung to it out of a desperate fear.

Fear of what? I have no idea. Part of me screams in protest at the mere thought I had gone through with this, but the empty bedroom closet is a relief. It gives me room to grow, to re-find myself. It gives me room to — metaphorically and physically — claim back some space in the life of Gerry.

I had lived for this woman for many years, and during the ten months between February and December, I was consumed by her and her illness. So much so that, now that she is dead, I find myself aimless and listless and not sure if it's all worth it.

But with her clothes now off to people who can benefit from it, and the infinite possibility of an empty closet now in the master bedroom, it feels like I can make the first tentative steps in moving on. I can find direction and purpose, and I can turn this whole big fucking mess called life into something of value.

25

Present day update: July 2021

Speaking of dreams…

The good dreams, where it's like a chilled visit just like in the old days, have gone. The dreams have turned into ghastly nightmares. I've had several of them now, all of them along the same central theme: We've broken up. Andrea has left me, and nothing I can say or do would sway her otherwise. She's resolute in keeping me at arm's length, and no amount of promises and pleading would persuade her to take me back. In these dreams I'm crying, weeping, begging her to please give me, us, another chance. But she always shakes her head stoically and tells me nope, it's over, no chance of that happening.

These dreams are killing me. And on days like today — a freezing winter's morning as I'm finishing up my manuscript — I almost wish they would. They are so intense in their emotion that upon waking and the realisation that she had died, and not broken up with me, is a fucking relief! These break-up dreams leave me battle-scarred and exhausted, good for nothing except self-pity and carbohydrates.

God, I'm so tired. But I'm so afraid of the dreams that may come should I fall asleep.

26

12 April 2021 – Day 121

It was the four-month anniversary of Andrea dying, and what I've noticed is that, in a way, it's worse now than when it was fresh. When it was fresh, the shock 'protected' me. And then, as the shock wears off, the endless practical matters were a great distraction. But now there are no more urgent practical matters to sort out, the shock is gone, all that is left is this glaring emptiness that is totally void of meaning. But I've said that before.

And this is still a constant thing for me. Lion King, Camus, and Frankl references aside, I'm still trying to find meaning in it. It's still a roller coaster of "ah, I finally got it!" and "Nope, no I don't."

'Meaning.'

I am lucky enough not to have a regular job, and that is maybe part of the problem. Every day I get up with just about nothing to do, and all day to do it in. This is new for me. I'm not one to have the luxury of boredom. But boredom has been rearing its head. Oh, I've enough to do, and enough I *want* to do, to not allow idleness into my life, but the issue comes in that everything I do feels as pointless as fingerless gloves.

Those new manuscripts I'm working on? Bah, Humbug! The launch of *Defining Giulia*? Big fucking deal! The photos I took that still need editing? A tedious, joyless task.

I find everything so damn *shallow*. A handful of good people stand out, which tells me there's still substance in the world, but the bulk of…well, everything, will be out of its depth in a puddle left behind by molten ice cubes on the kitchen tiles.

This is not how I want to engage with the world.

I continually ask myself why I feel this way? Why am I so frustrated and pissed off and devoid of humour and — gasp — judgemental of everything? I'm the most non-judgmental person I know. (I mean, who am I to judge others, right? Me of all people!) Then the answer hits me like a sponge-covered VW Beetle hurtling at me at forty k's an hour: *Gerry, your wife fucking died! A ten-month war with cancer which you lost. Of course you're in a bad place, and it's only been four months! I'd be worried if you were traipsing through life singing 'The hills are alive with the sound of draught taps.'*

I cannot say I'd been through hell and back. Because I'm not back yet. But that handful of good people I mentioned above? They are showing me that there is a way out. And again, I quote Churchill: when you are going through hell, keep going.

So that's my agenda: keep going. And thank you to all of you who are helping me to keep on going. This is a lonely battle but knowing there's people there I can chat to every so often makes the journey just a smidgen easier, and so much more worth it.

27

6 May 2021 – Day 145

I was sitting on the phone, chatting to my father, having a jolly good time about how well cryptocurrencies are treating us, when there was a hoot at my gate.

What now?

It was a courier, delivering boxes.

What boxes?

And then it dawned on me: the paperbacks for my new novel, and the reprint of the old one. (Available directly through me, and in both paperback and Kindle through Amazon. Shameless punt. Sue me!)

There is something truly magnificent about opening a box of paperbacks with your name on it. It's one of the better feelings in the world. I've had many great experiences I can — and probably have — bore you to tears with, but a box of paperbacks with your name on it?

It's right fucking up there!

Except when it isn't.

In 2015, I published my first book: *From Snapshot to Hotshot*. Because the information in it is out of date, it is now out of print (maybe I'll rework sometime). But let me tell you, when I realised this thing was going to be published, albeit only in e-form (Do you have any idea how expensive it is to print 200-odd 6x9 pages in full colour!?), I was joyous. For the annual *Photo and Film Expo* I put a hundred-and-fifty copies of my book on branded memory sticks, and that's how I sold them. When the box of sticks arrived with my book and name on it, Andrea was on hand with a bottle of bubbly and a grin. The first one out of the box I gave to Andrea. It was hers. The dedication page said so.

In 2018, when my first printing of *Discovering Leigh* arrived, Andrea was on hand with a bottle of champers. We ceremoniously opened a box, and the first book out of the box I gave to her. Literally the first of the first editions. I loved doing that, giving my wife, my champion, my first book.

A year later, I published another book: an abortive ghost-written / co-written memoir that ended in a copyright dispute and bad feelings. But before the bad feelings set in, it was the same procedure: Andrea popped a cork, and the first one out the box was hers. She earned it. She put up with this cantankerous bastard while he slogged his way through someone else's life story.

But with *Defining Giulia*? No champers, no corks, no Andrea. A hollow victory. Here is the greatest thing I've ever written, and I'm opening up that box alone. My greatest achievement, and no one here to hug me and kiss me and tell me how proud they are of me.

I've got many great friends, all who are proud of me and happy for me, and I am profoundly grateful for them. But at the end of the day, a pat on the back from a friend is not the same as a smile from a wife.

I'm saddened by a strange contradictory feeling of celebration and happiness, contrasted with a profound loneliness that was always here, but made vocal by a courier delivering a celebratory box.

Cheers, Sweetie. Thanks for supporting me while writing this book. And the one before. And the one before. And the one before. It will be so weird writing the next one without my constant companion and eternal champion. But I know you'll be here with me to slap me upside the head and go, "Don't be daft!" when I muck up, and tell me, "Well done" to celebrate my victories.

28

20 May 2021 – Day 159

I know when the best day of my life was. March 20th 2015. I know that no matter how glorious life gets, nothing will ever be as great as that day. Even if I win the lottery three days before being announced the winner of the Pulitzer, and hearing Tilda Swinton won best actress for a role in one of my screenplays*, nothing will come close to that awesome day.

And I'm okay with that.

And I also know what the worst day of my life was. It was not the day Andrea died. That was number two. The worst day of my life was before she died, when I was the one to be the bearer of the final sentence: it's over. Even if a train accident cuts off all my limbs and a Kardashian wins the Raspberry for worst actress for a role in my screenplay, it may suck, but will never be as bad as that day.

And boy, am I okay with that!

And I also know what my second-best day was. May 30th 2018. The day I published *Discovering Leigh*. An evening at *Skoobs* (A boutique bookstore championing the indie authors, subsequently closed down thanks to a small pandemic you may have heard of), about a hundred people present, both friend and stranger, and selling out all the books I had for sale. I autographed boobs! And not just Andrea's...We had chicken wings and beer at the after-party. It was awesome.

Just about three years later, I published the sequel. And it was one of the worst days of my life. Because there was no *Skoobs*, no boobs to autograph, no celebratory dinners, no wife by my side. Just me in my sweatpants at home with an UberEats dinner and two bottles of beer.

It sucked, man.

So, this is where I am. On the low end of the spectrum somewhere between bliss and misery. And it still sucks, man. Everyone deserves to be happy. Even me. Even anyone who lost someone so vital to themselves and their survival as Andrea was to me. So, how does a guy like me get happy?

I have a few guesses. Because here's the thing many people don't get, or don't want to get: happiness is a choice. As the great famous someone said: "If you want to be happy, then be." And even after everything, I still believe that.

I also believe in its corollary: Suffering is a choice. Yes, you read that right, too. Pain is a vital part of life, we cannot avoid it. But suffering? Suffering is a psychological construct to make a virtue of pain. Pain isn't virtuous, it just is. This is the thing with the choice of happiness: you do not need the absence of pain to choose it.

It's an amazing contradiction: you can be in a state of absolute misery and still be happy, all you have to do is choose it.

Here's the caveat though: you choose to be happy the same way you choose to be a cardiologist. You don't simply snap your fingers and its done. It's a process which may take years.

And this is where I am on this sunny autumnal morning: in the process of choosing happiness and trying to figure out how. Stephen Duneier (Google him, fascinating man) credits his status as a fascinating guy — and his transformation from being a below average man to what he has become — to one thing: "I started becoming an active participant in my decision making".

Man, that's deep!

It means that I — and all of us — have the responsibility of making our own decisions. And we need to happen to life, not let life happen to us.

I cannot afford to let life happen to me.

For years, all I've been doing is holding on for dear life to a towbar while the pickup truck is speeding over the gravel road of life. There comes a time when you either have to let go, or figure out how the hell you are doing to get up on that truck, and find your way into the driver's seat.

As said, it's a process.

And it brings with it another great contradiction: you have to take your happiness seriously.

How you do that, I do not know. All I know is that I don't want to feel the way I do right now for the rest of my life. I owe Andrea my happiness. It is all she ever wanted for me. To 'blame' her now for my unhappiness would be a great injustice.

The only person responsible for my happiness, is me. I want to choose. I just do not know how.

I have a suspicion it may be in the words I am writing right now.

*Screenplays?

Remember I said earlier I'm 'hitting the books and studying'? This is what I'm learning at the moment. I'm teaching myself how to do screenplays. Will anything come of it? Probably not. But it's fun!

29

12 June 2021 – Day 182

What is the worst thing about losing somebody you love so dearly? The irony: there are many 'worst things'. Grammatically: "You know what the worst thing is about watching your wife get cancer and die? Well, it is…"

Except, that I can make it about literally anything. I can repeat that 'the worst thing' statement two dozen times and they will all be true. It's difficult, nay, impossible, to say what is the singular 'worst thing'.

But this afternoon, I can tell you what my current 'worst thing' is. My recurring dream which I mentioned earlier. The ones where she keeps on leaving me.

These dreams leave me shattered, and emotionally glad that "She's only dead, thank God!" What an odd thing to say. But the force of the loss in these dreams is so intense that the waking realisation that she has not broken up with me, but had no choice in the matter and died, is actually a relief. Can you believe that? These waking moments of realisation are a welcome respite from the intensity of the dream, but the dream leaves me dazed and winded for a long time afterwards, sometimes for days.

…and leaves me wondering if the dream-Andrea is right. Was I a useless low-life piece of shit to her? I doubt myself. Was there anything I could have done better? Could have done differently? Been a better husband, a better partner? Logically, these questions make no sense, but emotionally they creep up and I cannot ignore them.

I am so tired. "In the mirror stands half a man I thought no one could break." I hardly recognise myself anymore. I've grown grotesquely overweight. My scale is broken, but I guess I'm up probably about ten kilos from when she died. I am succumbing to every single stereotypical symptom of depression in the book. Every day is a battle to find new meaning and not to drown myself in amber liquid from Scotchland. The dogs help. But my depression is now affecting them, and that makes me feel even more guilty.

This whole thing is the gift that keeps on giving. And so far, it has left me with almost no respite.

More than half a year has passed. I've still not been back to the main bedroom. I still battle to walk into that part of the house at night. Not because I'm scared of ghosts.

But because I'm scared one day, I will go to that bed and there will *not* be one.

30

21 June 2021 – Day 191 – Winter Solstice

Andrea died on the 12th of December, high summer in the southern hemisphere. Later that afternoon, I told my father, "I just need to get through the winter."

My father did not understand my concern for winter when the summer solstice has not even arrived yet.

Here's the thing: I fucking *hate* winter. Johannesburg has sublime winters, to be sure. The sun shines, it is 'warm' (comparatively speaking), the air is crisp and clear, it has many great things to say for itself.

I hate it.

The cold settles deep. In Europe, even outdoors in minus twenty-eight temperatures, I've not been as cold as I am right this second, indoors, at a balmy sixteen degrees. I do not know what it is, but the South African winter kills me. It is a 'different' type of cold than the European winter. The snow of Austria and the ice of Svalbard and the 'nothing' of western Germany may be a lot colder on a thermometer, but on the Gerryometer, it is orders of magnitude more tolerable. The European cold has never locked my bones and cramped up my muscles.

Winter is my least favourite time of year. Which, naturally, is why I love midwinter's day, the winter solstice. To me, it's a rebirth. While the cold is far from over, and spring still months away, the mere thought that tomorrow will be slightly longer, and will continue to grow slightly longer until December 21st , is balm on my aching soul.

So why was I worried about pre-solstice winter since December? Because Andrea was my warmth and comfort. She helped me, physically, during the winter months. My body next to hers during those nights when you have to pee away a scrim of ice in the toilet bowl every time you have to take a swazz, relieved my mental and physical aches and pains, and I could survive.

I worried about winter because I knew it would be the first one in a decade-and-a-half I would not have her comfort. The most difficult time of the year for me I'd need to deal without someone who could rub ointment into hands.

The winter of 2021 has been, physically, the most difficult season of my life. Because last year I had the distraction of having to fight for the life of my wife. I did not need to deal with the abuse of the cold because my attention was focused on a much greater battle than sore hands.

This year my hands are actually not that sore. But the pain is much worse. All I need to do is survive until the stinkwood tree in the back yard buds its first gentle leaves, and I'll be okay. And since the days are getting longer from tomorrow, I might just make it.

31

28 June 2021 – Day 198

This may be a long one, a trilogy in two parts.

Sometimes — often — I find myself in a weird surreal state where I'm in that space DiCaprio speaks of in *Inception*: how do you know you are dreaming? (Relax, this is not about dreams again!) To wit: If you just find yourself in a place and/or situation without any recollection of the events preceding it or how you got there, Buddy, you're in a dream.

Sometimes this is how my life feels. Right now, in this big three-bedroom house with two dogs and a one litre Ford, well, it was *always* just like this. I do not have a memory of getting here. And my wife who allegedly died allegedly six months ago allegedly from cancer? Never happened. Just like in a dream where pain and emotions are so much more intense than in meatworld, so do I experience this almost dream-like intensity of continual sadness for a person who never even existed.

At least that's what it feels like. Either it was all a dream, or I am in a dream right now. This odd nebulous quality of life makes for zero certainty. As said: at least that's what it feels like. I find I have more vivid and colourful memories of a four-month long relationship I had sixteen, seventeen, years ago, than I do of the woman whom I spent virtually every single moment with for the last fifteen. My rational mind asks if this is a psychological coping mechanism: the loss is too great. Let's put the memories in a safe somewhere, lest they overwhelm me and splinter the mind. My mind allows me to remember that earth-shaking, mind-numbing, tooth-filling-melting, IQ-lowering, kinky, dirty, filthy bondage sex I had on a one-night-stand two decades ago, but won't allow me to remember a goddamn thing I did with my wife a mere eight months ago!

And this is where I quote Nick Cave: memories become monstrous lies. I was lying in bed one night, and — as before — all I remember are the arguments. The tense moments in our marriage. The times when it was really tough, and we both fought tooth and nail to keep it together. The physical and emotional strains we had to endure. I cannot for the life of me remember the good times. I know they were there, but all my mind throws at me are the bad ones.

At 3:00 I was awake, and I lay staring at the ceiling, the bad shit just keeps coming. The cancer. The blood. The stress. The arguments. And the death-scene repeating over and over and over. Rick Astley live on stage.

I tell myself there *has* to be good stuff. I mean, we were together for fifteen years and highly in love! Why do I only get the bad shit? Let's go *find* the good shit. Actively go looking for them.

I recall a selfie I took of the two of us at the A-Ha concert last year. One of the last times I ever saw her with long hair, just before we shaved her head for chemo. Even A-Ha, a great day, ended up being a sad day. So, I rewind a bit more, and I find The Cure concert we attended. She was healthy then. We were in a good space in our relationship, her business was doing well, the future was bright, Covid was unknown, yeah man, this is where it's at! This is life!

The safe securing the good memories opened…

All the fun times came flooding back, hit me like a tsunami hits a Japanese nuclear power station: total Gerry meltdown in the best possible way. I cried myself to sleep in a tidal wave of good memories.

And this morning, I recall how we danced: Andrea and I grooving at The Cure, arms around each other's necks, looking into each other's eyes, dancing to *Inbetween Days*.

Do I even need to tell you I put on my The Cure concert T-shirt after my shower?

Thanks, Robert Smith. Your songs made me smile for the first time in months. Not an accolade The Cure gets credited with often, I'm sure.

32

9 July 2021 – Day 209

I had a shrink session a few weeks ago. I love my shrink, been with her for four years now, and she has the unenviable task of keeping me sane. And she succeeds! Which tells you just how damn fine she is.

She asked me an interesting question: "Are you lonely?"

And the answer to that question, amazingly, is, "No. I'm not lonely."

Except sometimes.

I live in a big house. It's huge! You can fit a family of four in here, arguably five, with comfort and ease. The irony is, I'm now sleeping in my office, I've not been back to the main bedroom since March last year. Two thirds of the house is going unused. I'm rattling around this house like a pea in a tin can. It gets a bit 'odd' at times, being all alone in such a big place. But it's merely 'odd', not weird or disturbing or spooky.

Yet, occasionally I get this pang of something I'm reluctant to call loneliness. Because it isn't generic loneliness, it is *specific* loneliness. I do not want someone, anyone, to visit me to fill the silence in this empty house. I want my *wife*! The emptiness can only be filled by one person, and that person…well, you know the story by now, I'm sure.

There's a rhythm, a language, a comfortable familiarity Andrea and I had. I miss that. I miss our private language. Yesterday I felt that absence with such a profound impact it was all I could do not to have a breakdown in the middle of Woolworths.

Andrea and I were both foodies, as my rotund shape attests to. We loved making and eating food, and always up to trying something new. I've not cooked anything (cooking as distinct from just making a quick bachelor meal) since Andrea died. I do not see the point in it. Yesterday I needed to stop by a shop to grab a few staples, and because of logistical reasons, I went to a large flagship store, not just the small one down the corner. And there it was: all these exotic and rare ingredients and fancy cuts of protein that one just does not get at your generic shops.

Boy, did that hurt! Andrea and I would have stacked the trolley full and spent the next three weeks making all kinds of odd and delicious food, critiquing it, sorting it into losers and keepers, and if and how we could improve on it.

I left with a bread, a pepper-steak pie, and some heat-and-eat veg. I missed the presence of my wife, but I realised here is now a door that has also closed. The food-value door.

I've got awesome friends. And I value them more than they will ever know. I love having them over and having great chinwags. I love the odd WhatsApp check-in and chit-chat. I can never live without them. But friends are just that: friends.

I'm not lonely; my friends keep me from being lonely. But there is an aching hole that no number of friends can ever fill.

And that's okay.

The Reluctant Widower
19 August 2021

Chapter 10 - Evil Glove Haul.

1

This publication is an experiment in the afterlife. It is a falsifiable and repeatable-under-laboratory-conditions test to see if ghosts exist.

The fact that Andrea's ghost is not here toppling chairs and breaking mirrors is testament that there ain't no such thing as ghosts.

You see, Andrea never wanted to be *that* woman. She was incredibly private and did not want anyone to know she had cancer. Only an intimate circle of friends and family knew. She told me "I do not want to be 'the woman who has cancer' or 'the woman who beat cancer.' I have cancer, then I won't, and then that's it. No need to make a song and dance about it." She never saw herself as a 'victim'. She did not let her cancer define her. She was particularly riled at the term 'Cancer Survivor'. "The fact that I survived cancer is just another thing. I do not want to be defined as a cancer survivor, I want to de defined as Andrea Heidgen, with all her complexities."

Well, we all know she did not survive. And now the woman who did not want to make a big deal out if it, gets the biggest deal of all made in her name: a whole sodding book.

I survived, though. Heaven alone knows how, but I did. And it hurts like hell. And I'd bet my beer money it always will. It never gets easier. But I'm learning to live with it. Despite earlier declarations — or hopes — I don't think I've made peace with it, but there is an uneasy truce, and I'd see that as progress.

A day or two after we knew it was over, I wrote her a letter and took it to her where she lay in hospital. It contained all the things I wanted to say but did not trust myself to say without turning into a weeping mess. The easiest way for me to say how much I loved her was to put it on paper. She read it, she cried, I cried, we hugged…Ugh, it was like a scene from a badly written romance novel.

Then she told me that I have her blessing if I want to marry again, and my response shocked me.

"No," I said to her. "I don't want to marry again. I *have* a wife. She may be dead, but she is still my wife." I know that may sound incredibly ghoulish, or like a load of bulldust with a smattering of cheese, but that's the way I see it.

My legal marital status may be 'widowed', but she's still my wife. I speak of her in the present tense, and use 'we' now as often as before. Seldom do I use the singular 'I'. "Our house. Our dogs. *We* have this Green Thing…"

'Seldom'. Not 'never'. A few months after she died, I bought a new television. I was watching cricket and suddenly the old one was too small for my middle-aged eyes. Every time I wanted to see the score, I needed to get up to go look. It was embarrassing, frustrating, and torturous on my knees. The only solution was a new telly. I set off and bought a humongous 4k wall-mounted screen. Hey, I can see the score again! And that became the first thing in the house that was 'mine' and not 'ours'. For the first time I said 'my' TV, and not 'our' TV.

As the weeks turn into months, months into years, and years into the rest of my life, I am sure there will be many things which I'll replace, the label of 'ours' will fall away, and be replaced with 'mine'. Just this week I broke the handle of one of our measuring cups while making blueberry pancakes. Soon our old and familiar blue measuring cup will be replaced by my unfamiliar one. There may even be a time where a few new things will enter my life which will again carry the label of 'ours'.

But Andrea will always be my wife.

Always.

2

I started Chapter Two by saying that I need to explain some backstory. This is where I close that loop. My greatest fear has always been growing old alone. I've no kids to smuggle booze into the old age home for me. With Andrea by my side, that fear was alleviated. And then, it became justified. It is my 47th birthday as I write this. And now I'm facing 'growing old alone' once again. And it is still a fear, but not as great a fear as it used to be. Because I'm taking with me into my middle-age — and hopefully my 100th birthday — fifteen years of memories, and the knowledge that I had a hell of a ride. A ride not many people can say they had.

All the fights, all the tension, drama, illnesses…they all took their toll, but none of them defined who we were. We were a team greater than the bullshit and disease that we had to face. Ultimately, we based our decisions and actions on our hopes and not our fears. We had each other's backs, always, no matter what the cost.

But her death now redefined who I am. I cannot sit here and say, "Her death does not define me" because that would be woefully inaccurate. Of course it does not absolutely characterise my life, but I cannot deny the profound impact it had on me.

Nor can I deny the affects the other close deaths had on me. Before my friends and lovers died, I was one man. Their deaths shaped me into an altogether different one.

And ironically, a better one. It's easy to become bitter and angry. Trust me, I know. I had my moments. But there comes a time when you have to take your happiness seriously, and choose. Am I going to be bitter, or better? Would her death — and indeed, life — have had any purpose whatsoever if I allowed myself to become a bitter old man? To 'wallow' in a chosen misery?

I can never deny the hurt. But I can choose to let it hone me, and not destroy me.

I can choose a better life for myself.

If not for my own sake, then for Andrea's.

Which may just be the greatest gift of all.

3

And well, that's it.

Apart from a few teas to dot and eyes to cross, that's my story.

"But Gerry," I hear you say, "That can't be it! It just... ends! Where's the rest?"

That's the point, Gentle Reader, that's exactly the point. It just fucking *ends*. I woke up on a Sunday morning and found a lump in my wife's breast. I woke up on a Sunday morning ten months later a widower. Neither Andrea nor I asked for it. Yet, we were lucky.

We got to say goodbye.

Several of you reading this never did. You just got *that* phone call, or walked into *that* room, or woke up in *that* bed, and out of the sweet blue yonder that was that: the end. The fucking end in all its blunt finality and repeated questions of "what do I do now?". To you who had to deal with 'that' situation, I do not envy you. Nine months of a life-or-death battle, and then a one month wait for death, is physical and emotional hell. But at least we got to say goodbye.

Gentle Reader, say what you need to say. Because *that* phone call *will* come. It's a guarantee. And if you are not the one receiving it, you will be its subject. So, say what you need to say.

My story of grief will carry on for as long as I breathe. But at some stage, this memoir has to stop. I cannot carry on with it forever.

As my Facebook entries of *The Chronicles of a Reluctant Widower* got more sporadic, I noticed I'm starting to repeat myself. How many times can I say I miss her? Or that I loved her? Or that I lived with her? Or that I laughed with her? I mean, c'mon, it gets boring.

Which is what an 'Evil Glove Haul' is. It is an anagram of that incredibly annoying yet ubiquitous 'Love Live Laugh' motto. As those who have seen my photography and read my novels will know, I have a 'thing' for gloves: an evil haul is just up my alley!

However, just because it is ubiquitous and annoying, does not mean it does not have a point. Loving and laughter is what life is all about. … and just because my entries have become repetitive does not mean they are not invaluable.

However, they are starting to become only invaluable to *me*.

Thusly, there comes a point where I have to draw a line under it all. I shall probably carry on with any insights or thoughts or ravings on Facebook as needed, but the memoir is complete. Anything I say more is indulgence and cannon fodder for my critics who already think of me as verbose and overly long. Best not to give them more ammunition.

I wish all of you who read this one metric fuck-ton of love and laughter, and a life of health, wealth, happiness, and cricket.

Take care.

Gerry.

Epilogue: The Ayahuasca Chronicles

1

I am a drug virgin. Apart from prescription medication and alcohol, I've never taken any form of drug. I have actually *held* a lit cigarette one or twice in my life, but that was under great duress and distress. Andrea was even worse. She would not even *touch* a sealed pack of cigs, let alone hold a lit one.

A big part of the reason for this was the era in which I grew up in. The '80s saw a great 'satanic panic', and everything, as in *everything*, that was not sanctioned by a very specific sect of the Christian church was the work of Satan trying to seduce you. If you were Presbyterian, that included the Baptists a block away, and if you were Baptist, that included the Presbyterians a block to the other side. Even innocuous things like Disney movies and surfing during the summer holidays were the work of Devil himself claiming your soul from the comfort of *Honey I Shrunk the Kids*.

And naturally, because of the new thing called 'crack' which made all the headlines, and Nancy Reagan's 'Just Say No' campaign, The Satanic Panic had with it a new cousin: The War on Drugs. (yes, yes, I know it was Nixon, but everything here came ten years later than the rest of the world!)

Young and impressionable me believed all this hooey.

As I grew older and my fundamentalism grew into agnosticism into atheism into a place where Dawkins looked positively revivalist, I saw the Satanic Panic for what it was: a level of ridiculousness that any grown-up should be ashamed of. However, in that same 'growing older' era, I also saw what drugs did to people who 'Just Said Yes' and it ain't pretty. My aversion to narcotics remained, though my libertarian stance intensified: you do you, just don't ask me to join. You wanna smoke your brain into an IQ in the upper fifties, be my guest. If you find your home in smack and blow, hey, who am I to tell you that you're wrong? But I'll refrain, thank you very much.

Besides, can you imagine *my* brain on acid? Holy crap...

2

When I was fifteen, I met a guy at a school camp. In South Africa — at least in pre-democracy South Africa — we had a thing called 'veld-school'. For a week they take all the city-dwellers and bus these kids to a rural location where you get up early and learn things about how nature around you worked. We climbed mountains and clambered over streams and avoided snakes and scorpions and learned how to make fire using only two sticks and a smuggled cigarette lighter. This was the only week of high school I ever enjoyed.

During this trip, I started chatting to a kid who I saw around the school but never had contact with. This was in 1990. Thirty years later, he is still one of my best mates.

I'm talking about my buddy, Juan. The one who I say I know he is enlightened because he fights tooth and nail in his denial that he is not. Yet, he has great wisdom and insight. For a few years after school, we laughed in the face of satanic panic by going to goth and alternative nightclubs together. Got drunk, played pool, and listened to Sisters of Mercy and The Offspring. Ah, the good old days.

However, Juan also joined the 'Just Say Yes' brigade, and his journey into drugs started with cigarettes and ended up in experimenting. Never cocaine and heroin, though. But as far as I know, he took just about everything else. His illicit drug experimentation phase did not last long, and by the time he hit forty, he even quit smoking. These days, on a Saturday afternoon at the pub, Juan has a two-beer limit. Bloody lightweight...

A few days after Andrea was told 'pack your bags, time's up', Juan came for a visit. The three of us chatted about anything and everything, except cancer and the terminal finality thereof. But we could see he had something on his mind and was trying to find a way to say it. After careful prodding, he told us he had had this extreme experience, and he believed Andrea could benefit from it: Ayahuasca.

I've heard of it. And that's about where it ended. During the drug-crazed '80s, 'education' meant telling you exactly what each drug was, what it did, how much it cost, and where to get it. No wonder the 'Just

Say No' thing flopped miserably! I knew what MDMA, cocaine, LSD, etc. was, and what it did. But Ayahuasca — or its active ingredient, DMT — was not even on the 'Just Say No' radar, let alone central.

Juan told us it was the most profound experience of his life, and that it is used 'off label' to treat depression. In particular, 'end-of-life anxiety'. This had our curiosity piqued. As Juan related his experience, Andrea and I looked at each other and we instinctively knew that our days of claiming the moral high ground of being 'drug virgins' were rapidly coming to an end.

The Queen of Google confirmed the anecdotal reports that this brew was, indeed, great for helping terminal people accept their fate. It seemed a great idea. What have we got to lose, right? Even Andrea's psychiatrist mentioned something similar to her previously, that there have been encouraging results with psilocybin. Or 'Magic Mushrooms' to you and me. (I'm so happy psychiatry is starting to look at these things. There's more to medicine than things synthesised in a lab.)

We never got there. As said, "You have six months to live" did not last four weeks. Andrea kicked the bucket way before we could even think of trying it.

But, as you may know, *I* haven't kicked the bucket yet. I am still very much alive, if not exactly kicking…

3

I did it.

I spoke to Juan, and he said that he thought it could help me deal with Andrea's death. Help me make peace with it. At this stage, I was in such a psychological mess, I would have tried anything in an attempt to make sense of it. And if Ayahuasca could help with 'end-of-life anxiety', maybe it could help for my 'carrying-on-with-life anxiety'.

As fate would have it, the next ceremony would be the weekend of March 20th . Does that date sound familiar? It should. It's our wedding anniversary. So, not an emotionally charged weekend for me in the slightest! The ceremony takes place over two nights: Friday night Ayahuasca, Saturday morning a dose of San Pedro, Saturday night another Ayahuasca, and then home on Sunday.

I have to admit, for a guy who never even smoked weed, this scared me absolutely shitless.

I had to prepare, both physically and psychiatrically. I was warned that I am not to be on any psychotropic medication during the ceremony, and

I had to be at least two weeks clean and sober from all substances. This was not just my psyche meds — I've been taking an anti-depressant and an anti-convulsant for years — but also alcohol. In addition to that, I needed to go vegetarian for two weeks, as well as several other things. Like no spices or oils in food. There are several reasons for this, most of which sounds like new age woo-woo to me, but I can see how taking something this strong while you have psychiatric chemicals coursing through your brain could be a recipe for ending up in a straitjacket in a room with soft walls.

The first person I tell is my psychologist. I did not beat around the bush, I just straight up told her, "I want to do Ayahuasca. What do you think?"

Her eyes lit up like she just won the jackpot at Caesar's Palace in Vegas and told me she thinks it's a brilliant idea. One down, one to go.

Next up my psychiatrist. Same thing. I told him straight up: "I want to do Ayahuasca, I need you to wean me off my meds." You know, you don't mess with psyche meds. You don't just quit cold turkey. Not a wise idea. I expected some pushback, but from my psychiatrist I get the same answer: "Wow, that is so cool!" And then he said: "Okay, on the condition that you come back and tell me all about it."

For the next several weeks, I go through the process of getting my system weaned off all psyche meds. It was hairy at times, not gonna lie, and I had many second thoughts, but I persevered, and a few weeks later I was clean and sober for two weeks, ready for my journey.

Juan and I take the drive to the mountain resort on Friday morning, arrive in the most beautifully scenic place in the middle of the Drakensberg. The tail end of summer, everything is green, the sky is blue, it is pleasantly warm. It's bloody paradise, it is.

The Shaman, a big Dutchman with a scruffy beard and a wear-faded *Nirvana* T-shirt named Johan Harlaar gives us newbies the lowdown on how it works, and what to expect. At sunset, we — twelve participants of the ceremony that weekend — depart for the ceremonial room: a circular hut with camping mattresses aligned against the wall like the numbers on a clock. We lay down and Johan begins his thing. After his initial 'prayers', he calls us each one by one and gives us a dose of Ayahuasca.

Jesus, that's vile. Okay, it's not quite as bitter and dry and 'orrible as some of the craft brew IPAs I've had, but it's close!

So, Drug Virgin Gerry goes and lies down on his camping mattress, pulls a blanket over him, and waits for the fun to begin.

Nothing.

Absolutely nothing. The strongest hallucinogen known to mankind does absolutely sweet blue fuck-all for me. It was a great disappointment. But hey, I tried.

4

Saturday morning — anniversary day — just after sunrise, Johan gives us a dose of San Pedro, which is not as vile as Ayahuasca on the palate, and now I am allegedly tripping on mescaline. Again, nada. This is a great disappointment. But the rest of Saturday is fricking brilliant, hey. The surroundings and the crowd make for a great day, and we take a hike. Through the fields we go for a walk, this city kid enjoying the fresh air and sight and sounds and textures of nature. At the end of the walk, we come to a stream, no more than a foot wide, coming from a 'waterfall'. Which means about ten metres of sheer rock and a bit more than a dribble of water cascading into a pool about a foot-and-a- half deep. Angel Falls, this is not.

But it's pretty!

I've always been a sucker for symbolism. I see this waterfall and stream as an opportunity. I stand on this side of the bank, and I say to myself, out loud, that old Zen koan: *A man cannot step into the same river twice; for it is not the same river, and it is not the same man.*

Very deliberately and considered, I step into that shallow foot-wide stream, and out the opposite side. And I turn back, and do it again, soaking my shoes and freezing off my toes. "I am no longer the same man," I say to no one in particular, but if some of the people heard me, I did not give a toss. It was time for a figurative rebirth.

And every birth needs a baptism.

I make my way to the shallow pool at the waterfall's edge where people are searching for pretty pebbles. I take off my shirt and give it to Juan. Again, deliberately and considered, I step underneath the tumble of the water, and I yawp into the skies. The water was freezing, not the type of thing I'd normally do. I am built for comfort, not adrenaline, but it seemed the right thing to do. I made sure I was well and truly soaked, and I stepped out of the spray, and called myself reborn and baptised.

My next life, one without Andrea, had its birth and baptism, and I felt cleansed.

I felt as if I could move on.

Even if the previous night's Ayahuasca and that morning's San Pedro did nothing for me, just this process of deliberately drawing a line under 'us' and now carrying on as 'I', on this highly symbolic day of our wedding anniversary, the entire weekend was worth it.

Boy, was I wrong!

5

I'm not religious, not even spiritual, but you know that. It is a famous song of mine and I make mention of it too often, even for my own comfort. But there is still a thing such as 'sacred', even if it has nothing to do with the supernatural. There are some things in life which need a certain level of respect, and definitely can do without nihilistic debasement.

Personally, my 'sacred' values lie in truth, beauty, and authenticity. I do not see the point in why any consenting adult should lie to another (That I write fiction, a lie by definition, is beside the point). I do not see the point of degrading things to the point of 'ugliness', and I most certainly do not see the point in lying to yourself. There are three people you should never lie to: your doctor, your lawyer, and, above all, yourself (As distinct from, say, the tax man, but I could be wrong.).

However, I have other 'sub-subjects' as well which I would respect. Chief among these is if you are voluntarily in another's space, treat them with respect, even if you do not like or agree with what they are doing. Like when we were in Prague and wanted to enter some of the historical synagogues, I had to cover my head. Some synagogues even had disposable yarmulkes for exactly this purpose. I felt slightly silly, but I put it on and entered the buildings. It did not turn me into a Hasidic Jew, it merely meant I honoured the rules of another's sacred space. With this attitude in mind, I head off on Saturday afternoon into a ceremony named the '*despacho*'.

It is an Andean gratitude ceremony. A prayer bundle-slash-offering of an expression of gratitude. As in not something I have the slightest bit of interest in. But I'm here, and I am in another's space, so I shall participate in the ceremony with the intention it was created with, even if I don't *believe* in it.

Johan sets out a large piece of paper on the grass and takes out several Tupperware containers (how holy!) full of various substances. We begin by placing leaves in the centre of the paper. Before each leaf, we are supposed to say a prayer of gratitude before we place it. I don't believe in prayer, but even an atheist like me can acknowledge and be grateful for things like two eyes. Without my eyes, I'm nothing. So, I say thank you to whatever there is to be thankful to that I have two eyes.

Enter the Tupperware: each of the substances represents something to the spirits. Sugar represents sweetness and love. Rice represents fertility and abundance. Beans for protection and abundance. Etcetera. And, a 'letter'. Each of us were to write a letter of that which we are grateful for. Coloured pencils are used to encourage the spirit of play. I play! I make up a silly poem which I cannot remember. But four lines in, and the playful silly poem turns into an homage to my late wife. I fold the paper, and because she would've loved it, I fold the paper into a little origami boat. The one and only origami skill I have, one I learned when I was seven. I write on the side of the paper boat 'SS Primlove', and put it in the *despacho*.

And there comes the waterworks. Holy crap! I have this moment, and I turn away and look into the sun, because on this day six years ago I married my wife under an eclipse, and staring at the sun seemed like an adequate way to remember that moment.

But it wasn't mere waterworks. It was one of those chainsaw sucker-punches to the gut, and I have myself a breakdown. I blubber and cannot speak. Everyone looks at me as if I'm having an apoplexy, which maybe I am. "It is my wedding anniversary today," I eke out through a throat way too tight to speak.

"Where is your wife," someone asks.

"She died three months ago," I say.

Johan just looks at me in stunned disbelief. "Why did you not say so! We could have made this so much more sacred."

I shrug. "It's not about me and my wife. I'm here as a part of a group. I cannot selfishly make this about me and my drama. It's a communal journey."

The reaction from the other people: "Bullshit."

The rest of the *despacho* ceremony became a funerary celebration for Andrea. Everything that was placed by everyone was in support of me, and to honour my wife.

This is one of the greatest honours that ever befell me.

When all the offerings and notes were placed, Johan folded the paper into a parcel, ready to be put on the fire we prepared. A literal burnt offering. It is the job of the Shaman to put this package onto the fire, but Johan handed the parcel to me. That honour befell me.

This part of the ritual I love in its symbolism — again, even if I don't believe a word of it. We form a circle around a fire, interlinking hands. But get this: with our backs to the fire. The reason is beautiful in its allegory: you do not get to watch the Gods feast.

I walk over to the fire with the *despacho* package, the only one of us seeing it, and I kiss it. "Goodbye, Sweetie," I say, and place it on the fire, watch for a second to make sure it catches flame, then I turn my back and take the hands of the people next to me, and I weep.

6

On the 12th of December, I kissed my dead wife on the forehead, and walked out of the room, and never saw her again. A few hours later, a hearse came and wheeled her away. I did not see it. I purposely averted my eyes.

And that was that. She is somewhere on a slab at Wits Medical, which is what she wanted.

We never had a funeral or a memorial service for her. It was all very 'clinical' at the end, and I just carried on with my life.

I never knew how important funerals are to the living until we had that impromptu funeral service at an Ayahuasca retreat on the day of our wedding anniversary. The day I symbolically gave myself a rebirth.

How vitally important it is to have a formal and ritualistic goodbye.

When it was all said and done, I told Johan that I got what I came for. I came for an Ayahuasca ceremony, which did nothing, but I got the most incredible gift instead: a funeral for my wife. I could skip that night's Ayahuasca and go straight home. I was at peace.

He gave me a smirk. "You think," he asked me cynically, knowingly.

After sundown, we returned to the ceremonial space, and I took my slug of the sacred brew which tastes of dry and bitter crap! The taste of it has categorically no redeeming features.

But the effects?

I lay back on my mattress, and Johan began to sing his *icaros*, and I waited for it all to be over so I could go to bed. I was knackered. I knew nothing would happen to me. Last night it was a waste of four hours of my time. This morning the San Pedro did nothing. I know how I'll react to this alleged most potent of hallucinogens.

Jesus, was I ever wrong!

That night, Mamma Aya rolled me. I did not just trip balls, I tripped fucking triangles. It was the most profoundly unpleasant experience of my life.

And I cannot wait to do it again.

If you have never done this, let me be quite clear: Ayahuasca is categorically not a feel-good party drug. It is so much more than that. I will not divulge what I saw and experienced during that Saturday night trip, but please take me at face value when I say that my wife dying was not the most profound thing that happened to me. A mere three months after that terrible December day, something even more life-changing and profound happened to me in a dark ceremonial hut in the Drakensberg. It was highly unpleasant and left me reeling for several weeks afterwards.

But it was invaluable.

This is not Gerry going: "Hey man, you gotta try this Ayahuasca shit!" This is not an endorsement. But I'd like to at least tell you I found *a* way, and if you are in a hole like I was, maybe you should seek the medicinal properties of this plant. This is not mere anecdote. There are several studies into hallucinogens generally — and Ayahuasca specifically — as a viable treatment for depression, all with promising results. Your milage may vary, but it is at least worth a consideration.

I have to put in my disclaimer here: don't be daft, okay? If you want to do it, speak to the pros, and for the love of all things sweet and caramel, don't go breaking any laws, okay?

7

Ayahuasca allowed me to make peace with Andrea's death. Living without her is painful. Living without her sucks hairy balls. It hurts like hell, and it is scary and confusing, and I'm still sitting here with a hollow pit in my stomach.

But I'm at peace with it now. I can sit with this pain and fear and confusion, and it does not consume me anymore. I'm not tra-la-la-ing though life like Mary fucking Poppins, I'm still seeing my psychologist twice a month, and I am back on my psychiatric meds.

But that weekend, which fate, coincidence, or just sheer luck, destined to fall on our wedding anniversary, was the best thing to have happened to me.

It allowed me to say goodbye to my wife.

It allowed me to say hello to me.

THE END

Johannesburg, South Africa.
12 December 2020 – 13 September 2021

Acknowledgements

If I were to thank everyone, I'd bankrupt myself on print costs. There are dozens of people who helped make this book a reality.

But some people need to be named.

Firstly, to Prof Carol-Ann Benn and Dr Ronwyn van Eeden: thank you for giving Andrea a fighting chance. And I cannot mention them without mentioning the fantastic support staff at the Breast Care Centre of Excellence and the Rosebank Oncology Clinic of Rosebank, especially Sister Una.

To Sister Mel Griggs: the way you supported me in the final days and hours, and especially immediately afterwards, is worth more than you can ever imagine.

To my beta readers: Lezzet, Phil, Sigrid, and especially Marianne: thanks for your feedback. It was invaluable.

To my editor, Tamsyn Bester, who helped whip my text into shape: thank you for sitting up with my is-es and ares and hasses and haves, and making my second-language English somewhat readable. And one cannot mention 'editor' without mentioning Flo Smith who always finds those annoying final bloopers nobody else does.

To Helen Holyoake, my publicist, who helped this volume get seen. Thank you. I know a thing or two about photographic lighting, and I've been told I can spin a yarn, but about marketing I know squat. It's good to have you in my corner.

To my Shaman, Johan Harlaar, who took my hand on my Ayahuasca journey: thank you for giving me an opportunity to make sense of what happened, and opening a doorway into myself. Johan died of cancer barely six months after my ceremony while this book was in rewrite phase. We spoke often, and he gave me his blessing in telling the tale of that fateful Saturday of which would have been our wedding anniversary. Johan has a CD out – search for his name on Deezer and Spotify and you can find the opening prayers and the rest of the Icaros he sang during the ceremonies. See links on the next page.

To the first-tier friends, second-tier friends, and the stragglers: Thank you for taking care of me. I needed that. Send beer. Visit more.

Very importantly: the absolute strangers who contacted me on Facebook to tell me how much my writing helped them. If not for you, this book would not exist. I am humbled by your response to my words.

Lucio and Rina, my lawyers, and buddies. Hey, even lawyers need friends. If I list what to thank you for, my editor will shoot me.

Kerron: thank you for being a grumpy old fuck and giving Andrea the best business partner I could have asked for.

Theresa: thanks for helping me set up the Christmas tree, Tree. You have no idea what that meant for me. I may call on you again.

Penultimately: my father, Charlie. He has become my best friend, and he shared the burden of carrying Andrea's death. Just because he does not feature much in the narrative, does not mean he did not, does not, feature every single day in my life. I love you, old man!

And lastly: Thank you to my wonderful wife. If there is even the remotest chance that I can explore time and space to find you again, I will. I love you.

Always.

6 November 2021 – Day 329

During the editing phase of this book, South Africa — you guessed it — bombed out of yet *another* Cricket World Cup…

Links

A list of various things mentioned in this book, just for context.

The Hungarian Puli
wikipedia.org/wiki/Puli_dog

The Breast Care Centre of Excellence
bcce.co.za

The Medical Oncology Centre of Rosebank
rosebankoncology.co.za

The Huset Restaurant in Svalbard
huset.com

Bidos Recipe
bit.ly/bidosrecipe

"Boob Soup"
bit.ly/boobsoup

Johan Harlaar's Ayahuasca Icaros
bit.ly/ayaicaros

A Star Called 'Prim'
software.star-register.com
Registry no: 75610-1949-1434079

And lastly: The soundtrack to our lives;
including songs mentioned in this book
bit.ly/PrimAndGerryMixTape

Reviews are meat and drink to us indie authors.
Please review my book here:
bit.ly/ChroniclesGoodreads

Printed in Great Britain
by Amazon

74489467R00122